IOWA BOY

IOWA BOY

Ten Years of Columns by Chuck Offenburger

Illustrated by Brian Duffy

Iowa State University Press – Ames

Dedicated to the people of Iowa in thanks for their warmth and willingness in teaching me, tolerating me and, most of all, talking to me.

© 1987 Iowa State University Press, Ames, Iowa 50010
All rights reserved

Composed by Iowa State University Press
Printed in the United States of America

No part of this book may be reproduced in any form or by any electronic or mechanical means, including information storage and retrieval systems, without written permission from the publisher, except for brief passages quoted in a review.

First edition, 1987

Library of Congress Cataloging-in-Publication Data

Offenburger, Chuck.
    Iowa boy.

    1. Iowa – Social life and customs. I. Title.
F625.035 1987   977.7   87–17269
ISBN 0–8138–0039–0

Contents

Foreword

Chuck Offenburger is the only 40-year-old boy that I know. There was a time, some years ago, when I thought he would eventually outgrow his "Iowa Boy" title and role as a columnist for *The Des Moines Register.* But now I'm convinced that Chuck can be Iowa's favorite boy when he's gray-haired and wrinkled. It just fits him.

That's the thing about Chuck's column. It fits Iowa like a pigskin glove. The column probably wouldn't work anywhere else in the world, but in Iowa, it's as much a part of the culture as the state fair. Great columnists fit their environment and their audiences that way: Chuck fits small town Iowa the way Mike Royko fits Chicago and Jimmy Breslin fits New York, New York. In a decade of writing for Iowa's statewide newspaper, the Iowa Boy has turned out more than 2,000 columns. In a typical year, he will put 40,000 miles on a car, averaging three days a week on the road in Iowa. He probably knows more about Iowa's back roads and backwaters than anyone living, and if there's a small town cafe he hasn't tried, or a weekly newspaper office he hasn't visited, I'd be surprised.

His columns appear in the *Register* four times a week—a grueling pace that would grind down most writers. But the Iowa Boy thrives on it, and probably would write six or seven columns a week if I'd let him. I won't, because I'd like him to last a long time. He's got a good thing going with the *Register*'s readers.

It's not easy to characterize the Iowa Boy column. It can be serious, funny, silly, outrageous or heart-warming, as the samples in this collection show. The range of subject matter is as wide as life in Iowa—everything from the pain of divorce to the search for the best cinnamon roll in the state.

Whatever else it is, it's always personal—in the sense of one Iowan talking to another, sort of like a backyard conversation. Chuck Offenburger is conducting a non-stop dialogue with his readers, in the neighborly, just-folks way that it's done along Main Street in Iowa's small towns.

It's not a one-way conversation. The readers respond. The most mail Chuck ever received on a column came after his poignant piece explaining his own divorce. He says he stopped counting at 375 letters. Many of them were from Iowans who had gone through the same painful experience; some of them turned to Chuck as a counsellor. He has that kind of relationship with his readers.

Mostly, though, the Iowa Boy column is fun. It's fun for readers and, more important, it's fun for Chuck. In fact, that's the main reason he gives for writing the column. As long as it's fun, he'll do it, Chuck says. "If the time ever comes when it's not fun, I'll just bow out."

I'm betting he will be the world's oldest boy before that happens.

JAMES P. GANNON

Introduction

I am a man with an Iowa soul.

I have been lucky enough to find a job with a newspaper, *The Des Moines Register,* that also has an Iowa soul. My editors, who have so generously allowed a reprinting of my columns in this book, have also generously given me the time and encouragement to roam about this state in the American heartland and to report the quirks, warts and glory that I think make Iowa such a warm, unique place.

Which brings up a story.

It hasn't been too many years ago that one of my bosses came to me and said that his boss was asking for a written job description for each of his troops. "Now, I think I've got a pretty good idea of what it is the Iowa Boy does," said the late Charlie Capaldo. "At least when I read your stuff, I usually say, 'That's an Iowa Boy piece for sure.' But when I try to put a definition on what it is you do, I have trouble putting the right words on paper. Would you write something for me?"

So I did. What I wrote for him is that it is the mission of the Iowa Boy to "report and reflect on the experience of being an Iowan." It seemed to satisfy all concerned. It also, on close examination, means I can do just about anything, as long as I can find a story in it that will be either informative or entertaining or both to a statewide audience of several hundred thousand readers of the *Register.*

There is the matter of the column name, which is also the name of this book: Iowa Boy. It is a name that makes the skin crawl on some of my more erudite colleagues. "Cornball," they say. Well, yes, it is corny, but I started with it, grew to like it and intend to stick with it—for a number of reasons.

I had been working at the *Register* as a general assignment reporter for five years before being asked to start the column in the fall of 1977. Two *Register* staffers, Gene Raffensperger and the late Gordon Gammack, had recruited me from my hometown newspaper in Shenandoah and convinced the *Register* editors to hire me. Gammack was a legend then as a columnist for the paper, and it was my goal to some day succeed him. When that opportunity came up, I was told I could name the column anything I wanted to but that the trend at the time was simply to put the writer's last name at the top of the column.

That is fine if your last name is short, crisp and memorable. But when your last name is Offenburger, a clunky German name that hides the half-Irish in me, you look for something shorter and crisper. So we were sitting around the kitchen table at home when my stepdaughter Janae Jaynes, then 7, came up with Iowa Boy. I went with it because it says exactly what I am, it's short and crisp and memorable, it's something people can kid about and thus is a conversation starter in interviews and, finally, because what could be more Iowan than to let your kid name your column? Janae was very proud at the time that her idea for the column name had been accepted. Now, a decade later, she is a sage 17-year-old and I suspect she thinks the name stinks.

It is a grand 10 years that I've had as Iowa Boy. There have been trips all over the United States as well as to China. More typically, though, the trips were into the countryside of Iowa, a state I've watched in one decade go from incredible prosperity to desperate economic woe and then, at this writing, finally begin to climb back to good times.

There have been for me brushes with the rich and famous, and there have been brushes with the poor and hopeless. Personally, there has been great fun and there has been some great pain—both of which I've shared with my readers.

In the summer of 1986, after I'd written how I'd knelt down and proposed to Michelle Peacock right in the middle of a Des Moines bike shop, the managing editor of the *Register,* Arnie Garson, came up to me and said, "Offenburger, you do some things that I'd never do myself, and if for some reason I did do them, I'd sure as hell never write about them." On reflection, maybe my boss was chiding me there, but at the time I took it as a compliment. And the reason I did was that it is my belief that communication—which is the business I am in—can only happen if the people trying to communicate are open and honest.

Iowans have been so open and honest with me as I've talked to them over the past 10 years that I can be no less myself, even when it hurts or is embarrassing. It's hardly ever been that way, though. Mostly it's been one grinning romp after another, and I hope this book reflects that.

There is one other thing I must say. Nowhere else in this book have I given proper credit to the person most responsible for making me whatever it is that I am today. That person is my mother, Anna Offenburger, a wonderful lady of 80 who still lives in Shenandoah. When I was 13 years old, she got a call from the boss at the *Evening Sentinel,* the newspaper in that southwest Iowa town. He wondered if I was ready to follow the example of two older brothers and write sports. I didn't want to do it. My mother made me. And then in that same year, the first year after the death of my dad, she spent hour after hour reading everything she could get her hands on, even going through old bound volumes of the *Sentinel* in the Shenandoah library basement to review what my brothers had written, to come up with words and phrases she thought would improve my writing. She remains today the critic I pay the most attention to — in writing and in life — as well as being my most faithful fan. I just know there has never been a better mother, and if you dispute that remark, the Iowa Boy is prepared to fight.

Some people, and one rooster, have been so special that we will never forget them. Here are a few.

LEGENDS

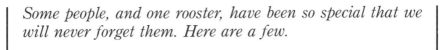

Chilling and thrilling memories of my connection with Dr. Martin Luther King, Jr.

January 1986

As I sit to write, it is the birthday of Martin Luther King, Jr., and we are headed toward Monday's first observance of a national holiday commemorating his life. It stirs some of my deepest, most fun and most chilling memories.

I knew King – not just through the news, as everyone did, but more personally through my brother Tom, who served as King's press secretary the last five years of his life.

My brother's time with him paralleled my time at Vanderbilt University in Nashville, so I was frequently in Atlanta, which was King's home, for visits. Let me assure you, it was pretty heady stuff for a college kid, especially one taken by the civil rights movement, to come face to face with King and his lieutenants and have them say, "Your brother is some of the best white folks we know."

Those of us in the family are always frustrated that we've never really been able to get brother Tom to open up about his experiences on his visits home. I remember one occasion when we were all determined we'd get it done, only to find him in a mood where all he wanted to do was drink Scotch and dance to Stevie Wonder records. He won out. Other times, he's been too occupied getting caught up on the exploits of his alma mater's football team, the Iowa Hawkeyes. I've goaded him to write a book about all he shared with King, but I think a lot of it is simply too painful for him to recall.

So I'm glad I have those recollections of a time when I was dropping in on them at their Southern Christian Leadership Conference office, hearing King preach in his church and – this is the chilling part – spending the whole night King was slain in Memphis in King's own room at the Lorraine Motel.

I look back on that night in 1968 almost in disbelief. It was late on an April afternoon when a friend, ashen-faced, ran into my office at the school newspaper in Nashville. "Oh God, Chuck, I'm so sorry," he screamed. "Doc King got shot in Memphis, and they're saying he's gone."

I tried to call Tom, who was in Atlanta, and couldn't get him. It was then my pal and I decided we would fly to Memphis. I can't remember where we got the money – Lord knows I didn't have any at that point in my college career – but we got it and went.

We arrived in Memphis to find a city on fire, literally. Everything in the ghetto was burning. Everywhere there were policemen in riot gear and National Guardsmen in those scary, tanklike personnel carriers. We had to pay a taxi driver an extra $20 to drive side streets to get past the police lines and drop us at the Lorraine.

King's aides still there – Ralph Abernathy, Hosea Williams, Andy Young, Jesse Jackson – should have put me on the run. However, when they recognized me as Tom's little brother, they pulled my buddy and me into the room where the suitcases and briefcase with the MLK initials were open on the bed. We stayed the night, occasionally stepping out on the balcony with them where King's blood was still in a horrifying pool. They pointed out the window across the street from which the assassin had fired.

We all went into periodic rages. We drank. We cussed. And we prayed. The phone never stopped ringing for Abernathy, who would succeed King, and the others. Brother Tom called, both to sob with me and scold me.

Morning finally came. King's people scooped their leader's blood into a jar and they all left. My pal and I left, too, flying back to Nashville and going to work on a special edition of our newspaper – all while our city and most others in the South began burning the same way Memphis had.

That was a King experience etched in my very soul. But it's not the one I hold dearest. What I like most are the stories I've squeezed from Tom about what a warm, wonderful and dedicated guy Doc was.

One in particular comes to mind. He and his father, Martin Luther King, Sr., whom everyone called "Daddy" King, shared the pulpit at a church in Atlanta. They had an agreement that no matter how busy they were with the civil rights struggle, and no matter where they were in the world, one of them would be back at Ebenezer Baptist to preach on Sunday mornings.

Tom told how many times, an exhausted Doc King would be winging it back to Atlanta late on a Saturday night and trying to write a sermon. Once he turned to my brother, moaned he was too tired to write anything and said with a sigh, "Tom, I'm afraid I'm just gonna have to 'whoop' one tomorrow."

What a national treasure.

[Tom Offenburger died after heart surgery July 2, 1986. His

funeral was held July 7 in St. Mary's Catholic Church in Shenandoah. Rev. Andy Young gave the eulogy and then led the congregation in singing "We Shall Overcome."]

Babe Bisignano plays golf and life the same way—in the rough

September 1986

Babe ("If I'm not in your column once a month people will quit
reading you") Bisignano had such a sore back last week that he
couldn't even play in his own golf tournament.

Some might suspect that Bisignano, the Des Moines restaura-
teur who readily admits he's a legend in his own mind, had only
himself to blame for his back problems. He wouldn't have them if he
didn't work so hard at patting himself there.

"No, it's golf," the 73-year-old said. "I took a lesson the other day
to get ready for my tournament, and then I went out and hit balls for
three hours. I tore myself up. What can I say? I'm just a terrible
golfer. The Lord has blessed me in so many ways, but one thing
He's denied me is playing good golf."

But He's certainly helped Babe put on a good golf tournament.
The fourth annual Babe-Mercy Classic was held on the beautiful
Echo Valley Country Club course Thursday south of Des Moines.
The 116 golfers paid $100 each to enter, and businesses threw in
enough more for "sponsorships" that more than $24,000 was raised
for alcoholism and drug addiction recovery programs at Mercy Hospital Medical Center. The four-year total of contributions from the
tourney is now pushing $100,000.

How ironic, you're thinking. Here we have an alcoholism treatment program benefiting because the state's foremost bootlegger in

Prohibition days is lending his celebrity to the cause. And it's not like the man himself, or his tournament and its accompanying parties, are dry. Indeed, Babe still likes enough Scotch in his cup so that his drink is Notre Dame gold. And the beer flowed on the golf course.

"He has that reputation among some people of being a rum runner who is nothing but an egomaniac," said Bill Maurer, Mercy spokesman, "but I'll tell you, the guy works his rear off on this."

How has it happened?

"I've had strong ties with Mercy forever," Babe said. "My wife got good treatment there before she died. After she did, I was talking to Steve Gleason. He's some big shot there. [Dr. Gleason is, in fact, medical director of the hospital's addiction program.] Well, anyway, I was telling this guy I wanted to do something nice for Mercy. He came up with the idea for the way to spend the money we could raise with a golf tournament, so I said, 'Let's do it.'

"I mean, look, what problem is there besides alcoholism that hurts so many people of all ages? Yeah, I drink too much myself sometimes, and yeah, I was a bootlegger and all that. But this is hurting people. Some of them are learning. The young people, God bless 'em, I think are starting to drink with some moderation – wine coolers and all that. And we're getting good laws on drunken driving. As far as I'm concerned, they can't make those laws tough enough.

"But I wanted to do something that would help people who are needing treatment. Besides, I love golf, even if I am terrible at it."

He's trying to do something about *that* problem, too. "What he does about that when he's playing," said Jim Rasley, a pal who is a big shot in Iowa golf, "is play 'Babe's Rules.' That means you can move your ball as much as you want as long as you can get away with it."

Indeed, Rasley told what must be the all-time story about Babe's shenanigans on the course. Babe not only confirmed it, he insisted on retelling it. "See, I was playing with Floren DiPaglia and a bunch of guys a few years ago," he began, "and it was a money game. Well, DiPaglia ain't no altar boy, as they say, and I always believe that when in Rome, do as the Romans. So he hits this shot into a deep rough, and we're over there looking for it, knowing if he can't find it, it'll cost him a stroke. DiPaglia gets kind of off to himself, and the next thing we know is he's yelling that he found it.

"I says, 'How could you have found it? I got it right here in my pocket!' True story."

Ah, Babe.

And we were no more than beyond that story when the hired driver of a stretch limousine parked in front of the clubhouse was standing at attention before us saying, yes, he would be off on his assigned errand.

And what was that?

"Going down to Mercy to pick up the nuns for the dinner party," said Babe. "Ain't that something? They take a vow of poverty, and then here we have a limousine with a bar and TV in it going to pick them up. Aw . . . let 'em have a good time on me."

Everybody else does.

My own graveside farewell to Iowa's "Music Man" — Meredith Willson

September 1984

MASON CITY, IA. — I suppose this might seem strange to some, but after composer Meredith Willson died at age 82 in June and was then buried here in his old hometown, I had this strong feeling that I somehow had to make my own peace with the passing of a man I never met.

A vacation that had taken me out of the territory kept me from the funeral. A business trip here the other day finally gave me the opportunity I needed to say my goodbyes.

Willson, as everyone knows, wrote *The Music Man,* a schmaltzy musical that had its roots in his own childhood. It's hard for me to put into words just what it is that the man and his show did for me. I've seen it a score or more times. I've nearly worn out my sound track album of it. Still, it thrills and touches me.

Perhaps what Willson gave me were directions on how to love Iowa: Appreciate its straight-arrow traditions. Tolerate its stubbornness. Exult in its neighborliness. Laugh out loud at Iowa, sure, but always with a genuine smile in the heart, never a sneer.

So I wandered out into Elmwood Cemetery to say thanks. I found the Willson family plot there under a lovely maple tree and sat on the headstone. On one side is a birdbath, on the other a sundial inscribed, "Time takes all but memories." I did feel a little out of place out there, thank goodness.

Then I wandered on down to the historic local tavern, Ransom's Cigar Store, the successor joint to the one that inspired Willson's line in the show about "kids peeking in the pool hall windows after school." I had a couple of beers, watched the good ol' boys shoot 8-ball and experienced a corny sense of communion with the spirits who peopled the mythical River City.

Unless you're one of those who look on taverns as dens of sin, you'd instantly recognize Ransom's as a wonderful place. It is clean, casual and properly pool hall dim. Behind the bar is a great talker, Bob Ransom, 47, the fourth generation of his family in the business. He is a rather controversial bloke just now, for he recently installed a jukebox for the first time, and the regulars, especially the older ones, are appalled.

Bob put me in touch with his father, Harley Ransom, 84, a high school classmate of Willson, for some history. The Ransoms have operated in their present location since 1950, the last of the five or six buildings they've been in since old Cort Ransom migrated here from Pennsylvania in 1868 and opened up. The actual pool hall that fueled Willson's imagination was the Pleazol, which the Ransoms ran from 1929 to 1950 before moving a couple of doors up North Federal to open their current parlor and resumed the Cigar Store name old Cort used.

"Meredith was a great guy," Harley said, "but a pool shooter? He'd usually stop in to see me when he came back to Mason City, but if he ever shot pool in our place, I don't remember it, and I would remember if he'd been any good."

Then I sought out the mayor, Ken Kew, 63, a great friend of Willson in later years. Kew is becoming almost as much of a Mason City institution as Ransom's. He was a radio and TV newsman here for years, then got into politics and is now in his third term and 11th year as mayor.

"We lost a great mouthpiece for Mason City when Meredith died," said Kew, who is quite a mouthpiece himself, having given 511 speeches (he keeps track) since taking office. "He always made sure people knew where he was from, and how proud he was of it.

There's been a clamor here to do something for Meredith—some want to rename Central Park or one of the streets—but I've decided not to do anything on the spur of the moment. I want to give us all some time to think about it and come up with a really fitting memorial."

I think it should include a statue, a fun one, of Willson in some sort of band director's or drum major's uniform, baton held on high. And below it should be the conclusion of Kew's seven-minute eulogy at the funeral.

"From this day forward," the mayor said so eloquently then, "whenever I hear thunder rolling across the skies like timpani and bass drums, I'll say to myself, 'There goes Meredith; he's leading another big parade.' "

That gives me goose bumps. Which is exactly the way a Meredith Willson character would react.

Hey, that may be it. That's probably why I was so taken by the man and his work, because even in real life, I'm nothing more than a Meredith Willson character—an Iowan.

There, I've found my peace.

He gave more than 11,600 assemblies in Iowa's schools – the first celebrity most of us ever met

April 1978

In Kenya, he was attacked by spear-throwing native warriors, their hair red with the blood of a lion. In Peru, he once awoke in a jungle hut to find himself eye-to-eye with an ocelot. He's shared quarters with a hairy tarantula. Al Bell has survived all that – plus a heart attack, open heart surgery and a stroke.

Most amazing of all, he's survived more than 11,600 assemblies in which he's told and shown Iowa schoolchildren the charm, wonder and adventure of faraway places. This is the 29th consecutive year of Al Bell travelogues in the small schools of the state. This year's schedule, like those of past years, includes more than 400 shows, sometimes as many as five in a day.

He's played to millions of Iowa kids. The oldest of them are now touching 40, but they still look back on him as a celebrity and remember him as looking and sounding a little like Walt Disney or Clark Gable. He did and does.

He certainly is a legend. He is now past 60, though he ducks the direct question about his age and says, "You're as young as you fool." Think about that and it'll make good sense.

William Allen Bell, Jr. was born in Lost Nation, Iowa, but wasn't there long. His father's bank went broke and his mother died in the same year. Bell spent his childhood "bouncing from one relative to another, attending 13 grade schools."

The way he tells it, he must have been a boy of spunk. "I was 10 years old before I found out my name wasn't Shut Up," he said.

But the quick lip has served him well. He "talked and worked" his way through Illinois Wesleyan College, where he met Rhea Morgan, now his wife of 40 years, the past nine of which she's co-starred in the productions.

His early career was in radio, and he was an air personality on WHO in Des Moines before joining in a venture to form an Ames station in 1948. "I was working 18 hours a day and hating it," Bell said. "I started examining myself, deciding what I really wanted to do. I knew I wanted to travel, that I liked kids [he and Rhea have four, all grown] and that I enjoyed photography. The travelogue idea just evolved."

He took two weeks in the fall of 1948 "and traveled all over Iowa, hitting 10 to 12 schools a day, asking if they'd let me do a presentation if I came up with some film and artifacts of some far-away place. Most of them said they'd try me once."

The following summer, he traveled the Alcan Highway in Alaska and Canada, shooting color movie film and interviewing to build a script. By the fall of 1949, he had 300 performances on contract.

"Time and distance meant nothing to me then," he said. "I might give a show in Essex in the morning, one in Spencer that afternoon and be over near Dubuque the next morning. I did whatever I had to to get started.

"Gas was cheap, and I'd run 90 miles per hour to get from one show to the next on time. I put 78,000 miles on an old Ford that first year."

In the 1950s, he moved his family to a farm near Stuart, and his children were schooled in Menlo. Rhea accompanied Al on the trips during the summer, and every other year they'd schedule a trip to a country where they were sure there'd be no danger and take the kids.

"When we didn't take them, we'd hire a housekeeper," said Rhea. "That worked out well, except one year when our oldest daughter, a precocious 14, fired the housekeeper and took over herself, while continuing to detassel corn. We about died when we found out."

Over the years, the Bells have traveled in 65 countries, preparing presentations on 28 of them (they've done shows on Alaska twice).

This year's feature is titled "Sons of Egypt," and for next, they plan on returning to Peru to redo their show on a primitive tribe of Indians that only recently abandoned head-hunting.

The Bells spend thousands of dollars making the trips. But they keep their fees to Iowa schools as low as possible. For years, Al charged students a dime apiece. "Most of the schools we go to now are the same ones we've been going to since 1949," he said, "and most now include us as part of their budget and don't charge the kids anything. They consider us as just part of their educational program, which is pretty flattering to us."

Their financial position is "comfortable but not more than that," Bell said. They travel Iowa in a worn and cluttered '76 Cadillac, pulling an Air Stream trailer that is their home on the road.

In the summers, when they're not traveling the world, they headquarter in the Iowa Great Lakes region. But they maintain a mailing address as Box 126, Ankeny, the town where two of their children live.

How long will they keep going? "Don't know," Al said. "We have no retirement plans."

Rhea would like to trim the schedule some, however. "We are getting older, and the travel gets harder every year," she said. "Because of his heart problems, I'd just as soon give up a little of the money we make if it means I can have my Al Bell a little longer."

His eyes do droop with miles and age, but the show seemed fresh as ever when we joined 171 youngsters at a Boone County elementary school recently. There would be 30 minutes of talk, followed by a 25-minute film, which opens with the clanging bell that has become the man's calling card.

A little cornball, a lot cultural.

"Hi boys and girls, it's a great day!" boomed Al Bell, wearing a robe and head wrap. He gave them a hip wiggle, rolled his eyes, and took them all to Egypt.

You don't always recognize a legend when he pops up unexpected (as Bob Ray found out)

April 1979

CENTER POINT, IA. – What we did here Saturday was undertake a new kind of political polling. Sort of. The surest thing about the whole caper is that Center Pointers won't soon forget the day the governor of Iowa sneaked up on them. And photographed them, for goodness sakes!

Now, the serious (and more conventional) polls all have been telling us how just about everybody in Iowa knows of – for that matter, approves of – Bob Ray, who is in his 11th year as governor. Everybody knows ol' Bob.

But the point we were working on here Saturday was if the governor walked right up to folks in an average Iowa town, would they recognize him?

Of course, we didn't trot him up here in a coat and tie and ask people, "Do you know who this man is?" No, we had him dress down in a light jacket, sweater, khaki pants and a flat cap. We slung a couple of cameras around his neck and told him to act like a *Register* photographer, to take pictures of people while they were being interviewed about what's on their minds as winter leaves and spring arrives.

And we made sure none of the 1,800 who live in this town, located between Cedar Rapids and Waterloo, knew ahead of time the governor was going to be here.

We flew him quietly in and out of the nearby Vinton airport. During the two and a half hours we were "working" Center Point, the governor's guard, Highway Patrol Trooper Dale Ward, was never far from his boss, but Ward had abandoned his uniform for blue jeans and a sweater. He went unrecognized by anyone.

But how about Ray?

Well, Clifton Hicks, 61, local garbageman, was tilling his garden when the press team approached him. He's had winter "right up to here," Hicks said while drawing his hand to his neck. The photographer made the camera whir.

And what would Mr. Hicks think of an idea of having the governor of Iowa issue a proclamation every year declaring an official end to winter? "That'd be a good idea," Hicks nodded.

And, speaking of the governor, what does Mr. Hicks think of him?

"Oh, I don't have any kind words for him at all," Hicks said. "I don't think he's got any smarts up here," as he pointed to his head.

The photographer started laughing. Uh, Mr. Hicks, meet Governor Bob Ray.

"I'm sorry I said that about you, governor," a stunned Hicks said after a minute or two.

"That's all right," said Ray. "I'm a big boy. I can take it."

Then there was Stan Primmer, the barber. (Everyone here calls him "Primmer the trimmer," naturally.)

He eyed the photographer the minute he walked in the door. But Primmer politely went ahead and answered the questions about spring while the photographer worked. Finally, Primmer interrupted the interview, looked at the man behind the camera and said, "That's a little unusual line of work for you, isn't it Bob?"

Martha Simanek, 71, who was working in her yard with her husband, Fred, 80, wasn't fooled a second. "Why, you're Governor Ray!" she said immediately. Thereafter, she had no enthusiasm for answering questions about spring. She and Ray discussed transportation problems for the elderly.

Jim Ramsey, who was building a garage in a backyard, looked up and said, "You're Governor Bob Ray, right?" He then went on to explain he's not really a builder, that he was "just doing a little moonlighting on a Saturday."

Said Ray: "So am I."

Then it was over to Elmer Imhoff, a Linn County Roads Department employee who happened to be walking down Main Street. He talked about the sogginess of the back roads, the wetness of the farm fields.

"You don't mind if I take your picture while you talk, do you?" asked the photographer.

"Who the hell are you?" Imhoff shot right back.

"I'm the photographer," said our man.

"What the hell's your name?" the persistent Imhoff said.

"Bob Ray," was the matter-of-fact answer.

Imhoff: "Well . . . you don't say!"

Mr. Imhoff, did we catch you by surprise?

"You sure as hell did!"

Kathy Sebetka was in her backyard, watching with considerable pride while the photographer attempted to take a picture of her children, Mike, 10, and Gloria, 8, flying a kite. She said she'd never before seen the cameraman.

"Bob, didn't you say you'd been in Center Point before?" the writer, carefully avoiding the last name, asked the photographer. The answer was yes.

"Maybe you saw him when he was here before," the writer suggested to the Sebetka woman.

"No, I don't think so," she said. "But we just moved into town from the farm. Maybe we weren't around when he was here."

The photographer, then, just didn't seem at all familiar?

"No, I don't think so," she said.

Surprise!

"He's Governor Ray?" she said, almost in shock. "O! That's terrible!"

Ray: "Well, I don't think I'm that bad."

Sebetka: "O! No. I mean it's terrible I didn't recognize you. O! My gosh! It's just that you don't expect to find the governor of Iowa taking pictures in your backyard!"

"Well," said Ray, "governors are interested in kite flying, too. In fact, governors are often told to go fly kites."

Little Tom Bach, 8, was romping down Main Street with a friendly dog when he was told the man taking his picture was the governor. He didn't seem much impressed.

"You didn't know governors take pictures sometimes, did you?" Ray asked him.

"No," the boy said calmly, "but I'm only in second grade."

The fact is, Tom, the governor is an accomplished amateur photographer. "It's something I've been interested in for years," Ray said. "Before I ran for office, I shot quite a bit, and I always enjoyed doing the lab work in a little darkroom we have in our private home in Des Moines.

"The first few years I was governor, I got completely away from it. I didn't think I had time. But I kept seeing things I'd like to photograph as I traveled around and finally I decided it was silly not to start shooting again. I did and really find it fun."

He warmed up for his assignment here by sharing photographer's duties with his wife, Billie, Friday night at the wedding reception of a friend of one of their three daughters. Then he came to Center Point and proved himself a first-rate lensman.

He did that, incidentally, to the feigned dismay of Warren Hannen, who encountered Ray in a coffee shop. "Oh, brother!" Hannen moaned good-naturedly. "When I go home and tell my wife the governor was running around Center Point shooting pictures, she's going to tell me I've just got to stop spending so much time in the tavern."

A requiem for the most famous rooster Iowa ever produced

December 1980

CHARLES CITY, IA. – Nothing is tougher than a death in the family at Christmastime. That is why Donna Weatherwax, 56, who lives on a farm south of this northern Iowa community, is grieving so.

"At least I can talk about it today," she said Monday morning. "I found him Saturday morning on the floor of the garage, and I just wasn't myself the rest of the weekend. But now I can even laugh about him again, especially as I think back on the fun we had together."

Yes, "Baby" is gone, the apparent victim of old age and cold weather. He and Weatherwax were not really kin, but they were sure the fastest of friends. They had been almost constant companions the past eight and a half years.

He was without doubt Iowa's most famous rooster, perhaps the world's. Baby's talent for crowing on command took him and Weatherwax to California where they appeared on the "Johnny Carson Tonight Show." There were some 20 other public appearances over the years, too. And there must have been 100 radio interviews over the phone from the farm here. The rooster and his pal were on radio shows in virtually all the states, as well as on two in Australia, two in Canada and one in Guam. I am not kidding.

"Crow pretty, crow pretty, crow pretty Baby," Weatherwax would say

softly. The bird's body would shake, its neck would extend and he'd crow a crow that'd bring tears to the eyes of those who'd been raised on farms but had moved on to alarm clock lives.

As long as Weatherwax slipped him a kernel of corn after each crow, he would keep it up almost indefinitely. That made him a four-time champion at the crowing contest held during the Dairy Cattle Congress in Waterloo.

Alas, the old boy was not himself the past year, and Weatherwax said Monday it was probably merciful he went when he did. "The arthritis in his hip was so bad you could hear it crunching when he walked," she said. "And he just wasn't getting enough exercise. The muscles were deteriorating and he had lost about two pounds from his prime. I don't suppose he would've been five pounds soaking wet in the last few weeks."

He seldom crowed in his final year, because he didn't feel good and because his beak was sore. The beak never stopped growing, and Weatherwax had to trim it several times. He was having toenail trouble, too, if that's what roosters call it.

There was a time when Weatherwax swore she thought Baby was the reincarnation of her first husband, the late Russell Weatherwax. "I know people thought I was crazy when I talked about that, but I really believed it," she said. "His mannerisms were so much like Russell's. Lots of people remembered how Russell, when he was happy, would throw back his head and crow like a rooster.

"But a couple of years ago, I found out that just couldn't be," she said. "I talked to Beatrice Leydecker—she's that great animal specialist in California. She's been on the 'Tonight Show,' too. She tells pet owners what their animals think of them. Anyway, Beatrice told me animals have a kind of ESP, and they act the way they think you want them to act. So maybe Baby thought I wanted him to act like Russell. Still, I'll never get over how much Baby's voice sounded like Russell's."

Weatherwax said she knows people "smirk" about how close she became to the rooster. "Maybe that's why I'm divorced, too," she said, noting that a second marriage failed. "I think the reason Baby took to me so was I happened to be in the hen house right after he was born," she said. "I was probably the first thing he saw. Later, his mother would chase him away, even though he was not really ready to be on his own. So he'd come follow me around the yard, and that's when I started giving him corn."

Weatherwax said that on Monday, Baby will "lie in state" in the garage until her brother gets here for Christmas and can help her dig a grave in the frozen ground.

Tributes were coming by mail and phone. "It's pretty obvious Baby gave a lot of people a lot of fun," Weatherwax said.

I know I am proud to have been a booster of this rooster. I will miss him. He was always good copy.

You've never heard of Clifford McMurry, but what he did is legendary

September 1983

PROMISE CITY, IA. – They come by the dozens now to see Clifford McMurry's rock. They marvel at it, in fact.

You see, there are some things man simply must do. Things that seem sort of crazy even. But they dare us in some weird way that ultimately lures us to the task. There are those guys who scale the Sears Tower in Chicago. There was the woman who swam twice around Manhattan Island. And people ride bicycles all the way across Iowa each summer. Some things just must be done.

For 41-year-old Clifford McMurry, the challenge this summer was moving a rock. A big rock, mind you: a granite boulder 12 feet by 13 feet by 17 feet, weighing 200 tons. That's a very big rock.

McMurry, it should be said right here at the top, is no flake. He is a farmer, as solid as the rock itself. "A practical man," said his wife, Arlene, also 41.

"The rock sat in a deep draw out in my back pasture," said Mr. Practical, whose farm is three miles north of this south-central Iowa town of 150. "A glacial rock. Been there billions of years probably. My dad and all his brothers and sisters played on it when they were kids. I did, too. Only part of it stuck up out of the ground, but it was big enough they square-danced on it, and they say somebody once put a horse and buggy up on it and took a picture of it.

"I'd been thinking about moving it for a few years now, and when the drought hit like it did this summer, I knew in my lifetime I'd probably never get such ideal conditions to move it, the ground being so hard and all. So the drought was good for something, I guess. I wanted to move it from where it's always been out there up so it'd be next to my farm buildings. That's three-quarters of a mile, as the crow flies."

Of course, 200-ton boulders don't move as the crow flies. They move, or at least this one did, only after you line up three of those huge, rubber-tired earth movers and then string two-inch-thick cable from the machines to the rock. Behind the rock, you position two big bulldozers that *heave* while the earth movers *ho*. That's a force of 2,000 horsepower. It was only barely enough.

In 100-degree heat on moving day, July 30, the great tires were spinning, the diesel engines were screaming for mercy and 70 spectators were sweating in absolute awe. "It was a very emotional day," said Arlene, "a day full of highs and lows. It was exhausting."

You can bet it was also expensive, but the McMurrys won't provide details.

"The contractor and I agreed we wouldn't put out any figure," Clifford said. "He was able to give me a good price because he already had his equipment in the neighborhood on a road project. He said no way could he make that good a deal to somebody else, and, besides, I don't really think he's much interested in moving any more rocks like mine."

The rock was tugged, coaxed, pushed, cussed and pulled up a 300-foot Wayne County hill, then along a ridge through a pasture and a soybean field.

In the bean field, so much dirt was pushing up in front of the rock that they had to stop for a time. The earth movers scraped away two feet of the soft topsoil to expose the firmer subsoil. The friction was terrific when the rock was eventually dragged across that strip of clay. When a neighbor put his hand on the ground where the rock had just been, he had to snap it back because of the great heat.

Few believed ahead of time that McMurry would ever get the rock moved. "When my uncles and aunts saw the rock, with all the dirt dug away from it down in that draw, and realized how big it really was, there wasn't none of them said that thing could be moved," he said. "I got discouraged sometimes, but I never gave up."

Two earlier attempts had failed. In early June, five farm tractors with dual wheels and three bulldozers could budge it no more than 15 feet. Later, the three earth movers and two bulldozers moved it 100 feet, but then the mission was scuttled because all the smaller cables being used were snapping.

But on that scorcher in late July, they indeed had the thing moving along the one-mile route to a spot adjacent to the comfortable McMurry farm home. At one point, the huge machines had the rock moving so well that McMurry had to jog to keep up with it.

When they got it out of the fields and on a gravel road for the final few hundred feet of the trip, the last doubters caved in and began hailing McMurry's feat. On a videotape the family made of the proceedings, farmers can be heard yelling, "Go for it!"

"I'd been the talk of the county all summer," McMurry said the other day as he looked back on that magic moment when he knew he'd won in his struggle with the rock. "In fact, I probably still am. They were all speculating on whether or not we could move the thing, how much all this was costing me and whether I was crazy.

"I think the thing I'll remember the best about that point when we knew we were going to make it was something one of my neighbors, Paul Koch, said. I don't know whether you should talk like this in the newspaper, but this is what he said when we got the rock up on the road: 'Dammit, you're going to get that sucker up there!' I felt a lot of satisfaction right then."

And that sucker is up there now, something to behold. The McMurrys keep a spiral notebook out there so visitors can sign in and leave comments. One left the other day: "Only an Iowa farmer could have done this."

Clifford checks the rock often, not in fear of anyone stealing it, of course, but rather to look in wonder at a dream fulfilled.

Why did he do it?

"You know, it's hard for me to say exactly why I did do it," he said.

It just had to be done, that's all.

The one story that my predecessor Gordon Gammack never put in print

June 1979

There's talk that the recently released book *Gordon Gammack: Columns from Three Wars,* may wind up being used as a text in history and journalism classes. With good reason, too.

The collected reportage of Gammack, the *Register and Tribune* columnist who died in 1974 at the age of 65, gives keen insights into wars and the men who fight them. The insights are especially revealing for readers who were not yet born, or are too young to remember, when Gammack was writing about World War II, Korea, Vietnam.

But, alas, the book has a shortcoming. It lacks the very human story that unfolded in Gammack's own household in Des Moines while he was chasing GIs all over the world.

It's the kind of story Gammack would have molded into several columns—had it happened in some home other than his own: the woman coping with keeping a young family together while her man went off to war. And not just one war, *three* of them.

So imagine how it was one day in the spring of 1943. Keep in mind that Gordon, a young reporter, was exempt from military duty because he'd been blinded in one eye in a car accident. And remember that Kaye, who'd worked at the phone company, was not accustomed to being away from her husband. In fact, she'd never in her life spent a night alone until, after their marriage in 1940, Gordon began traveling on business in Iowa. The first night he was away, she had a friend stay over. And two other bits of background are important to this scene: Little Katy, their daughter, was barely 2. Kaye was pregnant.

Here comes an excited Gordon home from work at mid-afternoon to tell his wife he'll be going off to the war after all!

The reaction?

"I was thrilled for him. No kidding, I really was," Kaye Gammack, 64, recalled during a recent visit at her home here. "I knew it would be tough, but I also knew from the beginning that Gordy was a newspaperman, first and foremost. I always said I hoped things for him never came down to a choice between me and the paper. The big story of the day was the war."

Ah, she really took the news that well?

"I did *not* weep and moan and feel sorry for myself," she said. "But, remember, everyone was in the same boat then. There were a lot of women with children being left at home while the men went to war.

"It was a patriotic war, if you know what I mean, and everyone knew they had to put their shoulders to the wheel and do the best they could. I guess the one thing I had a horror of was the possibility of having the baby without Gordy being here," she said. "But the newspaper bosses agreed to let him stay until the baby was born. At the same time, they were anxious for him to get going. Finally, the doctor said if necessary, he could force labor.

"I'll never forget going in for a checkup at about the time I thought I was due. The doctor told me I was nowhere near ready to deliver, and I thought, 'Oh, no! Gordy might have to leave!' I went right home from the doctor's office, did the knee-to-chest exercises and scrubbed the floor. The next morning, Tommy was born."

Two days later, the correspondent was en route to his first war. He was gone, the first time, for a full year.

"I had it a little easier than most wives," Kaye said. "Some women wouldn't hear from their husbands for six weeks at a time. But the newspaper kept me informed about what Gordy was doing, and I heard from him regularly by letter and telegram. I didn't really worry about him, because he'd promised me he wouldn't take unnecessary chances. Besides, his bosses had told him a dead war correspondent was no good to anybody. I frequently reminded him to follow that theory."

She did volunteer work at the local hospitals when she could line up a babysitter. She went crazy trying to shop for groceries while simultaneously battling a "terrible two" and shouldering an infant. She went the better part of the year wearing leg makeup because nylons were in such short supply.

When she got up around 4 A.M. for the night feeding, she'd grab the just-delivered *Register* and read her husband's stories—written from all over North Africa, Italy, France. She clipped the stories and placed them carefully in scrapbooks.

For a time, she moved with the kids to a cottage at Lake Okoboji. The correspondent, meanwhile, was basing himself at a press camp in Italy.

"He wrote how he loved that, because he got to know the other correspondents," she said. "At one point, in a telegram to the paper, he mentioned how he was going off to some certain place, then he'd be 'coming back home.' At first they thought he meant Iowa, but then they found out he was referring to the press camp. That made me see red. I wrote him that if he'd been there so long he was calling that damned press camp 'home' then it was time for him to get back to Des Moines."

He returned.

"I thought he was home to stay until one night, someone at the paper slipped and said something to him about, 'When you go back . . . ' I blew up. But I got used to the idea, and it wasn't so bad."

He was home six weeks before the second trip to the European theater. The second stay wasn't as long as the first. Five years later, he was preparing to leave again – for the first of three short trips to Korea.

And just as in 1943, Gordon was wondering whether he'd get to see a new baby before he left. He delayed leaving and the newspaper editors fretted until Julie was born in August 1950. A day or two after the birth, the beaming father was gone.

"I guess when he was gone to Korea, that was the toughest time for me," Kaye said. "Katy was 9, Tommy was 7 and Julie was just a baby. It was really like I was a single parent. The two older ones made a lot bigger demands on me than they had as babies. I'd be looking around for reinforcement on my decisions about them, and there'd be no one to give it – except for the Dr. Spock books and the comforting advice of our family physician.

"God, how the kids fought. I'd try to keep the blunt instruments hidden away from them so they couldn't beat each other bloody. I swore there was no way they'd ever be friends, but darned if they don't like each other now. When Gordy would come home, that's when we really had to be intelligent parents. It would've been easy for him to avoid jumping right in as a dispenser of discipline, to let the kids play one of us off against the other. But we'd visit in letters about how to make the transition to a two-parent home when he got home, and he'd always step right in."

Then came Vietnam.

"He was in his sixties when I asked him to go [there]," Drake Mabry, a managing editor at the newspapers, wrote in a foreword to the book. "It was a request, not an order. The hardships can be overwhelming at that age. The decision was his."

Kaye recalled the assignment as one of "the biggest thrills" in both their lives. "It was a matter of being proud he'd still be considered for such a thing," she said. "It was like he'd been told he wasn't over the hill. It made us both happy."

The kids were beyond the battling stage during his three trips to Vietnam, but there was a different kind of difficulty for Kaye to face. "People our age were all couples again during Vietnam," she said. "I was more lonely. Friends were kind enough to keep extending invitations, but I felt a little awkward going to things alone, at least after a while. And in the later years of the war, it was so unpopular. It was more difficult making the sacrifices of being alone than it had been during World War II, when everyone was behind the cause."

Their time together after his final return from Vietnam was short. Lung cancer took Gordon in November 1974. But they continued to share what time was left with the many friends he'd made while overseas during three wars.

"I really think just about everyone Gordy met during the wars has been through this place at one time or another," Kaye said from the porch of the Gammack home located near Terrace Hill. "The conversations about the old times were always a lot of fun."

And those conversations are being renewed in the aftermath of the publication of the book, which is peppered with the names of those old buddies.

The idea for the book was daughter Julie's. She left a position in the Iowa Democratic Party to coordinate production and promotion of the work. She's 29, recently married and living in Des Moines.

Tom, 36, manages a record shop in Fort Collins, Colorado. Katy, 38, is a public affairs coordinator for Planned Parenthood in Des Moines.

The book was edited by Andrea Clardy, a free-lance writer formerly from Ames, now living in Ithaca, New York. It features introductions by several of Gammack's colleagues in journalism, in addition to the war columns.

"It was an exciting, but teary, experience for me when I read the first copy," Kaye said. "I couldn't take it all at once. But as I read through it, I remember the stories as they first ran in the paper. I recall what I was doing at that particular time, how old the kids were, what we were all going through.

"It's been thrilling, you know?"

Byron Godbersen has lots of toys – and they may get him yet

November 1983

IDA GROVE, IA. – All his adult life, Byron Godbersen has been living proof of the old saw that the main difference between men and boys is the price of their toys. His toys, always high-ticket items, have become especially costly lately. They nearly cost him his life – and they might yet if somebody doesn't talk some sense into him. Getting Godbersen to listen to something he needs to hear, but doesn't want to, has always been a problem for those close to him. It's even tougher now, a time when, according to his son Bruce, "he's just grumpy as the devil."

Godbersen, 58, as you must know, is Mr. Big in this northwest Iowa town of 2,300. He is the industrial genius who built a fortune on boat trailers and boat hoists, and then began spending it on castles, chalets, moats, towers, arches, knights in armor (albeit concrete armor), a shopping center, a palatial roller skating rink and other projects here.

Awhile back, he got into electric trains. He built an incredible layout, one that fills his whole two-car garage. Push a button and a huge board comes hydraulically down from the ceiling. On it, 18 trains run on tracks that rise six feet through a setting of towns, farms, valleys and mountains. The controls are in a console that looks like the cockpit of a small airplane.

Ah, airplanes. Godbersen has been a pilot for years. He flies a twin-engine Cessna and does it well enough that he was able to qualify again for a license after having triple bypass heart surgery five years ago.

But besides real airplanes, he also has become deeply interested in one-fifth-scale, radio-controlled model airplanes. First it was a hobby. Then he organized a company, Byron Originals, to build model kits that are now recognized as about the best in the world. You may recall he put on a fantastic air show here last summer when he and his fellow modelers had gathered for their annual convention.

Not long ago, he decided what he really needed was a one-fifth-

25

scale airport to demonstrate his one-fifth-scale planes. So on a hill behind his breathtaking home, he had his employees built a 600-foot concrete runway. He plans to add scale-size hangars, a control tower and even radio-controlled model fire engines and ambulances – all to make it more realistic.

The model airport challenged his imagination, in more ways than one. The more he thought about it, the more he wanted to try to land his full-size, twin-engine Cessna on that 600-foot runway. Landing this type plane normally requires 3,000 feet.

Everyone said he was crazy. He answered: "This is one of those things you just have to do." He did it, all right, on a morning when conditions were perfect. "I got it in there, used only 500 feet of the runway and never skidded it at all," he said.

He let it sit as proof he did it. But by the time bragging rights were exercised, conditions weren't right for a takeoff. In fact, experienced pilots told Godbersen conditions would never be right. An attempt to fly the big plane off the hill, they said, would be asking for disaster.

So he stewed. That evening, he climbed aboard his huge Honda motorcycle, rode up the hill and stewed some more. And as he did, he lost control of the cycle on wet grass and it dumped him against a curb. Six broken ribs, broken collarbone, dislocated shoulder, serious internal bleeding.

He spent a week in the hospital here. The internal bleeding became so bad he nearly died. Finally, he had to be taken by helicopter ambulance to a Sioux City hospital where, after a long stay in intensive care, his condition stabilized.

He is now home, recovering but suffering. "Bypass heart surgery was a Sunday picnic compared to this," he said. "I'm in agony with these ribs. Let me tell you, I almost throw up anytime I see a motorcycle. I don't know why I even messed with one. Damned thing about got me." On doctor's orders, he is also taking off 50 of what had been his 280 pounds. He's halfway there.

Meanwhile, the twin-engine Cessna sits on the hill. "Sometime in, oh, three or four weeks, when I'm feeling better, I'm going to fly it out of there," he said. "No problem. I'll be the only one who knows when the time is right. When it is, I'll do it. Yes, a lot of pilots are saying I shouldn't, but a lot of pilots have never flown off anything but 5,000-foot runways and don't know anything about flying off marginal runways. I do."

[Godbersen's employees later towed the plane from the mini-runway, probably saving their boss's life but making him mad as hell.]

The Everly Brothers, as they prepared to play their first-ever hometown concert in Shenandoah

June 1986

SHENANDOAH, IA. – You want to know how big a deal it is, this return next Saturday of rock 'n' roll Hall of Famers the Everly Brothers for a first-ever hometown concert?

There are several ways to measure it:

Everly fans from California to New York have ordered tickets and booked travel arrangements to a town they've heretofore probably never heard of.

As a 100- by 30-foot covered stage was under construction on the west end of the business district, a couple of rubberneckers driving past on Railroad Avenue ran head-on into each other.

The Reverend Edythe Stirlen, who is 92 but still active in the ministry, was asked some time ago if she'd perform a wedding July 5. "No," she said, "I'm sorry, but I'm going to the concert." Not only was she a radio evangelist on the same local station that carried the Everly family in the late 1940s and early 1950s, she also was their neighbor for a time. That was when they were living in a cottage that rented for $12 per month and which, said Stirlen, "was so small they had to go outside to change their minds."

Phil Everly, speaking for both himself and brother Don in a recent phone interview, said that despite the thousands of shows the duo has done, "this one in Shenandoah will rank right up there with our reunion concert in London two years ago as being something special.

"Of all the places you want to be at your best, it's in the old hometown. This is a little nerve-wracking. It's one thing to play a concert in New York or L.A. or anywhere else, but it's quite another thing for us to play Shenandoah. I know the people will probably be kinder than a lot of audiences, but still, we want our music to be the absolute best it can be."

This is where it all started for them, playing with their father, the late "Cousin Ike" Everly, and their mother, Margaret, on radio stations KMA and KFNF, which had been founded by those legendary nurserymen and promoters, Earl May and Henry Field. Back then, the Everlys were thought to show considerable promise, but they were really no more special than a bunch of other live entertainers who worked on those two stations.

Phil, now 47, was asked recently to consider whether he or Don, now 49, could have conceived back then that someday they'd be bigger than Earl May and Henry Field put together—bigger, in fact, several times over.

"Not only could I not have conceived that then," he answered, "I still can't make myself believe that now. Those two guys, they were the giants. They always will be."

Lest you think he is being overly gushy about the old hometown and the coming concert, you should know of the serious financial commitment the Everly Brothers have made here. Their share of the concert income is expected to be between $25,000 and $35,000. They are going to donate almost all of it to endow a just-created "Everly Family Scholarship" which will give college scholarships to Shenandoah High graduates and provide funds for needy grade school and high school students who can't afford equipment and supplies to participate in extracurricular activities.

"I remember what it's like to be a penny short," said Phil. "Funny to think about that now, but it wasn't then. We want to help. We don't want to take anything out of the community. We want to put something back in it."

And just as they are remembering what they call "our growing-up hometown," this community is remembering them.

U.S. Highway 59, the main thoroughfare on the west edge of town, has been given a second name, "Everly Brothers Avenue," and will be dedicated on the afternoon of the concert.

Artist Larry Greenwalt, who lives and works here but is known throughout the region, has painted two huge portraits of the Everlys, the way they looked when they left here and first found fame, to hang onstage under a sign that says simply, "Welcome Home." The portraits are done in the Shenandoah High School colors of maroon and white.

Finally, when it's all over, a monument will be erected on the corner of the property where the concert will be held. It will include a photo of the brothers, as well as the stories of their start here and of their return. The special nature of it is told in the fact that it will be adjacent to another monument on the same spot, that one telling how President Theodore Roosevelt spoke right there in 1903.

This is the work of 32-year-old Shenandoah businessman Bill Hillman, who, with an army of friends who volunteered to help, is making this whole homecoming event happen. Hillman is personally on the line for $100,000 with this project.

"I have two goals," he said recently. "The first is to break even and the second is to make sure that Don and Phil have a great time here."

As a boy, Hillman heard his grandmother (who is the Stirlen mentioned earlier) and others tell tales of the Everlys years here. He "always thought it would be neat" if they would come back and perform here, but he became almost obsessed with the idea after the brothers ended a 10-year separation in 1984 and began performing together again.

His first phone calls to their agents resulted in curt turndowns, but then he enlisted the aid of Jim Danielson, 48, a Shenandoah native now working in public television in Lincoln, Nebraska. Danielson was the Everly boys' tightest pal in their youth and continues to visit them frequently. Danielson contacted "Donald and Phillip," as he still calls them, and suddenly the Everlys' agents became more receptive to Hillman's frequent calls.

The Shenandoah date was placed near the start of a four-month-long Everly tour that began two weeks ago in Detroit. They will play Thursday and Friday in Minneapolis before coming here in their fleet of chartered buses.

The event has already brought worldwide media attention to Shenandoah, and CBS-TV is planning to have a news crew in the community much of this week.

The roots of the Everlys are being deeply probed. The stories will tell how their parents brought them here from Kentucky as infants, how they grew into clean-cut, well-groomed high school boys before live radio died and the family packed all of its belongings into an old, pea-green Chevy and left for Tennessee in 1952.

"We weren't all that special when we were in Shenandoah," said Phil. "We didn't stand out. We did all the normal things – playing ball, working in the fields, delivering papers – but we also happened to be kids playing on the radio. None of our friends thought that was all that unusual. They were used to entertainers being around. We were accepted. Nobody made fun of us for being musicians. Well, nobody did that as long as we could hold our own on the playground, and we could."

In the decades since they became idols with hits like "Bye Bye Love" and "Wake Up Little Susie," Phil has returned once, in 1958, when he stayed with Danielson's parents and had a long line of Shenandoah teenagers following him around town. Don, the more reclusive of the two, drove through Shenandoah once while on a cross-country trip but did not stop.

They have welcomed Shenandoahans backstage at some of their concerts over the years, including old girlfriends like Carol Lee Knittle Copeland, now of Mission, Kansas; Rosanne Rodgers Vincent, now of Des Moines, and Judy Knittle Rea, now of Red Oak.

"We were all very young when we dated," said Rea. "I don't think any of us girls had any idea the Everlys would become as famous as they are. When I've seen Don in later years, it's been fun to visit with him about old friends, and it's been a fun thing to tell my own kids that I dated him. But we're all different people now than we were then."

Indeed. Although Rea and Copeland plan to be at the Shenandoah concert, Vincent said she'd have to miss it to stay home in Des Moines "and babysit a grandson."

It's about the same for the Everlys as they approach the age of 50. Phil, who lives in North Hollywood, California, has two sons but is currently divorced after two marriages. Don, who lives in Nashville, has a son and three daughters and recently told a reporter he is engaged to a woman who would be his fifth wife.

Danielson said he has talked with both of them about their personal failures through the years, including the marriages, alcohol and drug problems and financial reversals "that all seem to go with fame and the entertainment industry.

"They've come through that," he said. "Now both of them are pretty straight people. As an old friend, I'm always telling them I don't mind their being rich, it's their being famous which is a problem. When we're together, we can't go out and do all the things together we'd like to, just because it's difficult for them to be relaxed and themselves when they're in public. Hopefully it won't be as much that way for them in Shenandoah."

Ah, yes, Shenandoah.

Have the Everlys ever considered doing a song about the place? After all, it is, as Phil said, "where we were taught all those principles we still live by—honor, love, country, family, friends."

"Yeah, we've talked about it," he said, "but it's one of those things we'd have to sit down and write ourselves, and we hardly have a chance anymore to do that.

"There's another way to look at this, though," he continued. "Even though we've never written a song titled 'Shenandoah' or that had the name of the town in it, just about all of our songs have pieces of Shenandoah in them. It's so much a part of what we are that it becomes a part of everything we do."

A very brief look at the man who saved Davenport—V. O. Figge

May 1981

DAVENPORT, IA.—No discussion of the upper crust here would be complete without mention of the venerable and still very active V. O. Figge, 80. Chairman of the board of the powerful Davenport Bank and Trust Co., he came during the Depression when bank failures were epidemic and restored order in the financial community.

"There is no one like V. O. Figge," said Miss Hortense Finch, who has known him for decades. "He has built up great trust in the community. When my friends say 'Davenport Bank,' it's almost like they're speaking with reverence."

One of his past dinner partners described Figge as a total charmer. However, he has spent little charm over the years on reporters, who consider him something of a curmudgeon. So let's salute him this way:

V. O. Figge, local biggy,
Doesn't talk to press.
So for more about this man,
You'll simply have to guess.

Killing a caper that was threatening to make me a legend for something I'd come to hate

August 1986

Today I slay a 4-year-old monster. No more Roll Poll.

That's right—no more rating of Iowa's best cinnamon rolls. I appreciate the love you pour into your dough. I thank you for the extra pinches of cinnamon you've added just for me.

Your considerable effort expended in mailing and delivering them to me always leaves me awestruck. Your pilgrimages to the various homes of the great rolls I've selected have amazed me.

But, folks, enough is enough. I've had your cinnamon rolls right up to here. Will you still love me?

One bit of roll playing remains. As scheduled, I will judge the rolls August 14 at the Iowa State Fair. I will walk out there in the spotlights, take samples from 100 or more plates of rolls, crawl back behind the curtain and puke. Then I intend not to eat another cinnamon roll for a good, long time.

I came to this decision on days two and three of RAGBRAI-XIV. On day two, from Red Oak to Audubon, I was given 18 cinnamon rolls. I had them in my bike bag. I had them in two different vans. For crying out loud, I had an Iowa State Patrol trooper lugging them in for me. And when I got to my motel, lusting for a cold beer, who should knock on my room door but a wonderful lady with a great big cinnamon roll.

Day three began with breakfast at Gary's restaurant in Audubon, which has always had a glorious roll. I ordered eggs, ham and coffee. I got that — and a roll. I pedaled on over to Guthrie Center. On the way out of that community is the infamous (among bike riders) "Tank Hill," a particularly cruel climb, certainly the worst on our RAGBRAI route. Halfway up to the water tower — at a point where no cyclist in his right mind would stop — was a sign in front of a residence saying, "Sorry, Offenburger, no sweet rolls here." I was so thrilled that I stopped. The lady was kidding on the sign. She had a roll for me.

Just west of Panora, another roll — 10 inches in diameter — had been specially made for me. The Methodists in Panora had more. In Perry, someone gave me a plate of nine of them. My cycle mate, John Karras, was howling about it all. "Young man," he said, "I knew it was going to come to this. Why didn't you think ahead when you started this madness?"

So how did it start? I was snookered by a college sharpie. In 1982, one Jim Larson was an ISU student commuting to Des Moines from Ames for a summer internship at the *Register*. He was always marveling at the rolls he'd get each morning at a little beanery in Alleman. One day he brought me one and said: "You know, every restaurant in Iowa has these things. You ought to rate them, just like the sports guys rate basketball teams."

I fell for it. My erudite colleagues in the newsroom at first thought this was so much hooey. What are we doing with a columnist rating sweet rolls, they'd sneer, when there are Serious Issues with which to deal? Of course, that was before the carefully wrapped packages of Iowa's best rolls started arriving in the mail and by special delivery. Thereafter, they'd attack the platters like a pack of ill-mannered yahoos who hadn't been fed in a week.

Cinnamon rolls have been very, very good to me. They have brought me speaking engagements and other invitations. They have made me statewide chairman of the Iowa Restaurant Association's annual "Coffee Day," which raises money for retarded citizens. They have been my introduction to some of the warmest, sweetest people a guy could ever hope to meet.

Cinnamon rolls have been very, very bad to me. They have

bloated me. They have resulted in great controversy, like the time I screwed up the recipe of a state fair champion roll and had cooks all over Iowa standing in their kitchens as watery dough dripped from their countertops to the linoleum. Or the time when we named the wrong person as the blue ribbon roll baker at the fair.

I've had rolls made of nutritional, but boring, whole wheat dough.

I've had rolls with mashed potatoes stirred into them.

I've had rolls shaped like bicycles and naked women.

I've had rolls that melted in my mouth.

I've had rolls, not sufficiently cooked, that chewed like rubber.

Yes, I've had rolls right up to here.

It's not all good news out there. Some awful things happen in Iowa. When they do, they trigger wide discussion and examination. Eventually they become a fascinating, if painful, part of our lore.

LORE

Drinking, taunting and brawling, Butch Berenger dared all of northwest Iowa to cross him

June 1978

SPENCER, IA. – There are more than a few around here who think Donald Dean "Butch" Berenger, 44, is a man from another time. His lawyer, Mark Soldat, said Butch seems to live by, and believe in, "a sort of frontier justice." And Mike Patrick, 31, a beer truck driver who's tangled with Butch a few times, said Berenger reminds him of "one of those guys you see in old westerns, you know, the ragged guy who rides into town on an old brown horse after days on the trail, grabs a whiskey and then runs his mouth."

Check this one from Butch himself: "Anytime two fellas can't go out in the street, or in the backyard, have a good fist fight, then go back inside, forget it and have a drink together – anytime that can't happen without charges being filed back and forth – then they aren't real men to start with."

Butch has done lots of fighting. "Once I was in three fights in eight days, and I was on crutches at the time," he said in an interview. "But no one's ever tied me to no gun, or any other weapon. You ask people who know me and they'll tell you they never seen old Butch hit anybody with anything but his fists."

He's a big man, 6 feet 2 inches, 210 pounds. He's ruggedly handsome, with a dark complexion, steely eyes and black hair that's going gray. He has a barrel chest, huge thick hands and a long, bold stride despite foot structure so bad that a couple of toes stand almost straight up.

He's an odd-jobber, basically, who works when he must. He said, "One of the proudest things I've ever done in my life is work for Herman Gustoff & Sons Salvage Yard in Spencer off and on for 20 years."

He once told a jury he "just exists," and he now lives alone in a three-bedroom house on the east side of Spencer. He slurps great quantities of beer. "Once I start drinking, I'm likely to drink all night and all day, maybe three six-packs or a case in a day," he said.

He's encountered romance. Marriage? we asked. Butch, after a long pause, answered: "I would say I've been married approximately six times."

His most recent marriage started when a magistrate read Butch and the bride their vows in Butch's bedroom. Why there? "That's where we wanted it," he said. The relationship was an intense, often stormy one. "Once she tried to make me stop fighting some guys by smashing me over the head with a beer bottle. That smarted, made me mad, too." That marriage ended in divorce a year ago.

Butch has done his fighting, all right, and as a result, he's spent lots of time in court—which he fancies as a place where lesser men do their battling.

The northwest Iowa *Morning Herald* reported here last Sunday that since July 1975, there have been 49 charges brought against Butch in the Clay County Magistrate and District Courts. Most of those charges related in one way or another to drinking or brawling, and Butch has beat most of them. From seven to eleven of the charges are still pending, court officials say, explaining it's difficult to keep tabs on the stages of all the different litigation against Butch.

"It's a joke around here," says Billie Schomaker, 39, a Royal farmer who's fought Butch. "When he goes to court, guys bet that he'll get off one way or another. And he usually does."

Of course, the *Herald*'s study of the records covered only the most recent three years in the man's history before justice. It's a fair statement, said County Attorney Ron Barrick, that Butch, over say the past 25 years, has been arrested "dozens and dozens of times." Butch, however, says that's "going a little too far . . . just dozens would be closer to right."

Study the records and you'll find that in all that time, there's been only one serious rap—a felony, they call it—that Butch didn't elude. That was his 1968 conviction for breaking and entering a garage in Gillett Grove, a tiny town in the southeast part of the county. Butch was sentenced to 10 years in prison. He served 18 months before getting paroled.

Butch wins in court, said Barrick, "because people will file charges against him and then refuse to testify, or we'll file our own charges and people will refuse to cooperate as witnesses because they fear him."

Butch, naturally, disputes that. He says he wins because the cops and the public file unjustified charges against him and because the prosecutors up this way "are just terrible. . . . Old Barrick is a nice enough guy, he's just a bad lawyer."

Many times, he has represented himself in magistrate court, and Barrick concedes that "Butch can handle himself pretty well there." But when the legal action gets heavy, Butch seeks, and usually gets, court-appointed attorneys, who are paid from county funds.

Ostensibly, he's got lots of assets — a Cadillac, a pickup, a wrecker, a motorcycle, at least two houses and a tavern he operated in the small town of Rossie before he and his last wife split.

But Butch explained that while he's got "access" to a lot, he owns little — that instead he's just "affiliated" with those assets. What that means, he said, is "that a lot of times, I'll have done some work for someone, and they'll give me something that's in their name, even if I make the payments on it. That's just hog-trading, and you can't get by in this world without some hog-trading."

The city of Spencer is unconvinced about his indigency and has gone to court resisting Butch's most recent requests for court-appointed attorneys. That matter is unresolved. Clay County folks will tell you the fact that they always seem to end up paying Butch's legal bills really gets their goat.

Goat? That's another story. Butch has two of them, which until mid-week were penned outside his house. One's named Ron, after County Attorney Barrick, and the other's named Phil, after County Sheriff Phil Nelson.

There are laws against keeping livestock in town, but Butch figured he'd come up with a way around the law by posting a sign on the animals' cage saying they were genuine "registered racing goats," and thus not common stock. But he confided in the interview that he was just kidding everyone about them being racers. Ron and Phil, he said, "are nothing but just a pair of goats."

The city never did challenge their presence in his yard, and in recent days, Butch moved them to the country. "I got tired of looking at [them]," he said, "and they were starting to smell some."

Butch is obviously a character — and always has been.

He was next to the youngest in a Depression-era, Clay County farm family with 14 children. His father died when he was 7, and about the same time, the family moved from the Royal area to near Dickens, where Butch grew up.

Several of his brothers and sisters still live around the area, but you can learn little from them about Butch as a boy. One brother, Wayne, refused a request for an interview, saying that Butch is "making a fool of himself" by talking to reporters. Sister Helen, who runs a tavern in Royal, called him an unkind name and said, "He's not my brother; he's my mother's son." (Butch said he gets along "fair to middlin' " with his kin.)

Butch went to school through the ninth grade, he said, "tried tenth grade three times and couldn't make it, then quit and joined the Air Force," serving two years.

He draws a veteran's pension of $145 per month because of his bad feet. The rest of his regular income, he said, is $214 per month he receives because of a mental condition that has been diagnosed — and documented in court testimony — as "manic depression."

He said he once spent 60-some days in the state Mental Health Institute at Cherokee, where "they were trying to get me proved criminally insane, but I left that place the same person I was when I went in."

The stories about Butch are legend in Clay County. They have him bashing cops regularly with his fists, sassing nearly everyone and being barred or unwelcome at more than half the county's taverns. "The stories are all inflated," said Butch. "There's no way one man could do all I'm supposed to have done."

All of the law enforcement officials who were interviewed agreed.

Said Sheriff Nelson: "I walk down the street and people say, 'When are you going to do something about Butch . . . he's killed so many people.' Well, most of it turns out to be gossip, with no substantiation at all. The gossip is hurting us. It's made a mountain out of a molehill. But he is a big man, one who can be intimidating, and so the stories grow."

County Attorney Barrick: "From my standpoint, Butch is like a public nuisance, you know? He causes a lot of fights in bars and other small problems. The public looks at what he does cumulatively, but as a prosecutor, I've got to look at each incident individually, and other than the one felony, he hasn't done much that we could really go after him on.

"People ask why we can't get him as a habitual criminal, but the Code of Iowa requires that there be two prior felony convictions before that's possible. And people talk about the police being afraid of him. I don't think they are at all. Sometimes it takes several of them to control him, but they don't hesitate to control him when that's necessary."

Nearly everyone agrees that Butch is a much different person sober than he is drunk. Even Butch agrees. "I can go out and drink all day and have a lot of fun," he said, "until someone will make a bad remark about me, my ex-wife, anything. They'll get me all riled up and hyper. When you get that way when you've been drinking, it's hard to tell what you'll do. Sure, I'm dangerous to a certain extent. Anyone is when they're provoked or aggravated."

One of the more "serious" stories you hear about Butch is that while he was "affiliated," as he says, with the tavern in Rossie, he once ran a man out of the place by starting a chain saw and coming at him.

Two eyewitnesses confirmed the story, but both said Butch seemed to have no intention of really using the saw on the man. "Butch knows what that would mean," said one witness. "He knows the difference between a felony and a misdemeanor. He was just scaring the guy."

Butch was "involved" in one death, as a driver in a two-car accident here in 1973 in which the other motorist died. Authorities say they intensely investigated rumors that Butch had been drinking heavily that day but could produce no witnesses or evidence to indicate that the incident was anything but an accident.

"It was just one of those things," Butch said. "They said I'd been drinking all day and I hadn't. I'd had maybe two to three beers, and that was all."

There's no question that Butch does a lot that aggravates people, sometimes even tickles them.

One businessman, who asked not to be named, told of seeing Butch moving from chair to chair in a local pub, kissing men on the cheek – "almost daring anyone" to resist.

And just last Sunday, Butch came driving down Spencer's wide Grand Avenue in his wrecker, honking his horn, while a dying cow swung from the cable on the truck's rear. "A farmer gave her to me," Butch said. "I just took her to the rendering plant." He did that *after* backing the truck up to the entry area of a local restaurant-lounge for a while and *after* inviting at least one man "to come on over for a barbecue."

What to do with Butch? We asked farmer Schomaker and beer truck driver Patrick – both of whom are reputed to have whipped Butch – that question. (Butch, incidentally, denied Schomaker has ever beaten him in a fight, saying, "That little . . . couldn't tie my shoes.")

Schomaker: "The best thing a person can do, especially if Butch is drunk, is get away from him. He's a big guy and he ain't scared of nothing. If you stick around, he's going to take a punch at you, no doubt about it."

Patrick: "I don't turn my back on him. But as far as to advise someone, well, everyone's got different physical capabilities. I do think he's like a child, craving attention, especially when you can get close to him. The thing you've got to be careful of is that Butch is like a time bomb on a teeter-totter; you don't know when or in which direction he's going to go off."

What'll happen to Butch, in the long run?

Butch said he has no idea.

County Attorney Barrick said he thinks he has an idea: "The obvious answer is sooner or later, he'll get his comeuppance.

"People eventually will get fed up with his behavior and his intimidation, and sometime, some guy will take care of him. Like I said, that's the obvious answer. But I think more about it and I'm not so sure. Butch knows who he can manhandle and who he can't, and he pretty well steers clear of the latter group. As long as he doesn't make a mistake . . . "

Down the road in Rossie, T. W. Black, who's 60 and has "known Butch since he was knee-high," said Butch's biggest problem is "his big mouth."

"But underneath, he's got a heart that's at least as big as his mouth, he really does. Maybe he'll wise up some with age. If he don't, something bad will end up happening to him. Butch, more than any man I ever knew, is in a position to make a choice about his future. He can end up being Public Enemy No. 1, or he can end up being a model citizen. He's not the kind that'll let someone make the choice for him."

. . . and then Butch got his

August 1978

"You might say there's a legend about me,
but you can't really be a legend while
you're alive."
    —Donald Dean "Butch" Berenger
    June 15, 1978

By his own definition, Butch Berenger can now be a legend. He's dead. Berenger, about 45, of Spencer, died Monday morning in a Sioux Falls, South Dakota, hospital.

The papers are saying he was a "noted brawler," but that hardly catches it. He was a character—some say a desperado—the likes of which you seldom encounter any more.

Just two months ago, his attorney was quoted as saying Butch seemed to live by and believe in "a sort of frontier justice." For years, Butch was the subject of the hottest gossip in Clay County, where he was arrested dozens of times for raucous behavior that cut the moral grain of modern midwestern society.

He acknowledged his reputation was that of a "notorious SOB," but he said he really felt like "a whipping boy" because of things he said he was blamed for but hadn't done.

There's no question he was well known. The word of his death spread through the county with speed normally reserved for the demise of only the most prominent citizens.

"Maybe there won't be too many who'll miss him," said one woman in Royal, a small town that was one of Butch's favorite haunts, "but still, it was an awful way for him to go."

On August 18, after a tavern argument, Butch was hit by a pickup truck in the streets of Royal. He was taken to Spencer Municipal Hospital, where he was diagnosed as having serious internal injuries. His condition gradually improved over the next few days.

Maybe there's a reason for what he did Saturday night, but it has not been publicly told. Some say it was just a matter of Butch being Butch. Anyway, he got out of his hospital bed, reportedly jerked out tubes that had been inserted in his body and signed himself out of the hospital – against medical advice.

Charles Earhart, the Spencer hospital administrator, said Butch had not been squabbling with the hospital personnel and that there was no apparent reason why he left.

But Butch took a cab to his home. The cab driver told his boss that Butch "looked pretty rough" at the time. A little later Saturday night, an unidentified friend took Butch to the Veterans Administration hospital in Sioux Falls, where Butch had been treated at other times in his life.

"He arrived here between 12:30 and 1:30 Sunday morning," said Barry Augustine, chief of medical administration at that hospital. "He was diagnosed at that time as having a coronary insufficiency due to a bowel infection. He needed surgery, and since our surgical suite is closed now for remodeling, we had him transferred to a private hospital in Sioux Falls, still as a VA patient."

Augustine said surgery was performed on Butch, but that his condition deteriorated until he died about 6 A.M. Monday. The official cause of death had not been determined late Monday. An autopsy was ordered, but officials said the results would not be available until sometime today.

Clay County Sheriff Phil Nelson said Monday he will hold open the investigation of the incident in which Butch was hit by the pickup until "after we find out why he died." Roger Munden, 25, of Royal, identified as the driver of the truck that struck Butch, has been charged with leaving the scene of a personal injury accident.

But Nelson said authorities are hazy on what led up to Butch being struck down. "We know there was an argument in a tavern and then Butch was hit, but we're still looking into the details," he said. "Some people weren't willing to say too much about it up till now, but maybe that'll change with Butch having died."

He refused to speculate whether there might be additional charges or whether existing charges might be dropped. "We just have got some follow-up investigation to do now," he said.

Clay County authorities, in interviews about Butch earlier this summer, said they often had been hindered in investigations of his conduct because witnesses feared testifying against the man.

Butch was born on a farm near Royal, grew up in Dickens and lived most of his adult life in Spencer. A large, ruggedly handsome man, he worked occasionally as an auto mechanic and hired hand at a local salvage yard. He said earlier this summer that he'd been married "approximately six times" and had a number of children, but in recent times he lived alone in his Spencer home.

He drank heavily and fought frequently, though he said in an interview he was slowing down with age. "Hell, I used to fight four or five guys at a time," he said. "Now, a lot of times, I tell 'em if they're going to whip me, they better be able to catch me first."

He said the many stories that circulated about his hijinks were "mostly inflated," and that, while he tolerated them, he didn't like them. "It'd bother anybody with fair judgment to be talked of, thought of, as bad," he said. "It bothers my friends and family more than me. It's hard on my kids. They get rode hard about me."

At the time of the interview in June, he refused to characterize his life as tragic. "Butch Berenger's life is whatever you want to make it," he said. "It can be sad, bad, pitiful, happy, proud—depending on what part of me you're looking at."

His frequent brushes with the law included one in 1968 that landed him in prison for 18 months on a breaking and entering charge. He got to know the local officers well. In fact, within the past year, he named two goats, which he kept penned in his yard in Spencer, after the sheriff and county attorney.

"There's good cops and bad cops," he said. "I've seen new cops shake like a leaf when they're writing me a ticket, for no reason. But it takes them a year or two to get the stuff out of their diapers before they can become good cops. The trouble with some of the older cops around here is that they'd stay up all night if they thought they could catch me [urinating] in the street."

He resented the trend in society of being quick to summon the law, saying men who couldn't fight, then shake hands and have a drink together "aren't real men to start with."

Although he said he never used weapons other than his fists, he was being prosecuted at the time of his death for going armed with intent in connection with a tavern incident last spring.

Butch drove a flashy Cadillac but eschewed other fancy trappings. He seldom dressed well, preferring blue jeans and cowboy shirts.

He laughed hard telling how he had gone to a Salvation Army store last spring to purchase "a Foreman and Clark suit for $6" to wear to his daughter's high school graduation.

"Everyone remarked how nice I looked," Butch said. "I told them, 'Look me over good now, because the next time you see me with a suit on, I'll have my arms folded and my eyes closed.' "

In a tiny town where everybody watches everything, "nobody saw nothing" when the bank got robbed

January 1978

In towns the size of Burnside, a community of maybe 100 southeast of Fort Dodge, the popular saying is that everyone knows everything about anything that's going on at a particular moment.

Somehow, all that broke down about 10:30 A.M. Monday. Two men, wearing ski masks and toting shotguns, slipped into town, pulled off a broad daylight robbery of the Burnside bank, locked teller Kathy Rosenquist in the vault and slipped out of town again — apparently, and almost incredibly, without anyone seeing them or their getaway vehicle.

Soon after the robbery, area law enforcement officers reported that the take was "about $10,000," but later in the day, officials of the Union Trust and Savings Bank, the Fort Dodge bank that operates the branch in Burnside, said they'd been advised by the FBI not to comment on the amount taken.

Authorities said late Monday afternoon they had little to go on in the investigation, other than that the two robbers were young, about six feet tall, and that they wore dirty green coveralls in addition to the ski masks.

M. L. McClurg, the vice-president and security officer for the Fort Dodge bank, agreed that "it seems unbelievable that the two men could get out of that small town without being seen, but that apparently is the case. And, as they were leaving the bank, they couldn't have missed a customer that was coming in by more than a few seconds," he said. "They were very professional."

As a spokesman for the Webster County Sheriff's Department said, "The job was obviously well cased."

Indeed. Besides teller Rosenquist, there are two other employees who are regularly on duty in the Burnside bank. But manager Dick Freed was not working Monday. "He was taking a routine physical examination," said McClurg, "but I just don't see how the two holdup men could possibly have known that."

Gary Knopf, the other employee, left the bank shortly after 10 A.M. for coffee at the Burnside Grocery and Coffee Shop, not more than a few hundred feet down the street. That left Rosenquist, 24, an employee for about two years, alone in the office. She refused comment late Monday on what happened, other than that the two men entered the facility and told her "they'd shoot me if I didn't do exactly what they said."

Bank officials said money was taken both from the vault and the cash drawer at the teller station. Rosenquist was then locked in the vault, where she remained "for not more than five minutes," according to bank officials.

In another unusual twist to this unusual case, the first person in the bank after the robbery was Rosenquist's father, Seibert A. Stewart, 59, a farmer in the area. "I was going in to do some banking and say hello to my daughter," Stewart said later. "I looked around and couldn't see anyone, but I could hear a sort of pecking or pounding. I figured someone must be doing some building in there somewhere. I knew that Gary normally goes to coffee about that time, so I decided to go on down to the coffee shop."

As he was leaving, Vera Mollenhoff, 74, another customer, was coming into the bank. "I'd left my husband [Clarence] in the car, and I was hurrying in because I had to get to a hair appointment in Fort Dodge," she said. "Mr. Stewart left and I was standing and could hear all the pounding, so I called out for Gary, thinking he was back in the bank somewhere.

"I heard Kathy yell back to 'let me out of here.' I yelled to ask where she was, and she said 'in the vault.' I went over and asked how to open the door, she told me and I got it open," Mollenhoff said. "That poor girl, she just looked like she was going to collapse," Mollenhoff continued. "She was crying a little and was screaming, 'I've been robbed.' She was real white."

Mollenhoff said teller Rosenquist ran without her coat into the 10-degrees-below-zero weather toward the coffee shop to notify Knopf of the robbery. There, Rosenquist encountered her father. "I hadn't any more than got in the coffee shop than here comes Kathy yelling and screaming about the robbery," said Stewart. "I didn't get to talk to her much, other than to find out she was okay."

Around Burnside, the rest of the day, the locals were all shaking their heads about how the robbers and the robbery had gone unobserved. "I know it sounds funny," said Pearl Reed, who runs the grocery store, "but nobody saw nothing. And nobody remembers seeing any strange people around town the last few days. Everyone is pretty shook up about it."

On Saturday, there had been a bizarre attempted robbery at

Ida's Grocery in Callender, a town of 421 located less than 10 miles west of Burnside. But authorities said they doubted there was a connection between that incident and the bank stickup.

At Callender, store owner Ida Huedepohl said she was preparing to close about 5:30 P.M., "when this young man, I suppose about 25, came in, walked to the back of the store and then came back to the front. "He had his hand in his pocket like he had a gun," she said. "He told me this was a stickup and for me to open the cash drawer. I told him I wouldn't do it, that I work hard for my money and need it to buy the grocery supplies. I told him he could take all the groceries he wanted but that I wouldn't give him my money."

Huedepohl said the man "said he was serious, for me to open the cash drawer, and I told him I was serious, too, and that I wasn't going to do it. He just stared at me for a while, and then he left," she said. "It was scarey, especially after he left. Maybe I shouldn't have done what I did, but I felt like I had the Lord with me, so I refused to give him the money." She said as the man left, "he took his hand out of his pocket and he didn't have any gun."

If the Callender would-be crook was one of the Burnside crooks, which authorities said seems unlikely, he took on shotguns, a partner and a full load of audacity between Saturday and Monday.

They hated his guts but then came to understand why he torched a landmark

October 1985

WINTERSET, IA. – The Madison County Covered Bridge Festival, one of Iowa's grandest fall events, happens here next weekend, and 30,000 are expected to come see the structures and hear the stories that make this area's history so rich.

The past is fondly recalled. Yet many of the events that today seem warm chapters of history must have been regarded initially as pretty tough stuff: The notorious Jesse and Frank James holing up here before their storied train robbery near Adair. Another desperado escaping a posse by vanishing in the rafters of one of the covered bridges. Houses thought to be haunted by ghastly spirits of yesteryear.

And now, some are beginning to see how an ugly incident of two years ago – something that inspired the same kind of public hysteria and anger that the presence of the James boys must have triggered 112 years ago – may indeed become part of the community's treasured lore.

"The kids yell 'Bridge Burner' at me," 23-year-old Steve Mead said Thursday, bowing his head and speaking ever so softly. "Some of the older people treat me all right, but a lot of them hate my guts. I'm sorry I caused that. It hurts."

In the wee hours of October 8, 1983, the day the 14th festival was to start, a drunken, heartbroken Mead poured a coffee can full of gasoline in the center of McBride Bridge, one of the seven covered spans still standing, and dropped a match. The bridge, which like all the others is on the National Register of Historic Places, was destroyed.

"When word got out, people just went crazy," said Curtis Allen, president of the festival committee that year. "We sent firemen out to guard all the other bridges. We were afraid someone might be trying to burn all of them."

Pat Nelson, another key organizer, said local people "talked about finding whoever did it and having a hanging. But as time went on and the story of why it happened began to come out, well, it made at least some of the people feel not quite so hard about it."

What came out in court was that young Mead had been dealt an especially tough hand in life. His mother died when he was 12. He grew up a shy, sad, lonely kid who rarely, if ever, had a date. He was as much of a stranger to happiness as he was to trouble.

But in young adulthood he met a woman whose marriage was on the rocks. Over a five-month period in 1983, he fell hard for her, often courting her in McBride Bridge, where the two of them carved their initials, as per the local custom.

Ultimately she dumped him to return to her husband, leaving Mead despondent and alone again. On the night of October 7, he saw her with her husband in a Winterset tavern and he "couldn't handle it." He drank too much, went to the bridge and destroyed the initials that recalled the romance—and erased a century-old land-mark, too.

A month later, law officers asked him to come in for question-ing. "I told them it was me, that I did it," he recalled last week. "It'd been bothering me too much to try to hide it anymore. I was ashamed, and I still am. I love the bridges. I've been around them all my life. They've meant a lot to me."

He was convicted of second-degree arson and given a 10-year prison sentence. After serving a two-month "shock sentence," the rest of his incarceration was suspended. A judge placed him on three years' probation and ordered him to pay the county $4,000 and to do 150 hours of community work.

Ironically, he wound up being directed by probation officials to do that work for the Madison County Historical Society, one of the groups most angered by what he had done to the bridge. The so-ciety has a lovely museum in a complex of buildings on Winterset's south side. One of the buildings is an 1856 brick home left to the group by a woman who died in 1982. There is a slow restoration effort under way on it, and it was on that project that Mead did his 150 hours of community work.

"We'd had other offenders sent to us in the past, but they had never worked out," said Wayne Breeding, 52, president of the so-ciety and owner of an antiques business here. "Steve did." So much so that when the court-ordered 150 hours had been fulfilled, the historical society hired him full-time to continue his work on the old home.

A strong bond has developed between Mead and Breeding, his boss. "When he first came to us, he was real withdrawn and unre-sponsive, but that only lasted for a short time," said Breeding. "What

I've learned about him amazes me. This is a kid who was essentially left on his own real early on. He spent the better part of one winter sleeping in an old car. And in the past few years, he'd been sleeping in some old deserted shack out in the country. I mean, he didn't have anything.

"He'd come to work all clean and neat, and I eventually found out that he was going to the city park every morning and washing his hair under a faucet out there, and that when he'd get done at work here, he'd wait until dark and take baths under a hose.

"He earned our trust, and we finally told him to go ahead and stay in the old house he's working on. There are some people around who can't understand how we could turn an important building over to him after what he's done. They've torn into us for helping him. But they just don't know him. Yes, it was a very serious thing he did, but there's nothing we can do about that now. He's trying to make amends, and we've decided to try to help him."

And for that Mead is grateful. "I feel like these people are behind me," he said. "I'm glad to have this job they've given me, not just for the money but because it's got something to do with history around here. Working on something like this makes me feel like I'm helping to pay for the history I burned up."

Will he take part in this year's bridge festival?

"No, no, I'll stay away from it," he said, voice growing ever softer. "When the festival comes around, that's when I hurt the most over what I did. One sad part of it is, I think as many people go out now to see the ruins of the bridge I burned down as go to see the other bridges."

And as they do, they're already beginning to tell and retell the sad story of why a young man, a loser at love, did it.

A "possessed" woman kills her own mother in one of Iowa's most frightening murders ever

August 1978

CHARLES CITY, IA.—Just *who* was it that so brutally murdered 58-year-old Phyllis Koppen in the bedroom of her Nora Springs home last March? A four-day trial that ended in Floyd County District Court here Thursday left the question essentially unanswered.

Oh, a verdict was reached. Koppen's daughter, Sandra Kruger, 37, of Spencer, who'd been charged with the killing, was found innocent by reason of insanity. There was no dispute by either side in the trial that the killer had come to Nora Springs in Sandra Kruger's body on that grim day.

But who, or what, controlled her mind? Who could conceive, much less carry out, a prolonged attack in which Koppen was smashed on the head with a ceramic cornucopia vase, then slashed and gashed with an eight-inch butcher knife—15 or 20 or more times?

Who could, after the woman already was dead, go ahead and make "religiously significant" punctures in her feet, hands and side?

Who could possibly sever the head of Koppen's poodle, Fritz, and place the head in a baby's crib, in what was portrayed in the trial as a sacrificial rite of fertility?

The jury, by choosing the verdict it did, recognized that Sandra Kruger was the actual weapon in this savagery, that the knife was a mere tool. So what person, or what force, manipulated the attractive 5-foot 2-inch, petite, blond weapon?

Maybe it was "Kris." For years, "Kris" had been just a nickname that Sandra Kruger used.

The most frightening thing about the Kruger case is that on March 5, without apparent warning, something boiled up in the woman's mind. Expert psychiatric witnesses at the trial here diagnosed it as an "acute schizophrenic break," and one of them characterized it as "the most severe kind of mental disorder."

Roger Ott, a Charles City attorney who defended Sandra, thinks it was a "possession"—the takeover of control of Sandra's mind by a sort of imaginary person who'd lived undetected in her brain all these years. He admits that is the thinking of a psychiatric layman grasping to make good sense of an unthinkable situation.

In an interview, he frequently referred to the possessor as "Kris," noting that he'd been told by medical personnel that in Sandra's darkest hours after the slaying, she seemed to be confused whether she was really Sandra or really Kris. He said one of the big questions jurors faced, though it wasn't put to them this way, was: "Can you convict Sandra for the deeds of Kris?"

There was no history of mental problems in Sandra's family and no hint that she was developing any. In her childhood in Nora Springs and in the first 15½ years of her marriage to George Kruger, a 42-year-old Spencer elementary school principal, Sandra was a quiet, apparently happy person.

Her brother, Junior Koppen, 40, now of Red Oak, said Sandra always maintained an especially close relationship with their mother. "They were more like sisters than mother and daughter," he said in an interview on Friday.

In fact, the whole Koppen family was close, even the brothers-in-law and sisters-in-law. Clarence Koppen, 60, works at a cement plant in Mason City. Phyllis worked at a Mason City dairy and had a sideline of making wedding cakes for Nora Springs couples.

"I think of the family as real Middle America," said a man who knows the Koppen clan well. "They're the kind who pitched horseshoes together in the backyard on Sunday afternoons, and the kind who made a big deal out of every birthday and holiday. They were always getting together."

The wrath of this Kris – this possessor of Sandra – brought sudden pause to all that happiness.

Attorney Ronald Noah, who joined Floyd County Attorney Roger Sutton on the prosecution of the case, told jurors the ordeal was "one of the most horrible incidents any of us are likely to encounter in our lifetime."

In the 48 hours that preceded the slaying, Sandra Kruger, who'd never been more than an average believing Christian, was consumed by religious fanaticism. Testimony revealed that on the morning of March 6, she attempted to drown herself in the bathtub of her home in Spencer but couldn't go through with it and told her husband "the Lord will be unhappy because I can't put myself to sleep."

George Kruger said that at lunchtime that day, Sandra fixed him a meal of nutbread, cheese and "bad-tasting" cooking wine. He said he got the idea she was preparing a "last supper." Later that day, she told George it was good for people to smoke cigarettes because smoking afforded time "to think about God."

That evening, she began reciting Biblical passages, even acting some of them out. George testified that when she recited a verse that contains the line "knock and the door will be opened," she began beating her head against the bedpost. And she concocted the idea that it would please God if she and George would go to sleep and die, he said.

What triggered Sandra Kruger? "We've talked about that in the family," Junior Koppen said Friday. "We haven't figured it out, and I doubt we ever will."

Defense attorney Ott said he's been told by psychiatrists that "it will take months and months of in-depth psychoanalysis to try to come to grips with what did set her off."

Prosecutor Sutton said he has a hunch about it, based on the feelings he developed in months of working on the Kruger case.

"All her life, she was Mrs. Nicey-Nice," he said. "She always smiled and took everything. She never challenged anything or anybody. Someone could have hit her over the head and she would have just smiled. I think she was so full of frustration that it finally erupted. It happened to be with her mother, but it could have been with George or anyone else she was around. She couldn't take it any more."

Testimony in the trial indicated there had been at least four points of stress in Sandra's life in the months preceding the incident:

Her frustration at being childless in nearly 16 years of marriage increased when her 25-year-old sister, Katherine Broderson of Kensett, had a baby.

She had been uneasy about the couple's move in the summer of 1977 from the Tama area, where George had resigned his position in the South Tama schools, to Spencer.

She was distressed when a dog she and George had had for 15 years had to be put to sleep in February.

The unexpected but natural death in late February of an uncle in Mason City seemed to have touched her deeply. She told George that on her way home from the funeral she found herself in deep thought about "why people die."

George Kruger was battling the flu when his wife was behaving so bizarrely in their Spencer home. He kept thinking, he testified, that "she would come out of it." When she hadn't late at night on

March 6, he decided help was needed. He telephoned Sandra's parents in Nora Springs, told them there was trouble and that he and Sandra would drive over the next day.

Why hadn't he acted sooner?

"George isn't a psychiatrist," Ott told the jury. "He'd never dealt with problems like his wife was having. He knew he had to make a decision on what to do, but he didn't know how to make that decision. He wanted help, so he went to the one person he thought was even closer to Sandra than he was—her mother."

About 2:30 A.M. on March 7, George decided the trip could not be delayed longer. The drive from Spencer to Nora Springs, which normally takes only two hours, required five. The tired, ailing George allowed Sandra, bad as she was, to drive part of the way and she put the car in a cornfield.

They arrived in Nora Springs about 8 A.M., only to find that Clarence and Phyllis Koppen had already gone to work, not having expected the Krugers to arrive until later in the day. George and Sandra drove on to Mason City, picked up a key to the Koppen house from Mrs. Koppen at the business where she was working and then returned to Nora Springs.

At mid-morning, Mrs. Koppen came home. George—saying he wanted to pick up clothing for himself and Sandra, as well as visit with friends who'd been in their home the day she started her odd behavior—soon left for Spencer.

An Avon lady who was a friend of Phyllis Koppen dropped by for about an hour in the late morning. But after noon, Sandra and her mother were alone in the two-story frame house on the east edge of Nora Springs.

The killing is said to have occurred late that afternoon. When Clarence Koppen came home from work about 6 P.M., he found his wife's body in an upstairs bedroom and found his daughter sprawled on a bed in an adjacent bedroom, the knife still in her hand.

Sandra was taken to a Mason City hospital, where, the next day, the authorities officially charged her with murder. Bond was set at $200,000 and a police matron was assigned to stay at the hospital with her. Sandra remained at the Mason City hospital for a week, spent seven weeks at the Iowa Security Medical Facility at Oakdale and in early May was returned to the Floyd County Jail here, where she's been ever since.

The psychiatric reports on the woman didn't change drastically from the first one that was done on March 8 by Mason City physician Robert Powell.

"This patient is under the delusions that God is talking to her," Powell wrote in his report. "[She thinks God] told her that she should kill her mother's dog to have children. God told her to kill her mother in order to save her mother's soul. . . . She is having strong religious feelings that she has betrayed God or He has betrayed her. The patient is insane or psychotic and is suffering from paranoid schizophrenia. She is very mixed up with these ideas of doing God's bidding and the gravity of the situation in which she finds herself."

While hospitalized, Sandra reportedly was given to "snarling" and "growling" and occasionally became violent to the point where restraints were necessary. But from the time she was returned to the jail here, Sandra has remained calm, subdued. She has talked little and stared blankly at the walls and ceiling around her.

The trial, conducted before District Judge Jack Frye last week, was a sensational one. Spectators, ranging in age from infancy to octogenarians, packed the courtroom benches. On Thursday, when prosecutor Sutton was making his final argument to the jury in the hushed courtroom, one man walked in, loudly asked for a place to sit in the back row and was soon arrested and charged with public intoxication.

The prosecution pushed a first-degree murder case; the defense was insanity. For all its complexity, the case came down to one point: Was Sandra Kruger capable of distinguishing right from wrong at the time of the killing? Expert psychiatric testimony was split on the question.

"There was a violent struggle with her mother," defense attorney Ott told the jurors. "Sandra carved . . . a religious symbol on her mother, even continuing after she was dead. Did she really know the difference between right and wrong when she was doing this to her mother?"

Co–defense attorney James Smith, a 30-year veteran of trial work who broke down at the conclusion of his final argument, told the jury, "This is a tragedy of the human family. What happened here is that Sandra brought disease into this family. It was a severe disease – like cancer, like leprosy. Would we – if a member of our family came in with leprosy – would we stone them, put them in prison, as we used to do? Or would we attempt to treat it? This unfortunate creature got a disease. Should we punish her for it?"

Prosecutor Sutton argued that "we admit the criminal act was the product of a diseased mind, but that's . . . not an excuse. The very essence of her belief – 'I will save her soul' – required her to plan, meditate, get the specific intent to murder. Her motive

. . . was to save her mother. Granted, that is pretty kinky thinking. . . . Should she be justified to commit murder because she thought she was right?"

The jury took the dispute, deliberated five hours and returned the innocent by reason of insanity verdict. Sandra Kruger's pent-up emotions broke when the verdict was announced. She sobbed and sobbed, first in the arms of her attorney, Ott, then in the embrace of her husband.

George Kruger and Sandra's two brothers and sister all testified in her behalf. Her father, Clarence, the most tragic figure in this case, was scheduled to testify for her but didn't.

"Dad came to the courthouse one day to testify," said Junior Koppen, "but it was just too emotional for him. He couldn't do it. Since this happened, he's never been able to bring himself to come over to the jail and visit Sandra, but eventually he will. He's just not ready yet. He's doing well, though, considering. He did tell us after he'd heard about the verdict that the jury made the right decision. It came out the way the whole family wanted it. It was the only way it could come out."

Sandra Kruger will remain in the county jail at least until Wednesday, when a hearing is scheduled for 9:30 A.M. to determine whether she should be committed to a state institution for further treatment.

[Sandra Kruger received extensive psychiatric treatment. A couple of years later, she killed herself.]

The common admiration between a slippery young criminal and a veteran sheriff

September 1977

GUTHRIE CENTER, IA. – It had been a long summer for Lester Petersen, 57, one of the longest he's been through in his 16 years as Guthrie County sheriff.

There had been four escapes in a year from the jail in the basement of the courthouse here, three of them in a period of a couple of weeks near the end of July.

But that's all in the past, he says, as he leads a tour through the reworked jail. He pats the new concrete that plugs holes where large windows had been. He proudly shows off new steel bars and refurbished locks on the cell doors.

"I'd be willing to give you a hacksaw and defy you to get out of there now," he says.

Sure, it would hold the average prisoner. But the question is, would it hold Scott Pote?

The mention of the name brings a grin to the sheriff's face. You might figure Petersen would have hard feelings toward Pote, a 16-year-old slip of a lad who was the premiere escape artist. He broke the jail three of those four times.

And it wouldn't be too surprising if Pote – now among the youngest of some 700 inmates at the Iowa Men's Reformatory at Anamosa as a result of his repeated brushes with the law – thought ill of the sheriff.

Not so, either way. There's a common admiration that's refreshing, at least as far as law enforcer–law breaker relationships go.

Says Petersen of Pote: "After he'd come back or get caught, he'd come in and put his arm around me and say there was 'nothing personal.' How can you get mad at a guy like that?"

Says Pote of the sheriff: "I like him a lot. When I was getting ready to escape, I always did think about him. If I'd thought he was going to get in trouble because of me getting out, I don't think I'd ever have done it."

Pote acknowledges he's no model teenager. In fact, in a telephone interview from the reformatory, he says he's probably right where he should be because of his past crimes – which he said include armed robbery, two auto thefts and some earlier juvenile raps.

"I'd never thought of myself as a real criminal," he says. "But when I look at all I've done, I guess I'd have to say I am one. I still think I can straighten out, though."

Sometimes, he says, he feels he's let his friend Sheriff Petersen down. "He's always tried to help me," Pote says. "He's been trying since I was knee-high to him. He and my Dad were friends, and Lester would come over to our farm at Yale, and he'd always pack me around."

Their "professional" relationship developed in the summer of 1976. Pote, who had been at the Iowa Training School for Boys in Eldora, tells of escaping from there and stealing a car. He was apprehended and taken to the jail here. It would prove no match for him.

See, Pote is just 5 feet tall. His weight normally has been about 100 pounds – though with the "three squares" he's been taking lately, he's ballooned to 125.

And he's mechanically oriented. "He's really a pretty slick little devil that way," Sheriff Petersen says. "If he'd ever take up studying mechanics, I think he could do just about anything."

In September of 1976, Pote began tinkering around with a fork and discovered that the lock on his cell door was defective. After a little manipulating, he says, "you could take something hard and skinny like a book cover and slip the cell door open."

He did so and walked into the hallway just outside the cells but still inside the main jail door. But that hallway was bordered by huge windows – about 4 feet by 6 feet – that had aluminum bars spaced about 12 inches apart. Pote easily was able to slither between those bars and run. Authorities nabbed him a few hours later at his father's farm. He was sent back to Eldora, leaving Sheriff Petersen and other officials in the dark about the defective cell locks.

And those pliable aluminum bars on the big windows? "We'd always known that wasn't a very good arrangement for a jail," Petersen says. "But we'd gotten along with them for years because an average-size man couldn't get out. Everyone was a little reluctant to spend extra money to correct the problem."

In the summer of 1977, Pote was released from Eldora, he says. In July, he was arrested in connection with the armed robbery, and he was back in the Guthrie County jail. This time, the cell door was chained shut.

Pote says he found a loose bar in a ventilator shaft and used it on July 25 to break the chain on the door, walk into the hallway and again wiggle through the window to freedom. He roamed for 17 hours before surrendering.

He was placed in the most secure cell in the jail, one in which he was virtually surrounded by concrete and steel. But on July 31, he found yet another way out. He says this part of his story will be news even to the sheriff.

"I'd asked another inmate – I won't mention his name – to cut a hole in a ventilator shaft in the ceiling of the cell," Pote explains. The hole, about 11 inches in diameter, was just big enough for him to crawl through, he says. I got up in the pipes, crawled along and dropped down in the hallway by where a refrigerator and some cabinets were. I hid around the cabinets and then I had these other guys in the back cells create a disturbance."

One of the officers, he says, "came in and left the [main jail] door open while he went back to talk to those other guys. I got up and ran out. I thought the dispatcher would be out in the front office, but whoever it was that night must have been gone to the bathroom or something."

Pote says he ran from the courthouse, walked to the edge of Guthrie Center and stole a van, which he drove to Perry. Seven hours later, Perry police spotted him and made the arrest.

As if Pote's slipperiness wasn't enough of a headache for Sheriff Petersen, he also had prisoner James Ellis, accused of forgery, to deal with. Ellis, a little taller than Pote but equally as slender, slipped through those aluminum-barred windows in the same period Pote was escaping twice. Ellis was caught later in Utah. He was returned here to face the original forgery charges as well as a new one – escape.

The sheriff decided he'd had enough. "I went to the Board [of Supervisors] and got permission to spend whatever it took to make the place secure," he says.

A recalcitrant Pote – who was removed from the aegis of juvenile court and processed through adult court – then told his friend about how the locks on the cell doors were so jimmiable. Now everything's been fixed, Petersen says.

The day arrived when Pote was to be transported to Anamosa to begin serving a 10-year term for the armed robbery.

"As they were taking him out," Sheriff Petersen recalls, "he came in to me and said, 'I don't want you to be mad at me.' I said, 'I don't hold no grudge.' I couldn't help but feel a little sorry for him.

He's so young, you hate to see one that young go that way. I felt like he could've about been one of my own kids.

"I really think if I wasn't sheriff and I had a farm or a place like that, I could work with him and straighten him out. I just doubt they'll be able to do anything with him at Anamosa. "In fact, I'd bet that one of these mornings we'll get a phone call from over there asking if we've seen Scott Pote around Guthrie County."

Pote says he doubts there'll be such a call. "When I said good-by to Lester that day, I swear he had tears in his eyes," Pote says. "That really shook me up. They can keep me from escaping from Anamosa if they really want to, and I want them to keep me. I don't want the chance to go. I want to get all this over with."

Iowa's small towns are even more of an identifying factor for us than is corn. They are our glory; they are our curse. Even in our larger cities, we continue to live what is basically a small town life. Why? Well, most of us figure out it makes more sense to live that way, and besides, most of us in the cities are really from small towns. What follows is a study of several of them.

SMALL TOWNS

There are lots of ways
to judge small towns —
here's how I do it

June 1986

I was up in front of an Iowa audience recently when someone asked a question that I've been giving a lot of thought to ever since. "With as much as you travel around Iowa," this person said, "and as many small towns as you see, how do you form your perceptions of how good some certain town is?"

My first inclination was to answer that if the residents I'm dealing with speak in quotable sentences and have an interesting story to tell, then I'll think it's a great town.

But wait, I thought. That's selfish and shallow. Upon reflection, I've decided the thing I'm looking for in any new place I'm visiting are signs of what I'd call livability. We'll get to some of my measures of livability in a moment, but first I want to share one of the most sage bits of wisdom I've ever come across on judging towns. It came from an old shoe salesman who used to travel Wisconsin.

"No town," he once said, "is either as good or as bad as you first think it is."

Isn't it the truth? Like so many others, I used to have this idea that Ottumwa is the pits. Then when we took RAGBRAI through there one summer and I got to know a whole bunch of Ottumwans, I radically changed my opinion. Not only do I think it's a pretty town, but also a gutty one that has done well in surviving far too many shock waves in its local economy.

Not everybody has the opportunity to get over first impressions, however. That's why I think any town that doesn't pay a lot of attention to the way it looks from the highways coming into it is in big trouble.

Flowers are important. Trees are important. And I think a town sign that is big, bold, attractive and catchy is a must. Most towns have slogans. Most of the slogans stink. Some towns don't have enough sense to grab a good slogan when it's given to them.

Seymour, for example, in southern Iowa. Why they've never adopted the one I wrote for them a few years ago is beyond me. "Seymour?" it went. "We've seen less!"

65

Okay, let's say you're now into the town. What should you look for as indicators of livability?

If it's a small business district, and there is more than one upholstery shop in it, you're in a very troubled place.

If the signs on the businesses have obviously been painted by the owners themselves, or their children, it's more bad news.

If there are posters up for political campaigns earlier than the most recent one—bummer.

What good should be looked for?

The most quirky little test I have for livability is if there is a dry cleaners, or at least some store that has a sign saying it has arranged for dry cleaning pickup with a laundry in some nearby bigger town. I don't know how I came up with that, but it holds true—if the town supports a dry cleaners, it's a viable town.

Another one is the local baseball diamond. If it's gorgeous, you've found a good place, one that cares for its young people and for tradition.

And speaking of tradition, another positive indicator is the presence of statues and/or monuments—not to some nameless soldier but to some specific individual who served the community well or to some historic event that happened there.

You want to see some industrial operations, but not one big one that clearly dominates the whole community.

Notice how those towns that in the '60s and '70s tied their stars to the meat packing industry are now, in most cases, left with big, ugly, empty plant buildings?

But if there's one factor that can sway a visitor quicker than anything it's a friendly gas station attendant. Local Chambers of Commerce should have seminars for these guys. They should hire as the seminar leader the man who runs the D-X station in Panora, 45 miles west of Des Moines. I don't know the chap's name, but I'll bet with his genuine friendliness, he does more for Panora by 10 o'clock any morning than the Panora Development Corporation, if there is such a group, does in months of meetings. He's a gem, and he's made me, and probably lots of others, believe the town is, too.

Take all of that above, and that's how it happens, or doesn't happen, for me when I come by.

Amber was a one-tavern town suddenly with two taverns, but at least bar hopping became possible

August 1981

AMBER, IA. – In this tiny village set northeast of Cedar Rapids, 1981 will be remembered as the year free enterprise awoke and flexed its muscles.

Well, probably only local students of the American system will remember it that way. The man on the street in Amber will just say it was the year it became possible to go bar hopping here.

Amber, population 89, is a one-tavern town – with two taverns. The white-frame, two-story buildings stand not 50 feet from each other, odd twins on a county road that is main street. Both have those Old West–style fronts with high facades and covered porches.

The older of the two is the Amber Inn, a tavern with a history some say stretches back 120 years. For the last nine years, it has been operated by Mildred and Lauren Tonne, 60 and 61. Mildred is the boss. They figured they pretty well had a hammerlock on the tavern and restaurant business here. "You don't find two bars in places this size," said Lauren Tonne. "People are usually glad if one can stay open."

But six years ago, Becky and Mike Folkers, now 34 and 36, purchased the adjacent building and opened an antique shop. Business declined and last August they auctioned off their remaining pieces. What to do with a big old building in little Amber?

"We decided to open a bar and restaurant," said Becky Folkers, the manager. "It was nothing personal against the Tonnes. It was a business decision. I know they probably aren't very happy about it, but it's a free country."

That's right, said Lauren Tonne. "I was a prisoner of war in World War II and I just longed to get home and get in the free enterprise system again," he said. "What I'm saying, I agree they have every right to open another tavern here, but still, I just don't understand it."

The Folkers' Heritage House, which opened in January, is shiny clean like a new place should be. It is tastefully decorated with antiques, including a bar and backbar moved from the Czech Village in Cedar Rapids. The older Amber Inn suffers in a cosmetic comparison — it frankly needs a good scrubbing — but there is an undeniable sort of 1940s roadhouse charm to it. Their prices for food, beer and liquor are almost identical.

Competing at such close range can be uncomfortable. "Some jabs go back and forth," said Becky Folkers.

One jab: The Folkers stole the Tonnes' cook. Lucille Joslin, 63, said to be a wizard in a kitchen, had been with the Tonnes since they opened. Her move to Folkers' was a lateral one. "I get the same wage," she said. "So why'd I do it? Let's leave that alone."

The cook's departure, said Mildred Tonne, "was a low blow."

Still, the competitors get along. In fact, in June they co-sponsored a street dance. And last week, Lauren Tonne wound up his birthday celebration by leading some buddies into Folkers' for drinks. "I went in there and said my wife had thrown me out of our place," he said.

How long can both taverns stay open?

"It's pretty rough on both of us," said Lauren Tonne. "But we bought our place for $10,000 nine years ago. The Folkers bought their place for $16,000 and now have sunk another $27,000 into it. With that kind of debt, I can't help but feel a little sorry for them, the economy being what it is. I'll tell you, a lot of good places around the area are folding, more of them all the time."

Becky Folkers said those figures are inflated. Both places might survive, she said, then added, "but one is bound to suffer."

Mildred Tonne sees a chance for both to do well. "If there's any place this small where two taverns could make it, it is here," she said. "The people around this area are German, Bohemian and Irish. They like to drink. Besides, there's nothing wrong with a little competition. It keeps you on your toes. It makes it more exciting."

Indeed. Next month, the Folkers will have their long-awaited official grand opening, complete with a wet T-shirt contest. Right here in Amber.

Burt is a community
that gives a darn,
and then gives another one

October 1986

BURT, IA.–It's been a couple of weeks, and only now am I beginning to sort out my feelings about what I saw in this little northwest Iowa town (population 600), about what I experienced here.

Months ago, I began receiving letters and phone calls from a woman named Alice Benck, asking me if I would come speak at some function of "Exceptional Opportunities, Inc." She said it like I was supposed to know what it was. I didn't. She seemed disappointed, if not miffed, that I didn't.

Now I know why. Alice Benck is a good heart who has given so much of herself to Exceptional Opportunities–a residential and treatment program for mentally handicapped children and adults–for the past 18 years that she can hardly believe it when she runs into people who haven't gotten the message she constantly spreads.

The message, I would learn, is this: "When you work with people who have these kinds of problems, you have to give a darn. And then give another darn, and another, and another."

Her persistence is legendary around here. "When it comes to this program," Howard Wycoff, the mayor of Burt, told me later, "what she decides she needs, she's almost always gonna get."

She got me. She got me good. She eventually made me realize that all those months that I was rather curtly saying, "Now, what is this program again and why is it you want me to come speak?" what I was really doing was hearing "mentally handicapped" and then tuning out. I wasn't giving a darn.

I was telling myself, like so many of us normies tell ourselves, that I'm too busy scooting around Iowa, too busy making the next buck, too busy worrying about Big Things to take time for something like a program for the mentally handicapped. I was falling into the same awful mindset that so many have on the mentally handicapped–the old "out of sight, out of mind."

What a schnook. For when Alice got me here, she first of all showed me one of the warmest, most wonderful evenings I've had in a long time.

Burt calls itself "The Little Town with a Big Heart and a Helping Hand." I now believe it. She walked me into a gymnasium filled by 900 people, and remember, this is a town of only 600. They were 900 people who've given a darn and continue to do so.

They had come together for an evening billed as "Homecoming '86" and explained as being a chance for the people of Exceptional Opportunities and for the people of Burt and the rest of Kossuth County to thank each other for being here.

"Without the hospitality, patience and love the town of Burt has given us over the years," said Alice Benck, "we wouldn't have this program."

And Mayor Wycoff: "Without Exceptional Opportunities, this town would be in a world of hurt. The reason they originally located it here was that we had so many empty buildings they could get cheap. If they hadn't come, I'd hate to think of how many more empty buildings we'd have by now."

Indeed, they celebrated. The high school band played. The community chorus sang. Coffee, juice and goodies were abundant. We all shared 90 minutes of fun and good feeling.

The next morning, Alice and others on the staff showed me Exceptional Opportunities, which is now out of the old buildings and into new, specially built ones. There are two schools, the living quarters and a Work Activity Center where five cottage industries operate. It's clean, cheery, busy and upbeat.

I got big, spontaneous hugs from a lot of handicapped people that for those several, regrettable months had been out of my sight, out of my mind, out of my conscience. There are 100 of these "clients" here, with handicaps ranging from just this side of profound to, well, hopeless. They are taught, treated with dignity, taken care of and flat-out loved by a staff of about 120, meaning the attention is almost always one-to-one.

It's expensive running a program like Exceptional Opportunities, which survives on government and private money that is donated, begged, borrowed—whatever Alice and the others have to do to get it.

I couldn't do it, I confessed to Alice Benck. I'd get to where I was consumed by giving a darn. I just couldn't work in a situation like this.

"Not everybody can," she said.

Thank God, I've thought to myself a hundred times since, for those who can and do.

Soul-searching in a little town after an ugly racial incident

July 1982

MASONVILLE, IA. – When you're an apologist for the small town way of life, as I am, it makes you sick to think about what happened in this northeast Iowa community of 150 people.

For what we have here is an ugly counterpoint to the stories about the loving, caring, friendly nature of our small cities. It was hate on display, although most locals refuse to recognize it as such.

Helping bring up the rear of Masonville's annual Independence Day parade, held this year on the brilliant afternoon of July 3, were some 15 men on horseback. They were a group of young guys from around the area, "good ol' country boys" someone has called them. They took advantage of the fact that, as are most small town parades, Masonville's is pretty loosely organized. All entries are welcome. No advance explanation of the entry is required, apparently.

Lyle Mersch, 69, was sitting on his front porch with three or four friends watching the parade when he looked up and saw the riders coming. Mersch recalled his reaction: "I laughed and said to the others there on the porch with me, 'Well, lookee here, the Ku Klux Klan is coming.'"

Indeed, it appeared that way. The riders were dressed in the white sheets and hoods Klansmen have traditionally worn in public. Some were pulling a wagon, which carried another man, a white man whose face was smeared with the dark grease football players use under their eyes on sunny days. That man, Dale Ryan of nearby Winthrop, was, as they say in the theater, "in blackface." He was playing the role of a black man about to be lynched.

"When we were planning this thing out, the other guys who wound up being the 'Klansmen' all knew how to ride horses," said Ryan, about 25, a mechanic. "I don't know about horses, so I played the black guy."

As choreographed, the entourage stopped when it was right in front of the stand on which the Masonville parade judges were seated. Many in the crowd estimated at up to 2,000 were within earshot as the "Klansmen" put on a little skit. What it involved, according to Ryan, was that "I broke away and escaped. Then the 'Klansmen' were yelling, 'Nigger loose! Get the nigger!' "

When you ask now about what the reaction of the crowd was to all this, you get mixed stories. Most say the crowd took it as a joke, and that subsequently, the press has blown the whole episode "way out of proportion."

That's Dale Ryan's line of thought. "We certainly didn't go over there to offend anyone," he said. "All the people know us, and they'd know we didn't mean anything by it. We just thought of the Fourth of July being a holiday about history. Last year, the group of us put on kind of a Civil War battle in the Masonville parade, as part of our history. Well, the Ku Klux Klan is part of history, too, and that's why we decided on that this year."

Has he had any regrets about what he did? "None until the press got ahold of it and made such a big deal out of it," he said.

Vernon Sands, who was visiting Masonville the other day, said he missed the parade here but has now heard all about what happened. "So what?" he asked. "I happened to be over watching Manchester's parade that day, and there was this guy who came through all dressed up silly like a woman. No one thought that was anything but a joke. So in Masonville they have some guys dress up like Klansmen and one guy dress up like a colored guy. What's the difference. It was a joke in Manchester and it was a joke in Masonville."

Others were plainly shocked.

"It was very unfortunate it ever had to happen," said Mike Francis, 33, who watched the parade. "I was in the service with blacks and know how sensitive they are about this kind of thing. Most of those guys who did this have never had any contact with black people. I honestly don't think they considered that what they were doing would be thought of as being racist. But right when I saw it, I thought to myself, 'Oh-oh, there's going to be trouble over this.' "

Leon Schlichte, a man in his mid-20s who was helping stage the parade, said he "didn't think much one way or the other about what happened, but I had a sister visiting from away from here and I tell you, she raised all holy hell about it. She couldn't get out of here fast enough after that."

There are no blacks living in this immediate area to be outraged. Ryan said he and his buddies had that fact in mind when they were planning their skit. Would they have gone to Waterloo, where there is a large black community, and put on the same display in a parade there? "No," he said.

One thing that makes their willingness to appear as Klansmen here somewhat amazing is the historical fact that the Klan is almost as anti-Catholic as it is anti-black. This area is predominantly Catholic.

Some older residents say they can remember the Klan terrorizing Catholics in this area in the first two decades of this century. "They burned crosses and threw bombs," said Dorothy McDevitt, 66. "My folks often talked about it."

Ryan pointed out that he and "90 percent of the other guys" involved in the Klan stunt in the parade are Catholic. "We know what the real Klan did to Catholics," he said, "but we still thought we could joke about it."

The local leader of the church, Father Al White, pastor of Immaculate Conception parish here, has not yet had his say on the matters of the past week. He left Masonville on a week's vacation the day before the parade.

"I think I might go to Mass somewhere else the next couple of weeks," said young Schlichte, anticipating the sermon today. "I'm afraid we might be getting a real scolding from Father."

It has been one tough week in Masonville, a folksy community where the men's restroom in the park is marked "Boars." It is too little, too pretty, too peaceful a place for something like this to have happened.

In many ways, it was almost like there was a disaster here, something on the order of the Emerson flood or the Sibley tornado. There was no official disaster declaration by the governor, of course, but there has been a semiofficial one by the media.

Local residents were at first intrigued, later piqued, at the presence of so many reporters. "The first day it was kind of neat," said Schlichte. "The second day, it was, 'Oh, more of them?' Before long, I think people in Masonville are going to get irate at all this. In a little town like this, we don't know how to cope with something like this."

What he says seems to be evidence that a social disaster—if that's what Masonville had—can be even more difficult to clean up after than a natural disaster. The Iowa Civil Rights Commission will send staffers soon, much like the Iowa National Guard might after a flood.

"I got a call from one of their people," said Masonville Mayor

Bill Alden, 54. "The man told me he wanted to come up and sit down for a talk with the council and the officers of the Community Club. He said they just want to find out what happened and to see if there's anything they can do. He was real nice about it, and I said we'd be more than happy to talk to them."

The mayor believes the town is being singled out and bad-rapped as a rednecked, backwater burg. He says racial views here are no worse, maybe better, than anywhere else in Iowa—a state, he reminds, where the ugly racial joke is too often standard fare in idle conversation.

"Masonville is a good place, and the people here are good people," he said. "We don't hate. A lot of the people don't have much experience around blacks, so maybe we're not as sensitive as we should be. If you go door to door, you'll find that on race, it just doesn't matter to most people here when they really think about it. Go ahead and do that—go door to door."

That's what led me to stop at the door of Lyle Mersch, the old-timer who had watched the parade from his porch. "It was a good parade," he said. "Now, if those had been real Klan guys, I don't suppose I would've been real happy, but I knew they weren't. You know, I thought when I watched that thing that they had one guy dressed up like a nigger. Did they? Let me ask here. Lucille," he yelled back inside the house, "did they have a guy dressed up like a nigger in that parade?

"Yeah, she says they did. But I never thought nothing of it until I heard on the Oelwein news that somebody had got all upset. Somebody's always got to throw a monkey wrench on everything, don't they? The way I feel in general is this—it's what my dad always told me. He'd say, 'Lyle, my boy, don't let a man's religion, politics or nationality interfere with friendship, but if any man treats you like an SOB, then you treat him back like a double SOB.' "

Religion, politics, nationality? How about color?

"That too," said Mersch. "I'm not agin nobody."

Just like the mayor promised: A sensitivity problem.

Well, this *is* rural Iowa.

A young California couple discovers Iowa hospitality at its finest

February 1987

KELLOGG, IA.—Have you been wondering why the publicly traded stock of Casey's General Stores—those convenience food marts rapidly taking the place of so many mom-and-pop operations in small midwestern towns—is soaring as it is? It's probably because of incidents like this one.

In Kellogg, a town of 650, a young man and woman, toting a video camera, walked into the Casey's late on the afternoon of Sunday, January 18. Store manager Carolyn Haws looked them over. Clerk Debbie Daman struck up the initial conversation with them. Haws said hello, too, and then got involved. Oh, did she ever.

The couple introduced themselves as Rob and Lynn Beaumont from Los Angeles, California. "They were good-looking young kids, I suppose in their late 20s," Haws said. "They said they'd met each other for the first time when they were 14 years old and then didn't meet again until seven years later, when they were 21. And about a year ago, they'd gotten married. They said they'd made an agreement that every seven years, they'd do something real special with each other. I guess getting married last year was real special, so they went out to eat at that famous Brown Derby restaurant out in California.

"Apparently they decided that night that seven years would be too long to wait, so why not make it an annual deal? They'd call that dinner at the Brown Derby their 'first annual 7-year trip,' and they started making plans for the second one. They got ahold of a big, national map, and then they got out a pencil. They said they both grabbed the pencil, closed their eyes and stuck it down on the map. Of all the places they could've hit, they put that pencil right on Kellogg, Iowa."

Rob Beaumont told Haws he works for an airline company and that he and his wife had flown in to Des Moines that afternoon. He explained they wanted to use their video camera to take some pictures around town and then planned to go find a motel room. Haws told them the nearest motels were in Newton, nine miles to the west. The man said they'd go there and then return for dinner.

"He said they'd come back and eat one of our 99-cent deli sandwiches, since that's all we really have to eat here," Haws said. "He said that their agreement was to 'make it legal,' they had to have a meal together."

So the California couple left, promising to come back shortly. Well, manager Haws and clerk Daman, both of whom must be romantics at heart, weren't about to let these young lovers celebrate with deli sandwiches.

"Debbie said she'd run down to her grandmother's house and get a card table and a good linen tablecloth," Haws said. "So after she did that, I went home and made a pan of lasagna." She also "fixed a pasta salad to go with the meal and a lettuce salad to have first. Then I looked around and found my Christmas candlesticks and a nice bud vase for flowers.

"We set it all up so that we had a candlelight dinner all ready for them over in one corner of the store when they came back in. We had wine goblets and everything. But you can't serve wine in a Casey's, you know, so we gave them gingerale and told them to pretend it was wine."

The Californians, as you might guess, were pleasantly overwhelmed.

"They really got into the spirit of it," Haws said. "They were shooting their video all the time. They were having fun, but they were doing it without making fun of our little town, even though there isn't a whole lot to do here. They promised to send us a tape of their film.

"I think they really had a good time."

On a Wednesday night, it is possible to get "too excited" in Parkersburg — just ask Pedro

May 1983

PARKERSBURG, IA. — I've just met a cockatoo named Pedro here. Wondrous bird. Pedro not only whistles the full tune of "Yankee Doodle," but he also does wolf whistles at 81-year-old Tena Huisman when she walks past his cage in the workshop. Tena giggles because she knows Pedro learned this woo-woo from her husband of 61 years, Bill.

Bill, she explains, is even more of a character than Pedro. Now that I have seen both bird and Bill in action, I believe her.

Every Wednesday night, as they have done for 17 years, the Huismans — and Pedro, too, for that matter — share the large shop building out behind their home with a whole bunch of amateur musicians. They come from all over northeast Iowa to this town of 1,968 near Waterloo for three hours of picking, grinning, singing and forgetting about the worries of their workaday worlds.

On my Wednesday night, they ranged in age from drummer Rick Huisman, 29, grandson of the hosts, to Ed Mulnix, 82, who drove over from Evansdale to play his fiddle and to wear a ball cap proclaiming himself to be "Ed the Old Fiddler."

If most of these musicians aren't too good, well, most of them aren't too bad, either. The music selection includes some bluegrass, country-western, spirituals, Mexican — oh, best we call it folk music and forget subcategories. The rules: No beer, booze, drugs, pop, coffee, food or misbehaving. Just music and fun.

Attention shifts around the room as first one performer, then another, breaks into an old favorite with the rest of the group joining in. Merlin Meyer, an Ackley farmer and accordion player, hits "Roll Out the Barrel." Tako Ubben, Aplington, who recently was "lambasted" after 22 years on the job in hard-hearted cutbacks at the *Waterloo Courier,* plunks a guitar and sings that to solve a lot of life's problems, "Throw Another Log on the Fire."

Around they go, to the likes of Meta Parker of Parkersburg on a small organ, Bob Hof of Liscomb on bass, Jeannette Burrows of Parkersburg on banjo, Jim Gould of Conrad on violin, Don Huisman, son of the hosts, getting ready for his all-night shift as P-Burg town cop by playing guitar, and others.

The real stars, though, are Pedro, whom everyone says hello to at some time during the night, and his pal, Bill Huisman, master of all stringed instruments "except the German zither." Master of cornball humor, too.

"Play 'Peek-a-Boo,'" someone yells at him, referring to a grand old song. He smirks, then answers: "I used to play peek-a-boo until I got so old I was getting more boo than peek, so I quit." Har.

This old ham used to be an auctioneer and crazy as he gets making music, it's not difficult imagining him drawing huge crowds to sales. He goes through several hats and a wig in the course of an evening's entertainment, always patting his scalp as he removes them and asking, "My hair look OK?" He's bald as a banjo cover.

When he plays seriously, he plays beautifully, especially fiddles and banjos. He dabbles in buying, selling and fixing instruments and has hundreds around the shop. He also makes some. Ever seen a mandolin made from a hubcap? Or a violin made from a Pella wooden shoe? Or a ukulele that's really a turtle shell? Hanging up over his cluttered desk is a genuine armadillo shell, which doubtlessly has a future as some sort of wacky stringed instrument.

There are also lots of birds in cages—fake birds, mechanical ones. Pedro's the only real bird around here. Anyway, Bill trips some secret switch as he plays, and some of these birds sing. Bill puckers, pretends he's the whistler and takes all the praise for this virtuosity. The crowd loves it.

It drives Pedro a little nuts. The whistling, the crowd, the music. It's all a bit much for a sensitive cockatoo. So at times during the jam session, Tena Huisman slips a cover over his cage. "Otherwise," she explains, "he gets too excited."

It perhaps never occurred to you it is possible to get "too excited" in Parkersburg on a Wednesday night. But you've never seen wild Bill Huisman put on his hillbilly hat, brim turned up, plumes of pheasant feathers, and play a guitar with just one of his hands. Woo-woo!

Sampling Spillville's unique heritage – including the composer Dvořák

June 1985

SPILLVILLE, IA. – If you have any appreciation of the past at all, I don't know that there's another town this small (population 417) in the state that can awe you as this northeast Iowa community can.

Spillvillians wear their Czechoslovakian heritage like a badge of honor, with conversation in some homes still being carried on in the Czech language and with most everyone carrying a decided accent in English. They tell Iowa's official arbiter of cinnamon rolls he's never really had pastry if he hasn't stuffed himself with their kolaches and rholickies.

But it goes much deeper, and the locals invite one and all to sample just how deep in this, the town's quasquicentennial (125th) year. There are activities going on all summer, peaking with a two-day festival August 10–11 that celebrates not only the town's founding but also that of gorgeous old St. Wenceslaus Catholic Church, built from native limestone and lumber.

Go into the grand old church, being restored to its original quaintness and splendor, and you will, if you have ever plied a keyboard, stand transfixed before a massive old pipe organ.

"The sound is so clear, brilliant, glorious," says Dave Anderson, a parishioner and music teacher at nearby Turkey Valley High School who often plays it. "But there's an even bigger feeling of history when you think of what fingers have played that thing."

He refers first and foremost to those of the great Czech composer Antonin Dvořák, who, weary of New York, came to spend the summer here in 1893. Dvořák, recharged by being among his countrymen again, turned out a half-dozen of his great works while here, but each day interrupted his work to walk up the hill and play the organ during Mass.

Ever since, the parish priests at St. Wenceslaus have become accustomed to classical musicians of various credentials dropping by and talking them out of the key to the organ so they can "play the instrument that Dvořák played." I feel almost sinful thinking what I'd do to be able to try my "Amazing Grace" on it once.

Downtown, you find the most amazing piece of city government–owned property in the state – the Bily clock museum.

Two bachelors, Joseph and Frank Bily, now dead 20 years, spent their lives' leisure time hand-carving more than a dozen wooden clocks that stretch to the ceiling and amaze you not only with their artistry but also with their little figures shuttling in and out of cubbyholes as new hours are chimed. When the brothers were alive, they would draw crowds to their farm home for 10-cent tours of the buildings in which the clocks were housed, spurning all offers to buy the exotic time pieces. They decided late in life that they would give all their works to the city of Spillville, provided the clocks would be housed and taken care of by the town in the charming old brick building in which Dvořák and his family lived during their long-ago summer here. Now, 30,000 visitors a year go through the museum, which is open daily from May through October and is tended by Rusty Poshusta and other guides.

City officials, like Mayor Ed Klimesh, really have no idea of the total value of the clocks. Klimesh says the city is required to pay a $6,000 annual insurance fee on them, if that gives you any idea of their value. But perhaps more revealing is that Poshusta says she has been offered a million dollars for just *one* of them. She declined, of course.

Gracefully linking past and present is an old wooden ballroom in a park on the banks of the Turkey River, the Inwood. The only way I know how to describe it is that it is a small town ballroom exactly like God intended small town ballrooms to be. Built in the 1920s, and still oh so active today, it can hold up to 900 and has seen not only every regional polka band, but also national acts like the Byrds and Buddy Holly. It's busy almost every Saturday night with wedding dances, and Lord only knows how many of the young couples first fell in love on starry Inwood evenings.

The ambitious mayor, Klimesh, who is 36 and an English teacher in the South Winneshiek Community Schools, gives the town more heady leadership than it realizes. He is as modern as his geodesic-domed home, yet as traditional as the kolaches he insists visitors sample.

"It's funny in a town like this," he says. "There is a continuing debate among residents about how far we should go in promoting tourism. We're all proud of what we have here, but there is somewhat of a reluctance to opening up to the point where we are overrun."

For this summer, though, he notes, Spillville wants to share.

Westphalia's anguish after a tough internal conflict goes public

October 1981

WESTPHALIA, IA. – There is a big hurt in little Westphalia, population 169. This is a very Catholic community, one in which the parish priest is regarded as the shepherd, the parishioners as his flock. To continue the analogy to a painful conclusion, many of the sheep now think they were led to the wolf. And contempt for a priest is not something Westphalians are comfortable feeling.

Then there is the Westphalia Volunteer Fire Department, 23 members strong, which exists as all such departments do: to protect, to serve, and to have a heck of a good time. Much appreciated, seldom challenged. Yet here they stood accused – by, among others, the priest – of violating Iowa's liquor laws. The firefighters went to court last week to "save our reputation." They won, but the victory was not all sweet.

"This kind of friction in a town this small is not good," said Mike Schechinger, 42, a firefighter. "It has ripped Westphalia apart. It was just a local disagreement that went too far. It's hard to believe it wound up in a jury trial in district court. It has undone all the good public relations the department built up over the years. We've even got some of our wives mad at us because we fought this when a priest was involved. Challenging a priest is a tough thing to have to do."

The fuss began last year.

It is common knowledge that in Westphalia, as in a string of other small, predominantly Catholic towns along the west side of Shelby County, the liquor laws of the state of Iowa have been winked at through the years. Church halls, often the largest buildings in town, have been used for dances and parties at which liquor was sold without anyone having procured a license to do so.

In May 1980, County Attorney J. C. Salvo of Harlan decided it was time to do something about that. Salvo wrote a letter to pastors of all Catholic churches in the county advising them that when booze is served or consumed at parties or gatherings on church property, there must be strict compliance with the law. He wrote that "as a fellow Catholic" he understood the traditions, but that the law is the law and, besides, "we must also be aware of the image that we display to our non-Catholic neighbors."

As Salvo's assistant prosecutor, Richard Schenck, pointed out, this wasn't an issue that "a teetotaling Baptist county attorney" could address, but Salvo had proper credentials for the fight.

Among the priests who took Salvo's warning to heart was the Rev. Michael Sims, the young—he is in his early 30s—pastor of St. Boniface parish here. He began a serious inquiry into the law and how it would affect parties held in the hall adjacent to the church.

Among the people who use the hall were the firefighters, who held at least two fund-raising events there each year—one a soup supper during the annual Super Bowl football game, the other a chicken supper in the spring. They would customarily set up a cash bar. Although neither the firefighters nor the parish held a liquor license, "We never thought what we were doing was illegal," Schechinger said.

But things were going to change. In the year or so of discussions on what the changes would be, the dynamics of small town living came into play. Here we had the firefighters, all of whom are Catholic, battling the priest, himself a fireman, and the firefighters and priest battling the governing parish council, which, naturally, included a couple of firefighters as members.

The question was not whether booze would be allowed in the parish hall in the future but rather whether a liquor license should be purchased and, if so, by whom. Maurice Dingman, bishop of the Diocese of Des Moines, which includes Westphalia, attended one meeting and attempted to straighten things out.

But the people of Westphalia proved to be intractable, remaining at loggerheads after a dozen or more meetings held over several months.

The outcome: No one purchased a liquor license, but the firefighters served booze at their chicken dinner in the parish hall in April. Schechinger testified he thought "everything was legally hunky-dory" because the event was called "a private party for firemen and their friends," even though 500 "friends" attended. The booze was given away rather than sold, although donations to the fire department were accepted in another part of the room.

About that time, Father Sims began feeling "I had been in Westphalia four and a half years . . . long enough." He requested a transfer, which came through in July. He now serves in a team ministry in Creston.

Also about that time, Salvo and Schenck began a long investigation of the chicken supper, an investigation resulting in the fire department being charged with dispensing liquor without a license. Father Sims was subpoenaed as the key state witness, a role that he said was "very difficult for me."

"I know a number of people in Westphalia think Father Sims pressed the charges, that this was his baby," said Salvo, "but that's not true. I'll tell you why I went after this. We had all the other parishes in the county agreeing to abide by the liquor laws, and then all of a sudden Westphalia pulled this 'private party' deal. People from the other parishes were coming back on me and saying 'Hey, is the law different for Westphalia than for us?' I had to do something."

The case was tried on Thursday before a jury of four men and four women. After four hours of testimony, the jury deliberated for two and a half hours and found the fire department innocent. Foreman Jerry Ahrenholtz, who at one point wore a fancy cowboy hat in the jury box, said the jurors "just didn't feel they proved 'er beyond the shadow of a doubt."

Said prosecutor Schenck: "In one way we were quite surprised at the verdict. But in another way it wasn't totally unanticipated, considering the nature of the defendant. We were charging a volunteer fire department, an organization that is generally very highly thought of."

Salvo had said in his final argument to the jury that "the case is nothing more, nothing less, than a question of whether liquor was dispensed illegally."

But in the early aftermath, Westphalians already were discovering that the case was much more than Salvo said. It really was a case of one kicking oneself in both shins.

One pool hall
that even a
mother would love

September 1981

OSCEOLA, IA. – You know how mothers are about their sons and pool halls. Well, Van Dyke's Recreation in this southern Iowa town of 3,750 is the kind of a pool hall your mother wouldn't mind – no booze, no beer and a large sign over the front table saying, "Please, no profane language."

It isn't that Wynette Van Dyke, 50, for three years the proprietress, is bluenosed about the common vices. She'll take a drink, and she's been known to utter an indelicacy now and then.

But she regards her business as being something of a community center. "If I put beer or booze in, I'd make more money, sure," she said. "Then I couldn't have the kids in here. And the language? I admit we bend that rule quite a bit, especially when this one guy named Red Cottrell gets to playing. He's a pistol. But pool halls have always had such roughhouse reputations, I figure it doesn't hurt to have the language controlled, just a little."

Van Dyke's is a traditional-looking place. The building is 100 feet from entrance to alley and 25 feet wide. There are old ceiling fans and a dark, oiled-wood floor. There are five snooker tables and one 8-ball table. Wooden benches are along the walls, just below the racks that hold the 100 house cues and 50 or so privately owned ones. (The cue that has the rifle scope mounted on it was made as a gag for Cottrell, who always complains he can't see well enough to shoot a good game.)

The regulars start coming in as soon as the door opens at noon. One of the first on hand is Arlo Harger, about 70. He buys a bag of peanuts and takes the same seat every day near the front table. Players on that table don't have to bother recording their scores on the chalkboard because Harger keeps totals in his head.

Walter Utley, 67, a retired farmer, comes in early, too. "I've never played a game of pool in my life," he boasted. Yet, he spends most of the afternoon racking balls, collecting the money (20 cents per player per game) and running after pop and candy for the other customers. Why? "Something to do," he said.

"He works harder here than I do," said Van Dyke of Utley. "And all he'll take for pay is a free bottle of pop and one candy bar every day. Can you imagine someone working for that in this day 'n' age?"

Van Dyke began talking about how "I can almost set my clock by when some of these old guys come in here." She had no more than said that when Bill James walked in. "Wild Bill!" she said, almost scolding. "You're five minutes late. Do you have a good excuse?"

The snooker games start and stop as team combinations form and re-form. It's not all older men. There are a lot of nightshift workers at local factories, so a good many young men wander in to play in the early afternoon.

The kidding that goes on during the games is friendly, sometimes loud. Some of it is directed at Van Dyke. "Yes, I take a lot of ribbing from them," she said. "So I devil them right back, too."

She has a standing bet with the youngsters. "If they whip me in pool, the game's on me," she said. "I'm not much of a shooter so there's been an awful lot of free pool played in here the last couple of years."

She acknowledged that financially, the business could be better. "But I see those older men come in and see what this place means to them," she said. "They can spend all day in here without spending any money at all if they want to. There's a lot more good that comes out of here than money."

She said she is firm in her resolve not to serve beer and to keep the language reasonably clean. "I had a Foursquare minister in here shooting snooker one night," she said. "It really means something to me to have the kind of place a man like that will come in to."

A night in New Hampton's naughtiest motel room

November 1981

NEW HAMPTON, IA. – Business travelers like myself come to treasure the few unique hotel and motel rooms, those that have their own character. We know the good ones around Iowa.

For example, we always ask for one of the upstairs corner rooms when we are at the Manning Hotel in Keosauqua. They're beautiful. We can tell you about the bidet in the Presidential Suite at the Des Moines Marriott. Unusual. There's the Presidential Suite at Stouffer's Five Seasons Hotel in Cedar Rapids. Handsome indeed. We like the refurbished Blackhawk in Davenport. Very nice. And we know about the tub-for-two in the Heritage Suite at the Hyatt Des Moines. Tra-la, tra-la.

But now I'm one up on at least most of my fellow travelers. Why? Because the other night, I stayed in the Swinging Bed Room at the Mohawk Motel in New Hampton, population 3,940.

Let me set the scene. The Mohawk is a nice little 10-year-old motel located on the southwest edge of the business district. There is a utilitarian feel to the place, probably because one wing of the motel is given over to an electric motor repair shop and a dry cleaning establishment. The owner of all three businesses is Bart Townsend, 58, who is widely respected as a hard worker even if people do tend to wink about his Swinging Bed Room.

The key furnishing in the room is, as one might expect, a swinging bed. Installed six years ago, it is a normal mattress riding on a frame of massive wooden beams salvaged from a barn. Heavy chains stretch from each corner to the ceiling, suspending the bed about two and a half feet above the floor. The slightest motion by someone resting on the bed makes it start gently rocking to and fro. For special decorative effects, Townsend put large mirrors on three adjacent walls and the ceiling.

"I put the room together just as a gimmick," he said. "I didn't know whether it would be a popular thing or not. It's turned out to be very popular. It's used a lot by honeymooners."

That prompted an immediate question – who would come to New Hampton on their honeymoon?

"You'd be surprised," he said. "We get people from Minneapolis, and from Des Moines and Waterloo, too. And before they built a motel over in Nashua, we'd get a lot of couples who had their weddings at the Little Brown Church."

Aha. They would come to the church in the wildwood and then come to the Swinging Bed Room in New Hampton.

But business hasn't really lapsed since that competing motel was built. "The Swinging Bed Room averages being booked six and a half nights a week," he said. "Most of the business comes by word of mouth. People will call and say, 'We had some friends tell us about your room.' But sometimes we go through the wedding announcements in the papers and send out letters of congratulations that explain about our special rooms for newlyweds – we have the Water Bed Room besides the Swinging Bed Room."

A few years ago, Townsend stirred the community by taking out a large advertisement in the local paper, announcing that special rooms were available and that couples could use them for a fun night out.

"That got a lot of talk going around town," he said. "There was no immediate increase in business, but two to three weeks later, local people started streaming in. They really seem to enjoy themselves, which is great. A lot of marriages could stand something like this, you know."

Rates for the Swinging Bed Room are $17.31 on weeknights and $21.50 on weekend nights. Newlyweds receive a complimentary bottle of champagne.

So, fellow business travelers, here we have a truly different motel room. However, there are a couple of negative points I must make about New Hampton's Swinging Bed Room. First, the traveling man who stays alone in the room will receive some kidding if he stops at a local cafe or bar and mentions in conversation where he is staying. Take it from me. Second, the reading light is terrible.

Allerton shows the way
we all know
Thanksgiving should be

November 1984

ALLERTON, IA. – I've got a feeling the way they do Thanksgiving in this southern Iowa town of 650 is the way it's really supposed to be done.

This past, brilliant Thursday, whole families toting picnic baskets full of covered dishes and tableware began arriving at the spacious Centennial Building late in the morning. Inside, members of the Community Club were finishing carving 80 pounds of turkey and 38 pounds of ham the club purchased with proceeds from an Election Day bake sale.

And right after the noon whistle blew, some 200 people said grace and then sat down for their annual town Thanksgiving Day feast. Later, there was a brief message about the meaning of Thanksgiving, some hymn singing and a good deal of visiting. For the sick and elderly who could not make it downtown, plates of food were put together and delivered to their homes.

There is no charge for any of this. In Allerton, you see, they really do share their blessings on Thanksgiving Day.

No one can pinpoint when this neat tradition got started.

"Oh, I don't know – six, seven, maybe eight years ago," said Bob Wampler, 59, who with his wife operates Bob and Teressa's Country Store, a farm supply business, across the street from the Centennial Building.

"Teressa and I had been talking about Thanksgiving back then, and we knew a lot of people, especially older people, wind up being alone that day. You know, if you're alone on a holiday, it's not really a holiday. We decided we could do something about it."

That year, the Wamplers, who also farm, had an oversupply of chickens, squash, frozen corn and apples that would be perfect for pies. So they arranged to use the Methodist Church basement for Thanksgiving afternoon and said anybody who wanted to could come join their family for dinner.

"We had this at the church there for two or three years, and we couldn't handle more than about 35 people," said Teressa. "A lot

88   **SMALL TOWNS**

more were wanting to come, so we decided to move it on to the Centennial Building, and that's when our Allerton-World Booster Club took over supplying the meat. Everybody's been pitching in ever since."

For example, soon after Teressa had arrived at 6 A.M. to supervise final preparation of the turkey and dressing, in walked 11-year-old Jennifer De Bolt, asking if there wasn't something she could do to help. She spent the next couple of hours washing tabletops, setting napkins and filling and placing salt and pepper shakers.

Thursday's gathering was typical of recent years. The youngest person there was 3-week-old Brett Brown. The oldest was 93-year-old Edith Snodgrass. When Bessie Lowcock, 89, arrived, she answered all inquiries about how she was with, "No room to complain." But then she did complain just a bit. "I won't know anybody here," she said.

Wrong, said a 28-year-old man standing in front of her. "You know me, Bessie. I'm David Wampler, one of the Wampler boys," he said.

She eyed him closely, noticed his new beard, and then said: "Why, of course. I guess I didn't recognize you because of the way you're decorating your face."

Twice during the afternoon, Bob Wampler, who surely must have the last flattop in America, strode to the microphone in his flannel shirt, blue jeans and cowboy boots and addressed his fellow Allertonians.

The first time was to say the grace. "I used basically the same one I used last year, because I liked it and because no one will remember it," he said. "But because of the Ethiopian situation, I did add the line saying, 'Help us to be touched by, and to respond to, the pain and suffering of our brothers and sisters in foreign lands.'"

The second time, it was to deliver a bit of a history lesson about Thanksgiving, noting that aboard the Mayflower, there had been two men named Allerton. Then he closed with some thoughts on counting blessings.

"In the laws of mathematics, when you divide something, it becomes scattered," he said. "But in the laws of nature, when you divide something, it multiplies, and that's how it is when we divide our blessings."

Then the Reverend Dave Higdon, a Methodist from Lake Mills who married an Allerton girl, picked a spot under the huge American flag and led the singing of "We Gather Together" and "Come Ye Thankful People Come."

It was almost a tearful experience for a veteran Iowa-watcher, a firm believer in the folk goodness in this state. The community spirit in that building was alive, well, warm and caring.

The best definitions of our life here — "You know you're in small town Iowa when . . . "

June 1987

After all these years of roaming Iowa's highways and byways, I feel like I've almost qualified for a doctorate degree in what I would call Iowana. Of course, to get a doctorate, you need a thesis. I know what mine would be. It is the report from a project I became involved in six years ago — a fun examination of our life in this state that took the form of completing the phrase, "You know you're in small town Iowa when . . . "

In a sense, it's become almost the albatross for me that judging cinnamon rolls was before I resigned from the Roll Poll. For whenever I'm out speaking in Iowa, I virtually can't get away from audiences without someone asking that I do "the small town Iowa thing." So here it is in print.

The story behind it involves my good friend and journalistic brother John D. Field, editor and publisher of the *Hamburg Reporter* and the author of a very cosmopolitan column in that paper called "Country Tub Thumping."

It was Christmastime in 1980, I believe, when John found himself attending a rather dashing holiday cocktail party in Hamburg. Everyone was dressed up and behaving well. A local man walked up to Field and said, "That's a handsome new suit you're wearing there, John."

"Well, thank you," Field responded, "but the truth is elsewhere. This suit is five years old."

Field went home, thought about that, got up the next morning and called me. "It struck me," he said, "that you know you're in small town Iowa when absolutely everybody thinks they know when you buy a new suit. The more I thought about it, the more I realized we're on to something. Let's run a joint contest between our two columns, mine in Hamburg and yours in the *Register,* and have folks who really know complete the phrase, 'You know you're in small town Iowa when . . .'"

He had one more qualifier: "Look, since your column has a few more readers than mine, let's run the contest in your column."

"Fine," I said. "Then the grand prize will be on you."

Field: "Oh? And what'll that be?"

"A night on the town in Hamburg with the two of us."

So that's how it started. We launched our contest in the *Register,* using some completions of the phrase that Field and I made up. (We've been glad we did that, because as this thing has been re-printed and broadcast across the nation, Field and I have been able to keep track of it by recognizing the answers that were ours.) We held the contest open two weeks, during which more than 3,000 responses from Iowans were received.

We named an overall winner, a University of Northern Iowa professor named Dennis Cryer, who'd based the many answers he sent us on his boyhood in the small community of Treynor. And, yes, Field and I and Cryer went out one night and shot up the town of Hamburg.

In the years since, more and more ways to complete the phrase have continued coming to us from people in the state. At this writing, these are my favorites: *Oh, yes, you know you're in small town Iowa when . . .*

A night on the town in Hamburg sounds like a big deal.

You receive get-well cards after having a vasectomy.

You're born on June 13 and receive prizes from the merchants for being the second baby of the year.

Everybody in town knows who the father of the puppies is.

You don't need to use your car's turn signals because everybody knows where you're going.

You can charge your groceries.

Third Street is on the edge of town.

There is a widely followed race each spring to see who gets the first tomatoes from his vines.

And there's more here. There's no doubt you're in small town Iowa when . . .

You dial a wrong number but wind up talking 15 minutes anyway.

You can and do speak to each dog you meet by name and get a friendly wag in return.

During harvest season, you get run off Main Street by a combine.

You find out the airport is terraced.

The editor/publisher of the newspaper carries a camera.

Nobody looks twice when you ride a horse down the street.

After a major snowstorm, the farmers all have a race to see who can be the first one to get to town, sit in the coffee shop and talk about how tough it was to get to town.

The realtor advertises he'll show houses at night so no one will know you're looking.

Great fun, huh? Well, there's more to come. You know you're in small town Iowa when . . .

You're the local theater manager, and when it comes time to say the Pledge of Decency in church, everyone turns around to see if you're saying it, too.

It's hard to walk to work for exercise because it takes too long to stop and explain what you're doing to everybody stopping and offering you a ride.

You get married and the local newspaper devotes a half-page to the story.

You drive into a ditch five miles out of town and "the word" gets back before you do.

The same five people run everything in town.

People "let themselves in for a chat" just as you're stepping out of the tub.

You move to another house in town and the mailman doesn't have to be notified of the change of address.

You mistakenly write a counter check on the wrong bank and they cover it anyway.

And still more. You know you're in small town Iowa when . . .

Everybody knows whose check is good and whose husband isn't.

The winner of the "most popular" category in the local art show has entered a painted saw.

You go out for 15 minutes to clear a bit of snow the boy you hired to shovel has missed, only to have your husband come home from his office for lunch and say, "I hear you were out shoveling snow this morning."

Your extra chairs for family gatherings are borrowed from the funeral parlor.

The cop has a one-way radio.

Everybody knows your middle name and uses it, along with your first and last names, when they're scolding you.

The local radio station announces it will preempt its network coverage of Saturday's Iowa-Illinois homecoming football game so that it can bring you float-by-float coverage of the Pancake Day parade.

You can pick up the local paper and see printed evidence that people really care who had dinner with whom.

But most of all, you know you're in small town Iowa when people really care—period.

As my friend Max Rauer once said, "Who has more fun than people?" Here's a look at a bunch of Iowa's finest, every-day folks.

IOWANS

As a 9-year-old, Jason Conway had pretty well figured out the vicious circle

August 1979

It's good to sit for a serious chat with your kids. Especially if you can reach mutual understanding about what could turn into a problem.

So it was that Rob Conway, who lives northwest of Des Moines, sat recently with his 9-year-old Jason. Jason is grade-school chunky. Not fat, really, but stocky . . . maybe even firepluggish. His folks are mildly concerned. If he doesn't watch his diet, he could have a problem.

Rob, in a fatherly manner, raised the issue for discussion. Jason, as sharp as he is hefty, erupted in monologue.

"Dad, it's like this," he said.

"I'm bored.

"And when I'm bored, I eat.

"When I eat, I get fat.

"When I get fat, the kids call me names.

"When they call me names, I beat them up.

"When I beat them up, I get grounded.

"And when I get grounded, I get bored."

A stunned Rob Conway sat in silence.

"What was there to say?" the father, shaking his head, confessed later. "He said it all, didn't he?"

The boy knows the vicious circle.

The time a small town
editor tweaked me good –
and my sweet revenge

February 1987

SPIRIT LAKE, IA. – Many times in the past, people who have been skewered in the press have later come to ask me what response, if any, they should have made. After all, it is easy in the day or two after the attack to lose control of your bruised feelings, to want to go look up the author of the assault and rework his orthodontia.

My advice to the wounded has always been to rise above the passion of the moment, let some time pass, rethink it all and then go ahead in life, essentially ignoring what's been said about you. I always felt that was pretty good advice, until it happened to me.

There is, in this northwest Iowa town, a newspaper called the *Spirit Lake Beacon.* The managing editor is Brooks Taylor. Earlier this month, he used his column to carve me up good. Consider the headline on his piece: "Iowa Boy more like 'Iowa Bore.' " It got my attention, I'll tell you.

Taylor's opening: "The state's 'love affair' with *Des Moines Register* columnist Chuck Offenburger never ceases to amaze us. [Is it] that his trade has made him a celebrity? From this point of view, the quality of his column certainly wouldn't make him one. There are several *Register* columnists, one being Marc Hansen, who write circles around Offenburger.

"Maybe it's visibility. Offenburger seemingly visits every little hamlet in the state and accessibility is a great public relations tool. Whatever the case, he has the state by the tail. Every time he visits an Iowa town, he gains an advance front-page story and another story accompanied by pictures.

"Maybe the love affair with Offenburger signals that some Iowans have little to do with their time. Hopefully, no group in the lakes region is staging a contest to secure an Offenburger visit because we can ensure you that he won't merit a 48-point headline, two stories and a pair of pictures in the *Beacon.*"

I read it. And reread it. "Take that, big boy," I said to myself. "When you dish it out, as occasionally you do, you also must be able to take it."

And I was taking it quite well.

A week went by, and the next edition of the *Beacon* included several letters about Taylor's column, some saying his comments were on the mark and some saying he's obviously a green-eyed twit who ought to quit carping about such a nice young man in Des Moines.

Meanwhile, I was still rising above it all. Being cool.

That continued until Tuesday, when I was lunching in Pocahontas while on a northwest Iowa swing. The thought hit me that in another hour I would be in Taylor's backyard and that if ever I was going to do anything about what he had written, this was the time.

I had nearly talked myself out of that when I stopped in Milford to see my old pal, Herman Richter, the clothier and guiding genius behind the "University of Okoboji" promotions.

Thinking back now on what eventually happened, I must put some of the blame on Richter. After all, he has never been known as one to discourage foolhardiness. He has often told me, "I don't mind growing old, I just don't want to grow up."

Richter asked me how I was holding up after Taylor's recent barrage, and I told him I was being very mature about it. I'd no sooner said that than I realized Richter and I were looking wide-eyed at each other, asking ourselves, "Has it really come to this for us? Are we getting so old that we think maturity is admirable?"

Within minutes, Richter and I were off like a pair of guerrillas. We made a stop in the pastry section of the Milford Buy-Rite food store and sped on to Spirit Lake.

We parked behind the *Beacon* office, walked through the loading dock area and into the back shop. I sent Richter to Taylor's office up front, telling him to lure the columnist back down the hallway, where I crouched around a corner. When footsteps drew near, I jumped out to confront him.

Rise above it? Be mature? Be cool? Bullfeathers!

"Brooks Taylor?" I said. "I'm Chuck Offenburger. I agree with some of what you wrote. Marc Hansen writes circles around me. Small town papers shouldn't give me so much coverage. But one thing I dispute. I'm *not* boring." Whereupon I did a left hook with a cream pie and put it right on that sucker's face.

He spends 300 hours
a year sitting on a bench
and watching the
world go by

November 1979

When we first saw him, in August as RAGBRAI was passing through Deep River, he was just sitting there watching the passing scene. When we next saw him, on a slow-paced trip through the countryside in October, he was still just sitting there.

Donald Armstrong, 74, a retired farmer, sits a lot on the old, worn bench in front of the Deep River Garage. His nephew owns the place. Occasionally, the nephew talks the uncle into fixing flat tires. But when he's not busy, the uncle sits out in front—talking crops, talking weather, talking anything with anyone who happens by.

"Don't ask me why I sit out there," he said.

"Mr. Armstrong, why is it you sit out there?" we immediately asked.

"It's sure not to watch guys going up and down the street, I'll tell you that," he said with a wink.

Well, how much does he sit out there?

"I don't know," he said. "I don't time myself. But I do know I must've spent 16 hours on the bench the day the bike ride came through. I never saw anything like that. Fact is, I was having so much fun I called Ellen at noon and told her traffic was so heavy she'd have to bring my dinner down, that I just wasn't going to be able to get home."

And did she?

"She did," he said.

But how much is he out there?

"I said I don't know," he said.

Well, we said, let's try to figure it out.

Four hours on a nice day?

"Maybe," he said. Fifteen nice days a month?

"At least," he said. Five months of decent bench-sittin' weather per year?

"Yup."

That'd be 300 hours on the bench per season?

"I can't argue with that," he said. "Oh, I suppose maybe I would have to give or take 100 hours either way. But, whatever it is, I sure as hell waste a lot of time, don't I? Beats hell out of working."

Makes sense.

Lois Heskett stole
two cars in one
day without realizing it

February 1987

ESTHERVILLE, IA. – Lois Heskett demands that first of all I tell you that while she might be "a little nutty" and too frequently forgetful, she is not – and I repeat *not* – a car thief. That done, I'll relate to you the tale of how she stole two cars in one day without realizing it.

Heskett is a 15-year employee of Iowa Lakes Community College here. She now chairs the department of health occupations.

On a Thursday late in January, she was to drive from Estherville to Algona for an early morning chat with officials of Garrigan High School about a new health class. Heskett had made arrangements to take one of the college's cars, a 1975 blue Buick Riviera that some supporter had donated recently.

Now, before we go on here, you must remember that it is very common in many small towns for drivers to leave the keys in their cars and not to lock the doors.

So Heskett got to the college early, "when it was still sort of dark," went out back, got into a blue Buick Riviera and drove away to Algona.

"I should have been suspicious," she said, "because this was supposed to be a college car and there was no logbook in it. But the weather was bad that morning, and I wanted to get on to Algona before it got worse, so I didn't really take time to think about that."

When she got to her meeting, she was interrupted by a telephone call from Rose Bates, a secretary back at the college in Estherville. "I believe that you took the wrong car," said Bates. "You took mine." Hers also is a Buick Riviera, also blue but a much newer model.

Heskett was, naturally, embarrassed and promised to drive very carefully back to Estherville. She had to make an additional stop before she left Algona, "at the office of an attorney who'd done my income taxes. I had to sign the forms." She pulled into a parking place, stopped and—now mindful of the fact she was driving a friend's car—she locked the doors and took the keys.

She went in, signed the tax forms and came back out to leave for Estherville. The car she got into was a blue Buick and the keys were in it. Away she drove, not taking time to notice that this was not a Riviera but a LeSabre.

When she got back to the college in Estherville, she went immediately into the office, apologized to Rose Bates for taking her car, reached in her pocket and handed Bates her keys.

"I don't know whether Rose didn't trust me at that point or what. But she went outside to check her car," Heskett said. "She came back and said, 'I've been around this building four times, and I can't find it.'

"I went right back out with her and pointed it out. But she said, 'Lois, that's not mine!' It was then that I dug around in my purse and found a second set of keys, these marked with a tag saying 'Joe Bradley Cars.' "

Heskett immediately got on the telephone and called the Algona Police Department. Officers there confirmed that they had just received and put on the state crime computer a stolen-car report from Joe Bradley.

It seems that Bradley had driven a Buick LeSabre, which he had on his used car lot, to an attorney's office in downtown Algona, parked, left the keys and went in for a meeting. When he came back outside, the car was gone. After looking for it without success for a time, he called the cops.

Heskett, realizing finally that she had "stolen" not one but two cars that day, was powerfully embarrassed by now. "I told the Algona police that I'd drive right back over to their town with Mr. Bradley's car and pick up Rose's car," she said. "But they told me to wait a few minutes until they could get the stolen-car report removed from the state computer so that I wouldn't get arrested on the way over.

"I got back to Algona and gave the Bradleys their car. I asked them to take me out to Garrigan High School because I was assuming that that is where I'd made the mix-up. So they took me to the school, and we looked all over for Rose's car without seeing it. I was really starting to wonder what had happened. But right then, I remembered also stopping downtown, so we went there and found the car.

"I really feel terrible about it. You can imagine how much kidding I'm getting. I ask myself how I could have done such a thing. But my best friends are saying that if this could happen to anybody, it would be me. I guess that's the way I am."

Put three fairly militant young blacks in a small town barbershop discussion and race relations come into a warm, new focus

October 1981

Michael Easley, black Drake student: *"What really drives me crazy about all this is so many white people don't understand why we were mad."*

Dale Edwards, white Audubon farmer: *"You're talking to one of them."*

AUDUBON, IA. – Michael Easley and Dale Edwards didn't just happen to bump into each other at Sam's Barber Shop here and strike up a conversation about race relations.

No, they met at my invitation.

Accompanying Easley, 19, a sophomore from Des Moines, were two other members of the Drake University Black Student Organization – Veronica Blockton, 20, a sophomore from St. Louis, and Jeffery Smith, 19, a junior from suburban Chicago.

On hand from Audubon besides the 56-year-old Edwards were

Dorothy Kerkhoff, 53, a farmwife who is mother of eight children and chairman of the Audubon County Democratic Party, and Sam Kauffman, 45, the local oracle who owns the shop.

Sam's, on a prominent corner in this southwest Iowa town of 2,841, is my listening post, a little beachhead in the sea of public opinion.

I drop by every few months to see what people are thinking. We have a panel of regulars for our discussions – Kauffman, because he is a great talker; Edwards, because he is a farmer and every Iowa forum has to have a farmer; and a woman, because there must be a woman in everything these days, even barbershop bull sessions. (Kerkhoff was subbing for our regular, Norma Mountain, who was attending an out-of-state convention.) And, by shop rules, anyone who stops in for a haircut can also join the conversation.

In the past, we've covered sports, the sexes, politics, the economy – always applying as much wit as wisdom. This time, things were more serious. What had inspired this get-together, after all, was a bit of misguided flippancy that became a very unfunny racial slur.

It happened late last month at Drake in Des Moines. Jane Juffer, a sophomore from Sioux Center, wrote a story for the student newspaper about life in small town Iowa. In one part of the story, she was listing things many small towns do not have – "no movie theater, no shopping mall, no disco . . . "

Then she added this paragraph: "No blacks. No beatniks. No bedbugs, bedfellows (strange), or bralessness."

Black students were enraged. In letters to the editor and in a rally on the campus, they cited the Juffer statement as just another example of the racism of lily-white, small town Iowa. And in a burst of urban chauvinism, some black students dismissed small town life as "imaginary," one of them adding, "If [Juffer] wants to go back to her small town, she'll be OK. But I feel sorry for her if she thinks that small town is the real world."

Small town racism. Urban chauvinism. Worthy, important discussion topics for people who still hold hope that perhaps someday we might all learn to live together.

And so it happened that three young urban blacks and three older small town whites agreed to meet in a barbershop on an afternoon none will soon forget. It was tough, honest, fun, wrenching, revealing, frightening, civil.

Here was barber Kauffman, on the edge of frustration after

alternating among "colored" and "blacks" and "Negroes" all afternoon, finally saying, "Just what is it you people would prefer to be called?" Young Easley looked at his fellow students, looked back at Sam and answered: "Veronica, Jeffery, Michael."

Here was Chicagoan Jeffery Smith, uncompromising in his preference for city life with its ethnic and racial diversity, nevertheless admitting a growing concern about conditions in urban America—"more people, less resources, things more expensive, all of these contributing to the causes of crime and violence."

Here was Veronica Blockton, who grew up in tough St. Louis, saying she and most other blacks would be uneasy about stopping in a town like Audubon to buy something at a store. "There are the old jokes about getting lynched," she said. "I wouldn't really be worried about that, but, yes, I'd have at least a little fear."

Here was Dorothy Kerkhoff, asked if any one thing could quickly stop racism in the countryside, answering, "Brain surgery." Then she said with chagrin, "Several years ago a local minister had two young black children stay with him for part of a summer. Everyone thought they were so cute. If they would come back 30 or 35 years later, I'm afraid a lot of our people wouldn't think they were near so cute."

Here were all three students, absolutely astounded when businessman Wayne Crouse walked in the barbershop and everyone hailed him by his nickname, "Punk." Said Easley, "He doesn't care? Oh, man, in a city, we wouldn't call anyone 'Punk.' That'd be asking for trouble."

Here was Kauffman predicting (accurately, it turned out) that "the first thing people will ask me when this is over is whether I cut any of the blacks' hair. I guess there's some kind of curiosity about their hair texture. That same thing always comes up when a black is around here."

The point was made repeatedly that there is no more, and no less, racism in Audubon than in other small towns.

All six had strong doubts that a black family could live comfortably here, mainly because, as Edwards put it, "Birds of a feather flock together. . . . I think they'd miss being around more of their own kind." But, the Audubonites asked, could it really be better in the cities, places where, as Blockton said: "You have to watch your back?" Is there really less racism in the urban environment than in the small town one?

"The difference I think is awareness," said student Smith. "In cities, people are mixed in with people from so many different cultures. What happens is that they learn to accept other cultures. They become more sensitive about how things can hurt people from other cultures. The racism in small towns is bad, but I always imagine that it's probably unconscious. Things are said not with any real intention to hurt someone. It's just that the people don't really know about the different cultures.

"Being black, we know to live anywhere in America and become successful, we have to deal with white America. We *have* to. So we learn to accept your culture. But white America does not *have* to deal with black America. Whites can get their big house out away from everything and not have any contact at all with blacks, so they learn nothing about our culture."

Kerkhoff said she thought "we do get a little more exposure to blacks now through television than we used to." But Easley said the blacks appearing in the media are too often "just the athletes and criminals. There's more to us than that."

What to do?

"Most of us in this shop right now would agree that small town people need to realize there's more to life than what happens in their own town," said Kerkhoff. "But I'm afraid that's not the common feeling. Most of them probably feel that whatever they have is just fine, that there's no real need to know about how other people live in other places."

Can that feeling be changed?

"I think so," said student Blockton. "You start with the children, the young ones. They're always curious about everything. They're interested in what else is going on. What you have to do is get people who are aware of other cultures to talk to the children. That's how you start."

Kauffman acknowledged hard racial feelings in small towns but he said he has difficulty believing things are much better in the cities.

And student Smith agreed that, in a way, small towns are taking a bad rap. "They take bad raps in the same way other minorities do—blacks, Jews, women," he said. "You always hear small town people referred to as hicks. It's just a stereotype that you have to fight, like all the stereotypes blacks fight all the time."

It was when the discussion turned to stereotypes that farmer Edwards realized why the black students at Drake got so upset over what he earlier was calling "something that would have been a joke around here."

"Now it's starting to make sense to me what you got so stirred up about," he said. "No one likes to be stereotyped.

"Back in the '60s, we had a national cornhusking champion from here, Elmer Carlson. They flew him out to be on the Johnny Carson show. Now, this was a guy who never, I mean never, wore bibbed overalls. But when he got out there with Carson's people, the first thing they did was put a pair of old bibbed overalls on him for the show. I've never forgotten that. I was so damned mad. As far as I was concerned, they were mocking every farmer in America. God, I hated that. If that's how this was for you people, then I understand why you reacted like you did."

It was a nice way to close.

If you're sour, you'd never be admitted into the "Can't Come Crabby Club"

January 1984

RINGSTED, IA.—Time for another report on the social fabric of Iowa.

When those social organizations that have endured decades in this state are recognized, one that must be hailed is the Jack Creek CCC Club, which for 62 years has been meeting monthly in members' homes in Jack Creek Township near this small town tucked away in our northwest.

What's the CCC? Well, that's actually what brought me here, not the record of endurance, as admirable as it is. Yes, it was the name that got me: Can't Come Crabby Club.

"For years and years, that was kept real secret," said Mildred Dominy, whose mother was one of nine charter members. "Not even husbands or children were told. We just went by CCC Club. Then maybe 10 years ago, someone spilled it."

Club President Twila Olson said, "We still don't really advertise it much. We kind of keep it to ourselves." Yet, she admits after she moved here from Indiana seven years ago and joined, "I couldn't wait to write my friends back in Indiana and tell them the name."

And why not? As names of women's clubs go, the Can't Come Crabby Club is a classic. It's even better than another of my favorites, also known as a CCC club, the Calathump Comfort Club of the rural Calathump neighborhood near Allerton in Wayne County. And then there's the Stitch & Bitch Club of western Des Moines, but it's really in a league all by itself.

Carol McGarvey, a *Des Moines Register* writer who gave the S&B Club in Des Moines its name a few years ago, said, "It sounds as if we have a different operating theory than this club you've found in northwest Iowa. Apparently they go to their meetings to be pleasant. When our club gets together, we're there to get it all out of our systems before we go back home. Sometimes, in fact, we don't get any stitching done at all."

Back to rural Ringsted. Why did they name it the Can't Come Crabby Club way back there in 1921?

"We really don't know," said Dominy.

Does anyone ever show up crabby, or get crabby during a meeting, and thereby risk ouster?

"Oh no," said president Olson. "We all get along very well. And," said Dominy, "a remarkable thing is that it isn't a gossip club."

When I expressed mild disbelief at that, Olson 'fessed up: "Well, we do tell all the neighborhood news."

What else goes on?

The 21 current members, who range in age from 18 to 80, stick pretty close to the chartered purpose of the club, as outlined in the history and constitution. The Can't Come Crabby Club exists, those documents say in various places, "to be a source of entertainment, to be helpful to the community and to promote sociability with our neighbors." An early guide for what the meetings should be suggested that the women bring along "fancy-work or mending or just visit."

They gather at 2 P.M. on the first Thursday of the month at the appointed farmhouse. There is always a roll call, but it's never just the members saying "Here" or "Yo." Instead, they share. For example, once each member had to "tell of your first experience with a permanent." Another time it was "tell about your first crush." And the one this month was "tell an accomplishment of one of your children or grandchildren," a topic which, given the makeup of the group, could have consumed the whole afternoon.

But everyone cooperated with brevity, knowing full well that, as always, a brief business meeting, a program and lunch were to come.

The programs vary. Foreign exchange students have explained their homelands. Recently a retired army colonel, a cousin of one of the members, showed slides of his trip to Africa. "Our members really do a good job of presenting presentable programs," said Dominy.

Most members are musically inclined, so they have formed a side group called the Melody Maids who occasionally perform for other organizations. One song they sing was written by their own Pearl Fry. To the tune of "Auld Lang Syne," it opens this way: "We're members of the Jack Creek Club/that's called the CCC./We've celebrated 60 years/of loyal unity."

Loyal unity?

In 62 years, only one meeting of the group has been canceled, and that was a day when hub-deep mud on the back roads made travel impossible. There was another close call a couple of years ago when there was a horrible snowstorm on meeting day.

"We all used our four-wheel drives, but we could only get as close to Irene Fessler's house as the end of her lane," said Dominy. "We waded through knee-deep snow the rest of the way. When we got to the door, we found out Irene was sick in bed, but her daughter was there so we went on in and had club anyway."

The best auto body man
in Princeton is also
a leading opera singer

January 1986

PRINCETON, IA. – It's a fact that life in our river towns, like this little one north of Davenport on the Mississippi, somehow attracts the most eccentric type of folks.

So maybe I shouldn't have been as knocked out as I was upon discovering Paul Geiger, 41. The guy standing in bibbed overalls and a duck-hunting cap in his auto body shop is also a professional opera singer who performs at leading opera houses across the nation.

How goes it, this dual life – especially the part of it spent here along the river?

Well, first you should know what reviewers have said about his rich bass-baritone voice. "It has been called everything from 'a little bigger than normal' to 'the biggest voice I've ever heard,' " he said.

But around Princeton, folks say it's not *Paul's* big voice that rattles them.

"What Princeton people would say," said his wife, Ann, 40, "is that 'Paul Geiger is a swell guy, but that wife of his – oh!' I'm the one with the mouth around here. People were surprised when we moved here from Chicago six years ago. But now, I don't think they're as surprised that we've stayed as they are that we're still married."

Yes, more than a few of them have found themselves on the cracking end of the tongue of this woman, who is studying to be a court reporter and rides a motorcycle around town. She's high-strung and is "always one to speak her piece," said Mayor Dave McLaughlin, who added he still can't help but like her.

Said Paul with a grin: "I spend a lot of time smoothing over things she's roughed up, making her acceptable again."

What Paul and the mayor are getting to is that, after encountering Ann, folks think her opera-singing, fender-fixing hubby seems pretty regular. That, of course, is something of a delusion, and not just because he's done "Aida" with the Des Moines Metro Opera and other shows with companies in Detroit, Chicago, San Francisco and San Antonio.

"I don't know if people here think I'm eccentric," he said, "but I am."

An example might be found in the time he was chairman of the annual Princeton Days celebration. "We had an oversupply of automobiles with flatulent hardware operating around here then," he said. "I proposed that as a celebration event, we should have a 'Jump the Mississippi River' contest for hot rods, promising $1 million to the first one to land on Illinois soil. I thought we could get rid of quite a few of them." He acknowledged that most of the people probably figured Ann fed him that idea.

So just how is it that the Geigers have settled here?

He is a native of Beatrice, Nebraska, who was a voice major in his undergraduate studies at the University of Iowa and earned a master's degree in music at Northwestern University. She is a native of Burlington who went to the U of I, where she first met Paul, and then on to a job in Chicago, where she met him again and married him.

"We were wearing out on Chicago," she said. "My folks had moved to Bettendorf by then, and once when we were back visiting, we took a drive on the Iowa side of the river. We found this lovely old home in Princeton and decided to buy it and live here."

Auto body work is a trade Paul picked up between undergraduate and graduate school. "Work was hard to find then," he said, "so, I learned it to have something to do." He continues in it to supplement his opera checks, which run to $4,000 for a month's singing—when he has a show.

The word around town is that he's an excellent body man.

"That's because he's a perfectionist," chirped Ann. "Being a perfectionist is fine when it comes to music, but when it comes to working on cars, then it's the pits. We could starve to death by the time he gets a job done."

A few Princetonians have heard Paul sing. McLaughlin recalls a group "going into Chicago for one of his shows," and then there was the time "when he walked into the elementary school and sang 'Happy Birthday' to Joyce Brockhouse, our secretary." And he has done a couple of numbers at the community's Memorial Day services.

Occasionally, Paul launches into arias in his shop, but he's more likely to practice seriously when he's home—alone. "In close quarters, it really is quite noisy and not altogether pleasant," he said. Ann was more direct: "It makes my ears hurt."

There are few questions from locals about his operatic career, which he feels "is on the rise" after having roles for five months of 1985.

"No, here they talk to me as Paul, the body man," he said, "not Paul, the opera singer. But that's fine with me."

In defense of one Iowan's golf shot off the Great Wall of China

May 1984

So some people are upset about one of my traveling companions in China pulling a collapsible golf club out of his camera bag and hitting a shot off the Great Wall, are they?

Have you seen those letters to the editor?

Janet Ferson, of Des Moines, wrote in "disgust" that "in order to earn the almighty dollars necessary to purchase badly needed Western technology, China has had to open this monument to the abuse of insensitive, uncaring, 'ugly American' tourists. Is it any wonder that we find ourselves losing friends around the world? If we continue to show such disrespect for other cultures and peoples, we may find ourselves in a very lonely world."

Kathy Fuller, Waterloo, wrote, "What next? Perhaps hang-gliding from the Eiffel Tower?"

E. K. Nelson, Des Moines, added, "Friendship Force antics on the Great Wall of China were deplorable."

That's plenty for me, thank you. My answer, which I wish I could put in Chinese, would translate something like this: May you someday be served chopsticks with your soup. In the meantime, would you please lighten up?

It is time for me to rise in defense of one Stacey Henderson, the 51-year-old Des Moines stockbroker who hit the golf shot. Actually he didn't just hit it. He crushed it.

"Yeah, I wound up on it pretty good," he recalled Monday. "I hit it off the cobblestone, so I wasn't using any tee obviously. It took one hop and then took off. I'd estimate it went 400, maybe 500 yards." Fantastic shot—especially considering he did it with a putter—but as Henderson admitted, "Remember, coming off the Wall, which is really high, the ball took a big, big drop."

Let's move on from aesthetics to diplomacy. Stacey Henderson, who has been around the world a time or two, is about as far from being an "ugly American" as a guy can get. He has been on several Friendship Force trips. In China, I think he spent more time than anyone bending my ear about how people-to-people exchanges, like the Friendship Force offers, foster more international understanding and goodwill than a dozen presidential visits.

Many times, I heard him express sincere appreciation for the different culture we were enjoying, and I also heard him caution other Iowans about doing anything the Chinese would consider inappropriate or disrespectful.

So how did the Chinese people who happened to be visiting the Wall at the same time he was there take his golf shot? I reported they formed a "delighted gallery," and I'll stand by that.

Here's Henderson's recollection: "There must have been 25 or more of them nearby when I was doing it. There wasn't a dirty look at all. They were all smiling and laughing. I think they enjoyed it."

Probably so, according to what Neal Ulevich, a photographer and reporter for the Associated Press in Peking, told me. Ulevich was helping me transmit my columns from China back to the *Register.* As he read the one chronicling Henderson's golf shot, he said, "That's pretty good, but I'll tell you, the tradition is that at the Great Wall, absolutely everyone does something nutty. This wouldn't compare to a lot of them."

Now, letter writer Janet Ferson tried to turn around the situation. "Would a group of American spectators," she wrote, "form a 'delighted gallery' if Chinese tourists bounced Ping-Pong balls off the Washington Monument, the Lincoln Memorial or the Statue of Liberty? I think not."

Oh, I think so. At least I'd be delighted if I was standing there watching. I'd say something like, "Looks like harmless fun to me, folks, so let 'er rip, and let me laugh along with you. I couldn't be happier than seeing good visitors like you enjoying yourself in my great country. Can I help you with any information about the U.S.? And, by the way, do you have an extra Ping-Pong ball you'd let me swat off this tower?"

I do think, however, that Stacey Henderson deserves some criticism. He really should have stashed a second Top Flite golf ball in his camera bag. Then, after hitting one, he should have put the second ball down on the cobblestone, walked over to the nearest Chinese person, handed him or her his putter and said, "Your shot, friend."

In defense of young Allen Van Cleave, who among us men hasn't made a sap of himself over a girl?

July 1981

"Can't you think back to when you were a young kid and were away from home somewhere, saw some girl and absolutely fell in love with her? Then you go home and wonder who she was. I tell you, I feel young just thinking about it."
—Chuck Davis, 55
Iowa Falls newspaperman

He is in many ways a typical Iowa farm boy—described by one and all as handsome, as nice a kid as you could find, a hard worker at whatever he tries, never much of one for girls and a heart as big as a barn. That's Allen Van Cleave, 18.

A childhood fall caused a head injury that has made him a slow learner, though not an undetermined one. Probably because he is a year or two older than his classmates, he has never really joined in their social whirl.

He lives with his parents, Kenneth and Jo Anne Van Cleave,

and his sisters on a place between Jesup and La Porte City. The family bonds are strong.

Allen said he will not soon forget the day in late June when he, his mother, the girls and some friends made a trip to Adventureland, the amusement park near Des Moines.

He was with a buddy on the chair lift ride. He looked ahead to the next chair, and there she was. "I saw right away she had a pretty face," he said.

His mother would later describe the girl as "just a nice-looking, plain Iowa girl. Nothing fancy, but very pleasant and very kind to Al. Girls have never paid much attention to him, but this one seemed to enjoy his company."

As soon as they got off the ride, young Van Cleave walked right up to the girl and began talking to her. "I'd never really done anything like that before," said this boy whose devotion to honesty is total. "I didn't ask her name. I thought it was too soon for that. I was still a little embarrassed."

But they spent the rest of the afternoon together, strolling, talking, riding the rides at Adventureland. He recalled that in the conversation, she finally mentioned her name was Mary or Marian, that she was about 16 and was from Iowa Falls.

Then it ended, all too fast. Both families were leaving the park for home. Allen and the girl parted with a "Goodbye" and "See you again some time." He was well on the way back to the farm before it dawned on him that he didn't really know who she was.

A few days later, Frank McCord, manager of the Iowa Falls Chamber of Commerce, was surprised when he opened this letter:

"My name is Allen Van Cleave. I live at Rural Route 1, La Porte City, Iowa, 50651. I met a girl that is 16 years old and from Iowa Falls at Adventureland. I would like to contact her. Her first name is Mary or Marian, I'm not just sure which. What I would appreciate is having a picture of all 16 and 17 year old girls that have a name Mary or Marian with their telephone and address on the back of each picture. I'll pay the cost of the film you use.

"I am 18 years old and go to Jesup Community Schools and have a La Porte City address. I will appreciate any help you can give me in helping to find her. If you have a way to publicize this, I'll be happy to have her call me collect. Sincerely . . . "

His mother had approved of his sending the letter. "He didn't do it to bother the girl or embarrass her," Jo Anne Van Cleave said. "I could tell from talking to him he just wanted to find out if she remembered him being as nice as he remembered her."

McCord, recognizing "a sincerity" in the letter, wrote that he couldn't help with the photos but that he would turn the letter over to Iowa Falls radio station KIFG and to editor-publisher Chuck Davis at the *Iowa Falls Times-Citizen.* Both ran stories, but no Mary or Marian responded.

"I was afraid it wouldn't work," said the youth, "but I had to try something. She's someone special to me."

So that's the way it happened to young Allen Van Cleave, the same way it's happened to many others. Perhaps he took his search a bit further than most do. Because he did, he will undoubtedly face kidding that he has made a sap of himself, all over a girl.

But then, who hasn't?

The results of a contest to determine Iowa's absolutely worst-named 4-H clubs

May 1982

The Most Awful

1. Iowa Falls Jumping Jelly Beans, Hardin County.
2. Amity Jumping Kangaroos, Amity Township, College Springs, Page County.
3. Mormon Trail Vibrations, Garden Grove, Decatur County.
4. Poland Plowboys, Poland Township, Marathon, Buena Vista County.
5. Do-R-Best Eekamalla, Waukon, Allamakee County (Eekamalla? Spell it backwards and see what you get.)
6. Atomic Starlets, Denison, Crawford County.
7. Charming Cherries, Alta Vista, Chickasaw County.
8. Blairsburg Rustling Rascals, Blairsburg, Hamilton County.

9. Maquoketa Cavemen, near Maquoketa Caves State Park, Jackson County.

10. Deer Creek Wohelo, Deer Creek Township, Northwood, Worth County. (Take "Wo" from "Work," "he" from "health" and "lo" from "love." Put them all together for "Wohelo.")

Dishonorable Mention

Magnolia Hillbillies, Magnolia, Harrison County; Blairsburg Biting Bulldogs, Blairsburg, Hamilton County; Ames Mighty Muskrats, Story County; Le Martians, Le Mars, Plymouth County; Algona Eager Beavers, Kossuth County.

Pleasant Pluggers, Pleasant Township, Hardin County; Griswold Spitfires, Pottawattamie County; Buckhorn Busy Bodies, Buckhorn, Jackson County; Highland Happy Hustlers, Ruthven, Palo Alto County; Elk Antlers, Elk Township, Buena Vista County.

Royal Smurfs, Nevada, Story County; Tilden Tillies, Tilden Township, Cherokee County; The Funny Fuzzies, Ames, Story County; Freedom Flickers, Freedom Township, Hamilton County.

And Good Riddance

Clubs that, thank heavens, have changed names or gone out of existence: Gay Grant Girls, Grant Township, Franklin County; White Breast Lassies, White Breast Township, Lucas County; Palermo Money Makers, Palermo Township, Grundy County; Tenville Tooters, Tenville, Montgomery County; Fremont Farm Fairies, Fremont Township, Hamilton County; Mott Meat Makers, Franklin County; Earlville Untouchable Sweathogs, Earlville, Delaware County.

Mess with a man's coonhound and you're messin' with real trouble

November 1982

BLOOMFIELD, IA. – In the news last week, it was reported that a $1.3 million lawsuit has been filed in federal court in Des Moines over what's basically just another southern Iowa coonhound fuss blown all out of proportion.

The details of that particular suit don't concern me here. What I want to address is the larger question that arises every time one of these feuds makes news. At least it's a question that arises in the minds of those vast numbers of us who don't know a blue tick from a treeing walker. It is this: How can people get so screwed out of shape over dumb old hound dogs?

To seek an answer, I came to Bloomfield, a southeast Iowa town of 2,849, the coon-hunting capital of Iowa. The prudent visitor does not refer to hound dogs as being "dumb old" here. This, after all, was the site of several "world championship" coon hunts over the years.

There is just a whole lot of timber on the hills and in the gullies around here, and thus there are more raccoons, coon hunters and coonhounds than in other parts of the state. It's a country-talking, country-thinking subculture, one that was mighty busy last night when the two-month-long coon season officially opened.

It is also in this area where, over the past decade, the body of law dealing with coonhound disputes has been getting pretty well refined. There have been perhaps a half-dozen hound dog cases around here in that time. One of them was so intense it took a whole week in district court to settle – and they're still arguing it in the countryside.

Things have reached the rather revolting point where, if you really want to know about coonhounds in this territory, you can get information as readily from local lawyers as from coon hunters. Anyway, attorney John Martin has a pretty good story about how solid the bond is between coon hunter and coonhound.

"We were [questioning] the jury panel in a case over in Center-ville a couple of years ago, trying to get the jury picked," Martin said. "I asked this one guy if he had a dog. He said, yes, he had a coonhound. I asked him how he felt about his dog and he said, 'Mister, if you filled up this whole courtroom with gold, I still wouldn't trade you my hound for it.' "

My friend Don Piper, a mechanic who is wise in Davis County ways, said even newcomers around here figure out quickly that you can insult a coon hunter and he'll probably take it, but if you insult his dog, "you've spoken fightin' words." He said he's seen real nice fellows "get meaner 'n cat urine" over some slight of their dogs. (I cleaned up that quote just a little bit. My friend isn't accustomed to talking for publication in a family newspaper.)

And that brings to mind a piece of advice I once received from Dolan Thompson, who was dealing in hounds around here. "Mess with my dogs, and you won't need an attorney," he said. "You'll need an undertaker." I figured him a little radical, actually.

Why is it feelings are so strong? I did my research in farm kitchens, law offices, a medical clinic, a garage, the courthouse and the Long Branch saloon in nearby Drakesville. You find coon hunters everywhere.

My study reveals there are three things that make them get nutty about their hounds – money, skullduggery and love.

To get a good hound, one that will really tree a coon, you're going to spend $700 or more. That hound is going to enable you to take lots of coons, the pelts of which sell for an average of $25 apiece. I heard reports that some hunting teams of three or four guys have bagged nearly 300 coons in a season.

When there's the opportunity for big money – or at least a fair living – in something, there's bound to be skullduggery, too.

"Most dog traders are honorable," said Magistrate Rex Steinkruger, who has presided over a hound case, "but there's always a shady one around somewhere, too." A lot of good coonhounds seem to "mysteriously disappear" every year.

"A guy with a real good dog isn't likely to talk much about it," said farmer Kenny Swaim, regarded as something of an expert on hounds. "You might have 200 dogs in a lifetime. Only two or three will be really special. Those are the ones things seem to happen to. It's a worry."

His brother-in-law, Swede King, said no one ever seems to get caught stealing hounds. And lucky for the culprits, he added. They'd face justice in a county where they'd be thought of as lower than yesteryear's horse thieves.

And listen to Swaim's son, John, 26. With respect in his eye and a firm set to his jaw, he drew on the crackerbarrel philosophy coon hunters trade in: "An old boy once told me that a dog is the only true friend you can buy."

Best leave a man's hound dog alone.

A great place to study Iowans—the weekly small town junk auction

April 1981

CRESTON, IA.—If it is not an old axiom, it should be—you can learn a lot about Iowa by going to a small town junk auction.

I figure I picked up an additional three hours of coursework toward my advanced degree in Iowana by attending the regular Monday night sale at the J&C Auction in this southwest Iowa community of 8,429.

These things are as much sociology as they are sales. They operate on such important social tenets as "one man's junk is another's treasure," "never throw anything away" and, one obviously not always heeded, "you take a bath Saturday night whether you need it or not."

Just like in the state at large, you find a few well-heeled intelligent-looking people, a lot of average-looking people and a few grungy stupid-looking people at an auction. You can categorize them that way only by appearance, however; you cannot tell them apart by their purchases.

At an auction like this one, you come to appreciate the importance of the subtle nod of the head and the knowing wink of the eye—vital means of communication in Iowa society. Our strong inclination to humor is evident in the number of wife jokes ("Might as well sell this lawnmower 'cause I can't get the ol' lady to use it.'").

"Yep, people are funny," said Cliff Miller, 62, a big-bellied rough-talker who runs the place. "And they're gettin' funnier every day." He includes himself, of course.

His wife, Pauline, 52, who he claimed would not use the lawnmower, says Cliff's position at the auction is that of "the clown." He holds up items or directs attention to them as they are being auctioned, and he does it in a way that keeps the crowd in stitches.

"Lookee here, folks!" he once roared while waving a brassiere to be sold, "a double-barreled sling shot!" And when a toilet seat went on the block the other night, he held it in front of his beaming face and hollered, "We've got a beauty of a picture frame for sale!" To help move personal apparel during estate sales, he has been known to model girdles and wigs.

Miller stumbled into the auction business almost by accident 14 years ago. He ran it as a part-time job until he retired as Creston's water meter reader six months ago.

"I don't really understand why, but this is one helluva good money maker," he said. "You do have to work hard, but I'll tell you, if I'd started out in this business when I was 25 years old and stuck with it, I'm telling you I'd own three-fourths of the world by now."

He begins accepting items for the weekly sale on Tuesday mornings, lists them in the *Creston News-Advertiser* on Fridays and opens the doors for public inspection during the day on Mondays. Crowds of 200 or more will gather in the converted chicken hatchery by the 7 P.M. starting time. You see kids in diapers and old folks on canes.

Some in the audience are serious buyers, some are not.

"This is just my Monday night recreation," said Boyd Wenzel, 63, an Afton farmer. "Instead of going out, getting drunk and chasing women, this is what I do for fun. Oh, I might buy something and resell it at some other auction just to pay for my gas here and dinner. You can't find entertainment much cheaper than this."

The items for sale range from much sought after antiques to, uh, "well, let's just call this thing a 'gizmo,' " Miller said holding up a piece of iron. "To tell the truth, I don't know what the hell it is."

Auctioneer Marion Manley, the Millers' son-in-law, attempts to keep things moving briskly so he can have time afterward to change clothes before he begins the 11 P.M. shift as a Creston policeman.

"I guess the one thing I've really learned about people from running this place," said Miller, "is that they're damned honest. In 14 years here, I've lost a total of $4.95 in bad checks. Ain't that somethin'?"

Yep. We Iowans bring our integrity along when we go to junk auctions.

Only a Philadelphia lawyer could keep all this straight

October 1982

COUNCIL BLUFFS, IA. – Get that second cup of coffee and rub the sleep out of your eyes. Today we visit my favorite Iowa law firm, and it's not going to be easy.

To do so, we have to come *over* to this city on our state's west coast. Then we go *over* on the south side of the business district and find South Main Street. *Over* on the west side of South Main, you see the office. *Over* the front windows of the office is a big, arch-shaped sign. (All these *overs* are just warming you up for what's coming here.) Up on that arch, it says: "Over & Over & Over."

Over here in the Over law office, there are these Overs:

Oliver Oscar Over, Sr., 72
Oliver Oscar Over, Jr., 41
Oscar Oliver Over II, 41

I'm sure you can see why I like this firm. If you were of a mind to, you could do a piece of schtick here that would be to jurisprudence what that old "Who's on First?" routine is to baseball.

The first Over listed here is the father. The next two Overs listed are his twin sons. The son that's a Jr. is the namesake of Sr., obviously. The son that's a II is the namesake of his paternal grandfather, Oscar Oliver Over. And Oscar II's maternal grandfather's first name was Oscar, too.

More coffee, you say?

I'll make it easier on you for a moment. As my favorite law firm, this one wins out over the following other contenders:

The Dull law firm of Le Mars. When the Dull sons joined their father in the practice, why, a wag could've said the firm was getting considerably Duller.

The Marvel Law Office of Pella. I absolutely marvel at the name.

Moore & Moore of Morning Sun. This used to be Moore, Moore & Moore, but now they're less one Moore. He's more or less retired.

Marks, Marks & Marks of Des Moines. The Marks brothers, a-*hem*, are in practice with their father.

And, of course, the lawyering Lawyer brothers of Des Moines, who have their own firms. We have the James Lawyer Law Firm and the Law Offices of Verne Lawyer. Verne's partner, incidentally, is his wife, Vivian Lawyer. Her maiden name is Jury. She uses it. That means she's referred to as Vivian Jury Lawyer. (I am telling the truth, the whole truth and nothing but the truth.)

Now, if any of you honorees are feeling litigious, let me plead my case: I am *not* making fun of any of your own names or the names of your firms. People who labor under the likes of "Offenburger" never laugh at others on this count.

Let's get back over here to the Overs. You might think that fellows with names so similar might, over the years, have accumulated some pretty interesting stories to tell. Overall, that doesn't seem to be the case here.

Oh, there is one little thing we can go over. Back a few years ago, there was another partner in the practice, Bruce Fleming. Then the firm was Over, Over, Over & Fleming. But he left the firm to go it alone. That caused a lot of people in the legal community over here to start joking that this firm had become Over, Over, Over & Out. Get it?

The guy I talked to when I dropped by was Oscar Oliver Over II. It's easy to confuse them, of course, but the reason I'm certain which one I visited is that he was wearing one of those huge belt buckles formed by welding together three-inch-tall brass letters to spell "OSCAR." You've seen these buckles at truckstops, I know, but seldom on lawyers. However, if you go through this Oliver-Oscar and Oscar-Oliver thing a time or two, you begin wishing all of them would wear belt buckles with their names on them.

Or maybe they could just put their nicknames on them. Oscar is Ozzie. Oliver Jr. is Ollie. And years ago, some of them called Oliver Sr. "Oddie." Does that make it a little clearer? What's that? Well, have another cup of coffee then.

"People don't confuse any of us by looks or by what legal matter they talked to us about," said Oscar. "They just confuse us by our names. So when someone calls and is a little confused, the receptionist sorts it all out by asking whether the person talked to the one of us with light hair or dark hair, or whether they met us in the front office or the back office. Over the years, I'd have to say it's been fun having names like this. But on a few occasions, it's been a little trouble."

Each of the Over twins is married and has children. Each has a son. Each decided, with counsel from his wife, to go no further with the triple-O initials. So Oliver Oscar has a Todd Oliver. Oscar Oliver has a William Oscar.

And I have sort of a headache.

Josie Golwitzer becomes a real American

October 1985

Mary Hultman, a Shenandoah-based field-worker for U.S. Congressman Jim Ross Lightfoot, put it best. "We all do it—take our citizenship for granted," she said. "Then you run into someone like Josie, someone who cares so much about this, and it hits you between the eyes."

She was talking about Josie Golwitzer, 62, of Carroll, who this morning will be officially sworn an American by a federal judge in Cedar Rapids. Josie will cry. For the last two years, any time the subject of citizenship has come up, she has cried.

She did it a week ago when she emerged from her citizenship test at the U.S. Immigration and Naturalization Service offices in Omaha with news she had passed. She had been so nervous that Lightfoot called the INS and asked them to do all they could to put her at ease.

"Josie was crying, all right," said Hultman, sent by her boss to provide additional comfort. "And the woman who'd driven her down from Carroll was crying. And I was crying."

Josie's friends back in Carroll weren't crying. They were praying. She'd asked prayer groups from the various churches to go to work for her during the hour she was being tested.

A whole bunch of those friends were to board a Greyhound bus at 5 A.M. today to go to Cedar Rapids for Josie's biggest moment. They at first feared they weren't going to be able to. The cost of a bus trip was too much for their retirement incomes.

So they prayed some more while Alice Iverson, who runs the Retired Senior Volunteer Program office, where they all hang out, got on the phone. Iverson's calls eventually reached Fred Dunikoski, Greyhound president, in Phoenix, Arizona. He heard Josie's story Friday, turned to subordinates and said, "Let's do it." Free bus.

Josie's story is an amazing one.

She grew up in a horrible time in Naples, Italy. Her mother died when Josie was 12. Soon after, in the early '40s, German bombs were wrecking the city—she once dug her father, buried to his neck, from the rubble of their home. A brother, an Italian soldier, died in a Nazi concentration camp. At 18, German soldiers rounded her up with other teenagers and were trucking them to another prison camp, but she managed to jump from her truck at a checkpoint and escape into the darkness.

Then she met American serviceman Fred Golwitzer and married him. He came back to his home near Carroll in 1946. She followed a few months later. It was tough for Josie, raising seven children while Fred, a hard man, farmed and drove a truck. He died in 1981.

In 1985, she began considering her first trip ever back to Italy after her letters of inquiry about her long-lost family there produced news a brother was still alive. But when she went to the courthouse to begin paperwork for a passport, she was told there was no record she had ever officially entered this country.

"I said, 'What? I am citizen. I vote twice for presidents,'" she recalls now in still-broken English. "But no record. No country for me." It turned out her husband had never registered her as having come here. And search as she did, Josie could find none of the official paperwork she'd had.

Her friend Iverson said Josie refused to think of traveling to Italy before becoming a U.S. citizen. So for months, the two of them battled the bureaucracy for a chance at citizenship. Immigration officials required something indicating how she'd come to this country. Meanwhile, Josie lived in fear "somebody arrest me for not s'posed to be here."

A breakthrough came when, in a final search of all family records, Josie found a picture postcard of the hospital ship that had carried her to the United States. Immigration officials found documentation that that ship had been used to transport war brides like Josie and told her to come take the oral test.

"Only thing I mess up," she said, "was when they ask who president is. I practice so hard, but always it comes out 'Oreaganal.' The nice man at test said, 'We make him Italian for this day.'"

Today, Josie Golwitzer's dream happens. "To me, means everything," she said through tears Monday. "Forty years without country. Now I have home."

And also today, Lightfoot has arranged for a flag to fly over the U.S. Capitol in her name. Friday, he will personally present it to her.

"I'm just little old lady," she said. "All this for me? Do I dream and wake up to be not true?"

It's true, Citizen Josie Golwitzer.

A special poll that determines which subgroup of Iowa society is the most screwed up

February 1986

I don't know where in the sweet ether this one came from, but on a gray Monday, a good deal of thinking I've been doing on Iowa society at large has come to a weird focus.

It is on this point: If you divide all of us into our respective age and gender groups, who's the most screwed up? I'm talking errant behavior, insecurity, temper—a sort of basic Disagreeableness Index. If sociology doesn't have such a measure, it should.

To begin, the divisions must be made. I do it this way: Old men and old women; mid-career men and women; young adult men and women; high school boys and girls; pre-adolescent boys and girls; and finally, little boys and girls.

Now from my own experiences and from my close observations of how all you rascals are getting along out there, here is my, uh, Bonkers Poll, with No. 1 being most prone to social reprehensibility, and then calming on down to No. 12, the group that's found the calm in the eye of life's storm:

1. High school boys. Life's foul balls will be discussed more later.
2. Pre-adolescent girls. There should be a home for 13-year-old females. Parents could come visit, of course, but would bring their daughters back into the real world only after the girls have found acceptable hormonal balance.
3. Old men. Their struggles to accept retirement, and its re-definitions of self, lead too many of these old coots into either (a) a paranoid kind of philosophizing, or (b) a neighbor-stressing, almost malicious, genealogy.
4. Mid-career men. If they haven't convinced themselves they're dying, they're fractured by the realization they are never going to become the boss.
5. Young adult women. They have a devil of a time trying to decide whether to be seductive man-hunters or cold-hearted corporate climbers.

127

6. Pre-adolescent boys. It's terribly difficult to be cool around girls when what you truly enjoy is doing wheelies on an undersized dirt bike.

7. Mid-career women. They're painfully realizing that what they prepared themselves to become isn't meshing with their true destiny, which, of course, they've just discovered.

8. Young adult men. Most are trying to learn how you can go out with the guys and drink every beer in town, then keep from blowing breakfast in front of the boss at tomorrow morning's sales meeting.

9. High school girls. They're probably not as good as they seem, but when you compare them to what they were at 13, then look at them against high school boys – my goodness, they're nice.

10. Little girls. Dolls says it all.

11. Little boys. Give 'em a ball, a hamburger and/or a mud puddle, and they feel whole.

12. Old women. It should be obvious why they live so long. The Almighty looks at the rest of us and realizes how satisfied He is with them.

So, woe to high school boys. I was one myself. What can you say about yourself when you're at an age when the only two things you can really do well are grow zits and belch?

What! – someone's arguing? Well, then, why are these guys' car insurance rates the highest? This indictment is actuarially sound.

Look at them. They don't know whether they're worthless because they're athletes or worthless because they're not. They can't decide whether to get their hair cut long, short or short with a long tail over the collar. They can't decide whether to wear hunting boots, penny loafers or high-topped sneakers, and if they've opted for the latter, it's a question of whether to tie the laces or not.

Around girls, they're at their behavioral best, although if one winds up with a date in a dark car, he can't decide whether to ask to hold hands or just go ahead and try to impregnate her. Around parents or adults, they do imitations of bricks. Around each other, they go into this hilarious jive that has them strutting, preening and slugging each other on the shoulder muscles.

They say *"all riiight"* and *"you know"* more than any other societal group. They are also the group most likely to leave hair grease stains on the family room carpet. And they are the humans most likely to wear muscle shirts and, in moments of triumph, jab the air with their fists in such a manner as to expose their armpits, of which they seem inordinately proud. The balance here is that these dudes probably also have the best dreams.

Yes, high school boys are conclusive proof that God has a sense of humor.

From RAGBRAI to a Rolling Stones concert to a centennial celebration in a town of 7 to a prom date with a 17-year-old high school girl—it's been a decade of fun events in Iowa. Let's look back at some of them.

EVENTS

Why RAGBRAI has become one of Iowa's few truly major league events

July 1986

I suppose it's the same for any kind of Big Deal in which you find yourself deeply involved, but each year at about this stage of RAGBRAI preparation—we launch the beast Sunday in Council Bluffs—I find myself losing my ordinarily healthy perspective on it.

Nitpicky last-minute details become so overwhelming I begin to wonder whether it's all worth it. Is this thing really as special as I've thought?

So Wednesday morning, while pedaling a loop northwest of Des Moines, Dr. Offenburger conducted a therapy session with bicyclist-columnist Offenburger. Our conclusion, not surprisingly, was, yes, it's worth it, and, yes, RAGBRAI really is special.

Think about it with me. How many truly major league events do we have annually in Iowa? Hawkeye football is one. The Iowa State Fair has always been one. And RAGBRAI, I'd argue, has become one, too.

This year we've accepted 7,500 applications for RAGBRAI credentials, and we've said no to more than 3,000 others. When we start Sunday in the Bluffs, we'll have riders from all 50 states, and if tradition holds, about a dozen foreign countries. They'll spend $100,000 or more in each of the towns we stay overnight in, and Lord only knows how much they'll invest in lemonade, cookies and porkburgers between towns.

Why has it grown to such a level? Why has it become the biggest, oldest and most-talked-about bicycling event of its kind in the whole world?

There are four reasons, I think.

One is Don Benson. Recently retired as public relations director of the *Register,* he continues as the chief organizer of RAGBRAI. John Karras, my cycle mate and co-leader, always says RAGBRAI will last as long as Benson stays in charge of it—and no longer—and I think it's true.

Second, the ride is backed by a newspaper with a statewide circulation base. That's so important in spreading the information, not only to the riders but even more important to the people who live along the route.

Third, Iowa's geographical layout is just about perfect for a big bicycle ride. There is a fantastic network of paved secondary roads that are not only great for getting ag products to market but are also great for riding bicycles without challenging a lot of car and truck traffic.

And you also can't go more than about 10 miles in any direction in this state without encountering another small town. Ten miles is an hour's ride on a bicycle, and most bikers like the idea of riding an hour, taking a break in some new community, then riding on to another one.

The chief reason for the ride's success, though, is the unabashed friendliness of Iowa's people—those thousands who feed, water and entertain the riders every year. A RAGBRAIer who has a problem and stops to ask for help suddenly finds he's getting attention from an army.

The friendships that are born on RAGBRAI every year are another reason it's all worth it. I think that happens because no matter who or what you are back home, once you start RAGBRAI, you're just another bicyclist, haunted by the same problems every other bicyclist has—sore rear end, sunburn, aching muscles and a vacillating psyche.

Shared experiences promote good conversation, and it suddenly becomes insignificant that one person is actually a hog farmer from rural Iowa and the other is a brain surgeon from New York. The sense of community that develops among these people all thrown together for one week is intense. I mean, here I am going into my fourth RAGBRAI, and I still don't know how to change a tire. Yet, I have no fear of being stranded. Somebody coming by will not only know what to do but also will volunteer to do it. RAGBRAI itself becomes another small Iowa town. And you know how I am about small Iowa towns.

That's what leads me to what I think is the best thing that RAGBRAI does. It is bigger than most of the towns it visits. If the townsfolk are going to pull off the kind of reception they all want for us, they are forced to forget old differences, rally to the cause and work together.

In some cases, that hasn't happened for years. It's a wonderful exercise for those towns, and it often results in the emergence of new community leaders and a revived community spirit—ready to take on whatever projects come up years after RAGBRAI leaves.

That does it—I'm ready to go again.

An aging group of rock fans
attend the Cedar Falls concert
by the aging Rolling Stones

February 1981

CEDAR FALLS, IA. – Eleven of us gathered early Friday evening in the warm, comfortable family room of a new home near the University of Northern Iowa campus here. We were having a drink or two before throwing ourselves into the sea of 24,000 people inside the UNI-Dome for the concert by the Rolling Stones.

It was a cheery group of old friends, nearly all in their 30s. They had welcomed a journalistic interloper of the same vintage.

What a curious band of rock 'n' rollers we were. Sure, several of us had been neo-hippies in our college days in the 1960s. Some of us still refer to ourselves as "post-revolutionaries," veterans of the student uprisings on the campuses. We all liked our rock 'n' roll back then.

But look at us around this room, look at what we'd become a decade and a half later. Here we had a county attorney, a college professor, two elementary school teachers, a public relations man for a telephone company, a nurse, an advertising executive for a major industry, a housewife, a waiter, a columnist. We counted that we've given the world 10 children. A more thoroughly mortgaged group would be hard to find. Nice dressers. Great consumers.

Ready to rock 'n' roll again. I suspect some of our older children were snickering.

John Thomas, 38, the ad executive, told of the look of disbelief he received when he told a 22-year-old co-worker in Newton he was going to the Rolling Stones concert. "He told me he had 'great admiration' that a man my age could be doing this," Thomas said.

Our kids and the fans younger than ourselves do not recognize the heavy investment we have in the Rolling Stones. Consider Pat Jennings, 36, of Newton, the telephone public relations man. "It seems like I've always been listening to the Stones," he said. "In fact, in 1965, I think it was, I had a big idea of booking them for a fraternity party we were having at UNI. I got ahold of their agent somehow and found out the fee would be $80,000. Things didn't work out well."

Others recounted their own favorite Stones stories from the

'60s. We recalled the riots, war and fun Mick Jagger and the band sang us through. Indeed, the Stones carry a lot of emotional baggage for our generation.

But how, we asked as we bundled for the walk to the Dome, can the band that was so big back then still be so big now? How can UNI freshmen, some of whom weren't born when the Stones had their first hit, love the group as much as we do? Jagger, now 38, provided an answer during the show when he wailed, "Time is on our side, yes it is." It seems undeniable he is right.

The Stones show was an incredible blast of energy, color and, of course, sound. A mix of new songs and old.

One forgets, from one rock concert to the next, how much marijuana is being smoked nowadays. A sweet-smelling haze quickly filled the Dome. Did that bother the prosecutor in our group? "You just expect it any more," said Chick Neighbor, 35, the Jasper County attorney. "You see it everywhere, not just at rock concerts. I don't think I saw much more marijuana used during the Stones concert than I did at a Chicago Bears football game I was at recently."

We watched the band closely for signs of change brought on by the years. We saw a few, but nothing like the changes that have occurred in our own lives. It almost seemed unfair.

But Jennings put it in new light. "Think of it this way," he said. "We aren't the real young bucks any more, but most of us are still thought of as being young in our careers. Jagger and the Stones are our age, but they're thought of as being old."

A great show, it was.

"Yes," said Jennings, "something to tell our grandkids about."

Oh my, have we come to that already?

The crowning of the county pork queen

March 1978

RED OAK, IA. – In the never-ending task of hyping the hog, it is time to pick the county pork queen.

They did so here in Montgomery County recently. And in more than 80 other Iowa counties where there are pork promotional groups, they have recently done, or soon will do, the same.

In June, all these county queens will try to become queens of 11 pork districts in Iowa. Next January, the district queens will try to become the state queen, competing not only against each other but also against the queens of the various breed associations – the Poland China Queen, the Duroc Queen, the Chester White Queen, to name but three of eight. And there's a national pork queen, too.

Ah, commodity royalty! In Iowa, we carry it on into the domain of beef cattle, dairy cattle, sheep, even into soybeans – Hiya, Princess Soya.

But back to pigs. Now, praise to all porkers. And don't forget we said that.

But, if you surveyed the nation, how many high school girls would you find who would consent to wear a crown and satin sash heralding them as a pork queen? And how many women would eagerly involve themselves in an organization that exists to extol the glories of the hog?

Nationally, probably not many. But in a state that produces 28 per cent of the nation's pork, you find plenty. *Plenty who'll say without batting an eye that they dig pigs.*

"Some people see hogs wallowing in mud and think they're dirty and stupid," said Diane Gourley, one of the four queen candidates here. But she quickly added she doesn't think that way, and it was abundantly clear that none of the 50 or so women and girls who'd gathered in a banquet room of a nice restaurant here thought that way, either.

They are the Montgomery County Porkettes, the women's group affiliated with the 110 members of the county's Pork Producers. Their livelihood is pork. As the hog serves them, so do they serve the hog. The beast yields their income; it demands their labor and loyalty.

Debra Benskin, another candidate, said it well: "I know sometimes you don't like to go out with your husbands and fathers to work the hogs, but as my father says, this is what brings home the bacon."

All of the girls told how when it's hog-moving time on their home places, everyone from hired hand to homemaker gets involved. The Porkettes nodded knowingly.

But when the women of the pork industry come to the towns and cities, it's promotion that's important. Their blitz is aimed at all ages. It includes everything from baking pig-shaped cookies to sponsoring poster contests.

All the promotional efforts seek to make consumers want to eat more pork. The more consumption there is, the more income there will be.

And since pork queens help spread the good word, the faithful gather for the annual crowning. These queen contests produce queens of beauty, poise and personality who have at least basic knowledge about the animals and their products.

Pamphlets provide candidates with tips for preparing to face the contest judges, as well as the public. Tips like, *"It is better to discuss positive points rather than negative ones."* And, *"Do not discuss trichinosis unless asked; it is a clinical rarity in the United States today."* And, *"Be pleasant, happy and SMILE."*

The Porkettes recruit their queen candidates. "You know how it is with queen things," said Peg Lundgren, one of the organizers. "Not many girls want to rush out and apply. They have to be asked."

The Porkettes and the candidates, all attractively attired, lunched on cold salads and a main dish of green beans with ham and bacon mixed in. They sipped tea and coffee and chatted graciously. Socially proper–sized pieces of white cake – topped by a small, pink-sugar caricature of a smiling pig – were served. There was a review of spring's fashions, much of the apparel made at least partially from pigskin.

While it was all so pleasantly unfolding, three women acting as judges closely studied the queen candidates – Gourley, 17, Benskin, 17, Diane Herzberg, 18, and her cousin Karen Herzberg, 18.

There were private interviews with each. Samples:

Judge: *"Why did you decide to enter this contest?"*

Gourley: *"I guess I just want to represent the county for hogs."*

Judge: *"Can you name three breeds of hogs? I've just been dying to ask that question."*

Karen Herzberg, crisply: *"Hampshire, Chester White, Yorkshire."*

But the interviews proved inconclusive. "Usually there's one person that really sticks out like Bingo," Bernice Baier said to her judging partners. "But I don't think so here."

And so the competition moved into the five-minute prepared presentations by each girl on some phase of the pork industry.

There was a promise by one candidate that she would "not go hog wild" with facts and figures; there was the use by another of a pig hand puppet she called "Penelope" to help tell the pork story; there was a wealth of information about pork cuts, pork nutrition and pork by-products. "It is true," said one girl, "that the only useless part of the pig is the squeal."

Then it was Diane Herzberg's turn in front of the Porkettes. The girl, who works as a checker at a Villisca grocery and has been a cheerleader all through high school, erupted in a rush of arm-waving originality:

> *The Iowa Chop*
> *Just can't be beat!*
> *Over one inch thick,*
> *Man! What a treat!*
> *High in protein,*
> *For dieters a must.*
> *Tender and juicy,*
> *Iowa pork for us!*

She climaxed it with a "Yeaaay!" and a knee kick. Then she ended by telling the Porkettes to "eat pork today and you'll have something to cheer about."

The judges retreated to conference, reported back after the style show and announced that, while "this was one of the toughest contests we've ever had to judge," the $10 crown belonged to the cheerleader.

Diane Herzberg beamed as the crown was placed on her head and the satin sash "Mont. Co. Pork Queen" was pinned to her shoulder and waist.

Happy?

Yes.

Happy as, *as a hog in clover?*

Well, she smiled a lot.

The night the Des Moines Symphony played Corydon's town square—with church bells, fireworks and cannon

August 1983

CORYDON, IA.—Randy Popejoy, local appliance dealer, squirmed in his lawn chair in front of the bandstand on the courthouse lawn. He turned to his wife, Sue, and said, "I think I'd rather be golfing."

It was early Wednesday evening, ordinarily league golf night in the southern Iowa town of 1,818. But it also happened to be the evening the Des Moines Symphony Summer Pops Orchestra had come to help launch the 100th annual Corydon Old Settlers Reunion.

The powers here had wanted this centennial edition of their grand old celebration to begin with something really special. So they'd gone out and raised $10,000 to cover the costs of having the 55-piece symphony come for a free, outdoor concert.

After a big, gutty effort like that in a little place like this, it was darned near a command appearance for Randy Popejoy and everyone else in the territory: Be there, enjoy it, we paid a lot for this.

There actually was almost no chance people would not enjoy this concert that was about to begin. The program, which will be repeated this Wednesday night at the Iowa State Fair, was a lineup of old favorites beginning with the national anthem, moving through waltzes, polkas and an operatic overture to "American Salute." The windup—the "1812 Overture," complete with church bells, fireworks and cannon. The show was planned as a grabber, even for newcomers to symphonic music.

Whatever shred of doubt did linger about the music's appeal was removed two numbers into the program when conductor Dianne Pope turned to address the audience of 3,500. A delicious moment was at hand.

Here was this 40-year-old woman—a curio for those of a rural Iowa perspective. She wore a chic, poofy-sleeved, mid-calf-length ensemble that by itself would have been the talk of the town. Then there was what she'd been doing up there—flailing her arms, bobbing, weaving, gyrating—why, acting like a regular band director.

And as word had spread that this woman not only does this all over America but in Europe besides, well, the place was abuzz about how you don't find the likes of Dianne Pope on the Corydon town square just every evening.

She thanked the crowd for a warm reception and announced an addition to the program.

"You see, I grew up on an Iowa farm," she said, harking back to Onawa and building a strong bridge here. "I know this time of year, my father always wants rain. I noticed on the way down today that you need rain, too. We thought we'd play a rain dance for you. It's called, 'Unter Donner und Blitzen Polka.' That translates as 'Thunder and Lightning Polka.' If it rains in the next week or so, we hope you'll give the Des Moines Symphony at least a little bit of the credit."

From that moment on, Pope and the Des Moines Symphony owned this audience like they may never own another. A special feeling swept the crowd, and it lapped up over the stage, too. This performance became, as Corydon Times-Republican publisher Hugh Doty so aptly put it, "the biggest thing in Corydon since Jesse James robbed our bank in 1871."

It built toward the "1812." The orchestra handled the musical part of that one. A retired county employee did the church bells. Two volunteer firemen supervised the cascading fireworks. And the nine cannon were tended by a bunch of good ol' boys from around the area, a certain columnist from Des Moines and two lieutenants from the ROTC unit at Northeast Missouri State University–the latter wearing camouflage fatigues and firing a serious-looking howitzer. Asked what kind of cannon it was, one of them, Cindy Lindquist, 21, snapped like a drill sergeant: "An effective one."

The cannoneers, certainly more into guns than music, nonetheless got into the melodic flow. "I'm a Willie Nelson fan, but I'm starting to like this stuff," said Jack Ames of Weldon. He sells seed corn when he isn't wearing a Confederate officer's uniform and playing artillery.

Suffice it to say they put a charge to Corydon like it had never before had. And when Pope and the Des Moines answered with an encore of "Stars and Stripes Forever," it put a capper on one of the finest nights I've ever seen in a small town.

The crowd left on a real high.

Lois Keho of Allerton stopped to congratulate the cannoneers, who, she discovered, were as excited as kids at a carnival. "It's true what they say," she said with a smile at one of the men. "All little boys like to make noise."

Newspaperman Doty, aglow himself, said the best review of the evening was that "people are just grinning all over the place."

And Randy Popejoy turned again to his wife, Sue. "It was," he said, "better than golfing."

The best way to eat lunch in Cedar Rapids

September 1982

CEDAR RAPIDS, IA. – I'm a guy who gets around, and today I share a little secret from life on the road – the most pleasant way to spend a lunch hour in this state.

For starters, get downtown here. Now, you must understand that in this little caper, food is incidental. The ambience is the thing. But if you're as famished at noon as I usually am, then do what I do and drop by the basement cafeteria in Armstrong's department store. Tuna salad sandwich to go, please.

Walk south along Second Street until you get to the bank of plain, gray, side doors to the Paramount Theater. Find the unlocked one and enter. When you walk out of bright sunlight into a dark theater, you're going to immediately forget whatever was on your mind and start giving full attention to your next step. That's Paramount therapy at work.

After your eyes adjust to the dim light offered by a couple of bare bulbs on poles, ease on up through spooky corridors and take a seat in the balcony. Have a look around.

You are in one of 1,913 seats in one spectacular theater. It was built in the '20s as a movie house and has the rich, ornate trappings of that era, beautifully restored. Chandeliers, stained glass, mirrors, statues, gold, marble, velvet. This, the grandest of Iowa's old theaters, is a very sensuous place.

It probably would have fallen apart, as old theaters do, but wealthy Cedar Rapids financier Peter Bezanson bought it in 1975 and then donated it to the city. The performing arts had a home here.

By night, symphonies and great artists may command the Paramount. But during lunch hours, lesser-known artists take over. It might be Loren Frink, an engineer at Iowa Electric, or George Baldwin, credit manager at Armstrong's. Music teacher Al Erickson and secretary Jean Safley are among the regulars, too.

They slip away from their offices to come play the massive, mighty Wurlitzer organ that rises hydraulically from under the stage. It's not always available to them, since certain stage configurations mean it must be covered, but when it is available, well, there is no lovelier lunch for the sandwich-bearing sneak in the balcony.

These people do not play for pay or praise. They play for themselves, for escape. The idea that the huge theater is empty, or nearly so, matters not to them.

I told the 67-year-old Frink the other day that if a picture were taken of him at the keyboard, its caption would be, "Loren Frink in the Loneliness of the Paramount." Said Frink, almost cackling, "Well, that'd be OK, but you'd really want to add, 'He might be alone but he's not missing anybody.'"

Paramount janitors Owen Strickel and Ron Coppess are always glad to see Frink and the other players come around for the organ key. "When they play, it's like a fringe benefit for us," said Strickel. Added Coppess, "Once I was working around there while Loren was playing and I requested 'Indian Love Song.' You should've heard it. Real mellow."

Frink calls himself "a romantic old coot" who prefers ballads, old ones. "Why, if a song's not more than 30 years old, I don't mess with it," he said.

Baldwin is more into show tunes and marches. Safley prefers contemporary music, and Erickson plays anything and everything. Strickel says he can be working in the basement and "still be able to tell which one of them is up there playing, just by their different styles."

Ask nicely and these noon hour virtuosos might explore the full range of the 827-pipe Wurlitzer. Soul-shaking low notes. Teensie-weensie high ones. Sounds of gongs, drums, sirens and jalopy horns. As today's teenagers say, "Awesome, just awesome."

The organ is often in its lowered position beneath the floor when Frink and the others arrive.

"I clamber ungracefully down there, turn the switch so it starts to rise and then play like mad the whole, eight-foot trip up," he said. "Right then, in my head, I'm performing for a full house in the Paramount, with floodlights playing on me as I come up. This fantasy is very therapeutic, you know. I come over here from the office pretty tense. It's quiet. It's dark. There is no telephone. There is nothing to bother me. I start playing and lose all track of time. Then when I leave, I leave refreshed. Physically I might be a little tired from playing, but it's a delightful tired."

The fantasy performances do not always end in dead silence in the Paramount. "Yes," said Frink, "I've been surprised a few times to finish a number and all of a sudden, from somewhere way up there in the balcony, I hear someone applauding."

Guess who.

Never has a tuna salad sandwich been eaten in such glory.

A date with all the women—all at once—on a college campus

February 1982

WAVERLY, IA.—I have completed my research on the women of Wartburg College.

They felt I had slighted them in an earlier column about college women posing for cheesecake calendars. I noted that Iowa State and Drake women had already posed and said, rather carelessly, that if the craze continued, it might get to the point where we could even have a calendar of "Women of Wartburg."

Female Wartburgers responded, saying while they were not interested in making any calendars, they nevertheless wanted me to come look them over. On Friday, I did. I saw nearly all of them, from freshmen to faculty. I went to class and chapel with them. I ate with them. I took all of them on a "date" to wrestling and track meets Friday night. Later, we all went to the local hangout, Joe's Knight Hawk. They danced my feet off and beat me in a beer-chugging contest.

After all that, here is my two-point conclusion about Wartburg women:

As to brains: They seem to be sensitive, sensible and very bright, although I have to wonder about women who have put up with me in the gracious way they have.

As to beauty: Some caused my pulse to jump and my ears to turn red and made me want to say, "Ah-*woooooo!*" However, some others caused me to shiver and made me want to say, "Bow-wow."

This matter of bow-wow. I think socially, it could be a very slow spring for a lot of men on this campus. Why? Well, you might recall that the coeds have been referring to themselves as "Women of Wartburg" in my columns leading up to our date. They abbreviate it this way, "WOW." They even had WOW buttons made and sold several hundred.

A number of men, the rogues, have tampered with the acronym

145

and are calling the women "BOW-WOW"—"Basically Over-Weight Women of Wartburg."

Late Thursday night, a bunch of the men gathered in front of the cafeteria and began working on huge snow sculptures—two pigs and a woman with a paper bag over her head—planning to dedicate all of them to BOW-WOW. They worked on the sculptures until past midnight and then left, only to have a number of coeds come running out and mangle the sculptures with hammers and snow shovels. The men returned even later and rebuilt the pigs, which stood through the day Friday with "WOW" and "BOW-WOW" signs painted on adjacent snowbanks.

Other arrows were going through the air, too—none of them to be confused with Cupid's.

For example, Chris Donohue, a young man from Illinois, was telling me what would happen at a pie auction the campus Muscular Dystrophy Committee was sponsoring. "A Wartburg woman will buy a cream pie with the idea of putting it in your face," Donohue said. "But you don't have to worry. If she's a real Wartburg woman, she won't put it in your face, she'll eat it." (Incidentally, he was *wrong*. Sue Hanke, a junior from Colfax, put it on me with a flourish.)

"Our guys really do love us," said senior Candy Funk, of Graettinger. "They just show it in strange ways."

And vice-versa, it turns out. A little later, this same Funk was saying how "people were asking if we were going to introduce you to any men of Wartburg and we said we sure would—if we could find any." Then her friend Carla Stahlberg, a senior from Waverly, repeated the yarn of how "a man-eating tiger came to Wartburg and starved to death."

Funk, Stahlberg, Myrna Johnson and Michelle James, the four women who authored the letter inviting me here, were my escorts during the day. I learned a whale of a lot about Wartburg, nicknamed "The Wart" by the students.

For example, the American Lutheran Church–affiliated school has a couple of the neatest college traditions I've come across in Iowa.

One is "out-fly," a twice-a-year march by the student body to the president's home to ask for a day off. When the request is granted, it sets off a first-class hoedown.

Then there is the hoopla surrounding the yearly football game with archrival Luther College of Decorah. Following the game, the student body presidents from both schools meet at midfield, and the loser has to shed his pants and give them to the winner.

Our lunch Friday was another Wartburg tradition. We walked to Roy's, a diner just off the campus and had the "egg-cheese," a greasy delight Wartburg students have been eating for about 40 years. It's basically an omelet with cheese in the middle, fried in the same deep grease the hamburgers are cooked in, served on a bun with plenty of onions, pickles and ketchup.

"It's one of Wartburg's graduation requirements that you have to eat some certain number of these things before you get your diploma," said Al McNamar, the current owner.

Then we were back to the campus, discussing Wartburg women. Much of the talk was related to automobiles, since I had earlier referred to Iowa State women as the Cadillacs of coeds in the state and the Drake women as Fords. The four Wartburg seniors who wrote me claimed women here are generally of the Rolls Royce caliber.

True?

"Absolutely, baby!" said Doris Cottam, a sociology professor.

Pam Wegner, an English and theater professor, disagreed. "In this comparison of women to cars, you've talked always in terms of expense," she said. "I think of us more in terms of being very efficient. Maybe we're like a Honda CVCC."

Bob Vogel, the very popular college president, himself a Wartburg grad, said he wouldn't compare women here to a specific car. "That gets back to looks and, while the looks are here, there is much more to our women," he said. "The automotive term I would use for them is they are 'serviceable.' " He said he meant Wartburg women are open to the instruction and inspiration available at the institution and that they carry it far beyond the campus in the service of humanity.

Coeds I talked to throughout the day compared themselves to everything from a Corvette to a Jeep. I met Nancy Davis, the charmer who claims to be the Jeep, in the bar. She held up a glass and said, "I just stopped in for a lube job."

My four escorts finally decided the average Wartburg coed is a Buick Skylark. Why? "Carries herself well, is kind of classy, is sensible but still a little spunky," they said.

Late in the evening, one Wartburg man sought me out to have his say on the matter. "I've been reading where our alumni and some others have been kind of putting down Wartburg women," said

Reece Dodd, a senior from Geneva and a football player. "You hear about them being a little bit, you know, big. OK, we have our share of bad ones, but we have our share of good ones, too. Pretty ones, the kind you'd really like to marry. And you can have an intelligent conversation with women here."

As word of his remarks spread in the Knight Hawk, Reece Dodd found himself with no end of dance partners. There's a lesson in that, I'm sure.

A centennial celebration that brought 3,500 to Fiscus, a town of 7

June 1984

FISCUS, IA. — So here I sit typing on a table set up in the middle of the gravel road that is Main Street here, recording the sights and sounds of the day when little Fiscus, population 7, threw a centennial party that attracted thousands to this wide spot on the Audubon-Shelby county line.

How many thousands?

"OK, everybody!" screamed Laurel Nielsen over the public address system before the parade began. "We gotta get a crowd count. So either somebody come up with a number, or we're gonna make you count off from east to west across town."

The estimates ranged as high as 5,000 — actually, 3,500 seemed more plausible — but everyone agreed on one thing: Never before had so many people been in Fiscus. They signed in from as far away as California, New York, Texas, Canada and even Copenhagen, Denmark.

They came in herds from all over Iowa. A busload, with no real ties to Fiscus except a penchant "to have fun on a sunny afternoon," rolled in from Storm Lake aboard R. L. McLaughlin's customized old Greyhound coach sporting a sign, "Fiscus, Ia., Express."

They came for a lot of reasons. To see old friends. To see Floppy, the TV dog from Des Moines television station WHO. To see a daredevil named Olie Pash from Harlan do an aerial stunt show overhead in a snappy biplane. To see the dedication of a mammoth granite boulder as a historical marker bearing this slogan on a plaque: "Fiscus – Small on the map, big in our hearts!"

Many wanted a look at the new Fiscus "water tower," a 55-gallon drum perched atop a home-rigged trestle, looking for all the world like a mini-version of the standpipes that mark all our towns.

And I think a lot of them came to see what it would look like when a 140-unit parade, complete with two high school marching bands, wound its way through two oat fields, over a couple of gravel roads, past twin silos and right on by a team of apparently horrified draft horses that were used to jerk a few cars from the mud.

The parade finished on "Bert Street," which is the north-south gravel road renamed in honor of Bertha Armentrout, 72, who was stunned when she was named Fiscus Centennial Queen.

"I'm used to knowing everything that goes on around here," she said. "I didn't know about this." Imagine – a secret being kept in a town of seven!

In a great moment during the morning program, all of the Fiscussers were introduced on the stage. Taking bows along with Queen Bert were Jeff and Cheryl Swearingen and their children, Cheri and Mark, who were hailed as "Fiscus's Youngest Citizens." In the parade, they rode in a convertible marked with a sign, "We believe in the future of Fiscus!" And, of course, we can't forget Fay and Lois Lamberson, who were proclaimed forevermore to be mayor and first lady of Fiscus.

Let me add right here that as Grand Marshal of the parade, I was resplendent in my cutaway coat with tails, striped pants, spats, white gloves and top hat. I'm sure I'm the first guy ever to be this dressed up in Fiscus without being in a coffin.

They were afraid very early Saturday morning that the six months of fun and work invested in this event were going to go for naught. "It started raining at midnight, and rained for six hours," said Nielsen. "Believe me, I wasn't feeling very good about God or anybody else right then. I kept saying to myself, 'Hey, we're just a nice little spot in the road. What have we done so bad to deserve this?' I'll tell you, nothing is ever going to seem stressful again after this."

A decision was made to delay the parade one hour, with the possibility that the whole thing might have to be postponed or canceled. But the clouds broke, the sun came out and it turned into a beautiful day for a beautiful party.

Something wonderful is going to come from all this, I just know. Fiscus had staggered toward its 100th birthday like it wanted to give up and die. The population, once 57, dwindled to 7, and the last of the businesses were long since gone. The few people in town and the folks on the surrounding farms were all still friends, of course, but they were all going their separate ways.

"What we discovered after we decided to go ahead with this sort of crazy idea of having a centennial," said Chairman Everett Nelson, "was that it was fun getting together again and working on something. I think we're going to be benefiting from this kind of effort for a long time."

When the four-member Pocahontas County Medical Society meets, doctors from all over want to attend

September 1983

OKOBOJI, IA. – The closest most of you are going to get to attending a party where medical doctors are drinking beer, eating barbecued ribs and telling physicians' jokes is when you pay a bill that enables them to have one.

I got in on one here Thursday night – on an invitation even – and today I prove I'm the kiss-and-tell type. (Just a figure of speech there. I saw no kissing. It wasn't *that* wild a thing.) The event was the 28th annual gathering of the Pocahontas County Medical Society. This is a group that has only four – count 'em, four – members. But talk about a mouse that roared!

Every fall, the Drs. John Rhodes, John Rhodes, Jr., and Jim Slattery, who all practice in the town of Pocahontas, and Dr. Jim Gannon of nearby Laurens have a shindig here, a safe 50 miles or so from home. Over the years, it has become an evening of such good cheer that their "Okoboji Encounter," as they call it, has grown from barely filling a poker table to a blowout for which invitations are much sought after. Indeed, they kid now that there are such appendages to their organization as the "Sioux City Chapter of the Pocahontas County Medical Society."

Thursday night there were more than 100 doctors here from all over the Midwest, many having arrived in private planes. And in a coup of coups, the Pocahontas doctors also managed to lure no less than the president of the American Medical Association, Dr. Frank Jirka, Jr., of Chicago. I mean, this is a man who is the elected leader of 257,000 physicians, a man who spent the day before in the nation's capital and would spend the next day on the West Coast, helping shape the future of health care.

So, Dr. Jirka, what are you doing out here?

"John Rhodes, Sr., who is a good friend and a doctor's doctor, convinced me I had to come," he said. "Besides, I believe in getting out to the grass roots."

You don't get much deeper into the grass roots than a party thrown by a four-member county medical society.

"When my staff came back to me to check on this commitment I'd made," Jirka said, "they asked two questions—'Are you aware that's four members and not 4,000?' and 'Where the hell is Pocahontas?' "

The charge was led by the 66-year-old Rhodes, Sr., a jolly sort who set the dress standard for the evening with a straw cowboy hat and a "Go, you Hawkeyes" apron.

The ambience is like that of a college frat's fall stag. Golf, cards, drinks, ribs, steak and pleasant conversation that seemed to focus much more on football than medicine. Some say the party has become tamer as the Pocahontas doctors have aged. Said one visiting doctor, a man who has attended 18 "meetings," when asked for the highlight from all those years: "Well, it'd have to be the time I got in a fist fight here, because I won."

There is one serious part of the Okoboji Encounter. Each year, there is a medical lecture. They don't do it to satisfy continuing education requirements, which they probably could, but my suspicion is that it's far easier to write off a trip to the lakes on your taxes if you've done at least a little something more professionally related than drinking beer and hooting about the Hawks.

This year's lecture explored "Newer Developments in Inflammatory Bowel Disease." After sitting through it, I believe more than ever that doctors deserve the big bucks they make. How would you like to listen to a lecture on this topic, knowing full well you have an evening of drinking beer and eating barbecued ribs ahead?

The lecturer even used visual aids. When the X-ray of "a barium enema in a 25-year-old man" went up, oh! Only the fact it was in black and white instead of color enabled me to avoid fainting dead away. My colleagues in revelry, however, listened unflinchingly to 30 minutes of thoughts on "pancolonic ulcerative colitis" and related matters.

Then we went to the party. It was a gas.

A fashion show for women of "the fuller figure" (with free ice cream sundaes served afterward)

September 1980

CEDAR RAPIDS, IA. – No more trying to hide it. That was the basic fashion statement made at a style show for women last week at Killian's department store here.

I attended.

Every 10 years or so I try to get to one of these. It'd been about a decade since my last one – the La Femme Jamae Wig & Style Show in Shenandoah. I caught hell for wearing jeans and a sweatshirt that night, so this time, I knew enough to put on a sportcoat.

Recently, I'd been shopping around for a fashion show with a little extra, and when I ran across a Killian's ad for its event, I knew I'd found what I was seeking. It was the fall show for women of "the fuller figure." It was called "Fashions at Large."

But what really attracted me was that the ad said that after the show, everyone was invited to create her own ice cream sundae right there in the store. And the three rather large women pictured in the ad were showing just how a nice, tall sundae is constructed. They were also wearing some sharp-looking outfits.

"There is something I want to mention but not dwell on," said emcee and Killian's clothing buyer Ruth Hansen, 45, as she was wrapping up the show Thursday. "We showed an ice cream sundae in our ad for this event, and if that was offensive to anyone, I apologize.

"We've had the sundaes at the two shows we did for you last year, and we like to have them because we think it's fun. But we didn't advertise them last year. After our ad was in the paper the other night, someone called and said we were holding large women up to ridicule.

"We weren't. Each of us is a very valuable person, and we should be proud and grateful for what we are. Let's say, 'We love us the way we are.' "

All of that was intended as a statement about the ice cream sundaes. But what struck me was that it could also serve as a rather profound statement about fashions for women of the fuller figure.

Huh?

Well, as Hansen said later in an interview, until recently there have been no real fashions for large women. "When I started in this department seven years ago, all there were were dumb dresses, really cheap," she said. "We called them bullet-proof polyester.

"Things have changed. Now almost every designer cuts a large-size line. The manufacturers have discovered that large women love fashion. And these women are not as price-conscious because they're so thrilled when they find something they like that fits."

Added Gordon Rumpf, divisional merchandise manager: "America just forgot the larger woman for a while. But everyone — the designers, the manufacturers, all the stores — are waking up to the fact it's a big market. Do you realize that a third of the women in America wear a size 16 dress or larger?"

Hansen describes her customers as "ladies who do not feel they must get down to a size 8. As the fashions get better, the ladies become more confident. More and more of them are getting out of pantsuits and into dresses.

"They're enthused about fashion. It used to be it took some arm-twisting to get models for a show like this one, but no more. Now women volunteer because after being at a couple of our shows, they know it's fun."

Hansen said few large women quibble with the term "fuller-figured woman."

"In other areas of the country, they use other terms that I don't think are as nice," she said. "For example, in California, I know they refer to these women as 'the luscious large,' and in New York it's 'the large and beautiful.'"

The crowd of 50 or more attending the lunch-hour show was most attentive as models Nancy, Margaret, Holly, Carolyn and Esther paraded by in suedes, crepes, velvets, wovens and knits. Darned attractive styles, too.

After a half-hour of fashions and commentary from Hansen, the gathering broke to an adjacent room where the ice cream, syrup, nuts and whipped cream waited.

Most of the fuller-figured women partook. And why not?

As Hansen said, "Hey, let's hit it right where it is — there is absolutely nothing wrong with ice cream and topping."

Dropping in on a University of Iowa class in billiards — the "liberal" in Liberal Arts

April 1983

IOWA CITY, IA. — The school year is slipping away and I hadn't yet audited a college class, which I always like to do to stay in touch. So I popped in on a University of Iowa course that is listed in catalogs as Section 79, Department 10-21 — billiards.

There is a danger in visiting Academia and writing about something like this for the general public. The narrow-minded will start chirping about the punt courses being taught for actual credit in our tax-supported institutions. They're the same old mossbacks who always are yipping at Iowa State for those little creampuffs tucked away in the Home Ec curriculum. Those people never understand the "liberal" in Liberal Arts.

But I do, and that's in spite of the fact that, when it comes to pool, I'm from the Old School. In other words, I learned my game in a beer joint. My teacher was the late Harry Spargur, whom many of us called Harry the Hustler. He was no college man, unless attending an occasional football game makes you one.

Some will jump to the hasty conclusion that a guy like Harry would sneer at pool's being taught at a university. Hardly. Two things Harry always told us: (1) When we were cussing too loud, he'd growl, "Pretty rough language for a boy," and (2) when we were whining about school, he'd say, "Get that education or you'll wind up working in a pool hall like me." To think, if he'd hung on a few years more, what with his keen eye and steady hand and smooth stroke, he could've been a faculty member! Harry would love this course.

Now, I said the name of it is "billiards." You think immediately of the snobby, pocketless game played by rich men wearing smoking jackets and sipping brandy. Indeed, they give you a brush with that game here at the U of I, but mostly they teach 8-ball, straight pool, rotation and snooker. And as for dress and drink, it seemed to be all T-shirts, jeans, sneakers, Mello-Yellos and Cokes.

Instructors are primarily grad students in Physical Education. However, John Bowlsby, 27, director of the recreation center in the Iowa Memorial Union, where the classes are held, also teaches a couple of sections. You may remember Bowlsby as the great Hawkeye heavyweight wrestler of a couple of years ago. Gee, I hope he likes this column.

Bowlsby said billiards is one of the more popular of the minor Phys Ed classes. He said everyone is especially anxious for the appearance here soon of Sue Warnes, a trick-shot artist of national renown. Aha, visiting lecturer? "You could say that," he laughed.

Presiding at the class I attended was the youngest member of the teaching cadre, Chuck Meardon, a 20-year-old Iowa Citian, himself an undergraduate student. He is a sophomore in everything but pool, in which, believe me, even Harry Spargur would say the kid is a veritable professor.

When one of his students gets uppity, Meardon fetches a mop from the storage room and, using its handle as a cue, plays against the fool. Isn't that degrading to his students? "Of course," said the witty Meardon. "The mop shows 'em who's in charge. Teaches 'em humility."

He never loses. He was just one ball shy of skunking me, although I'm proud to say he felt it necessary to use his $400, custom-made Szamboti cue instead of that darned old mop handle.

He moves with cockiness and confidence among the tables, showing those in the class of 17 how to make a good bridge with the hand, to pay attention to where the cue ball might meander and how to use the cushions. "Some of the other teachers use group instruction," he said. "I teach table to table because different people have different abilities."

Meardon introduced as one of his most skilled students former Hawkeye basketball star Kevin Boyle, who is completing work on his degree. Boyle was much tougher in hoops than he is on the felt; I waxed him. "You've embarrassed your teacher," said Meardon to Boyle. "You wanna flunk this course?"

Few do flunk billiards. Meardon said of 20 students he had last semester, two were taking the course for actual grades. They both got A's. The other 18 were taking it on a pass-fail basis. The only two who failed did so because they never showed up.

Meardon is not paid for his teaching. Instead, he gets a financial break on his own university bill.

I asked if it had ever occurred to him to think of himself as "a faculty colleague" of, say, James Van Allen, the noted physicist.

"Dr. Van Allen doesn't have the same status at the university as I do," Meardon said, "but it's okay with me if you mention our names together."

A high society beer blast— the "victory party" of a softball team with Des Moines' biggest names on its roster

February 1983

It was revolting, darlings. Absolutely revolting.

Which means, of course, that the Mad Dogs will consider their fourth annual victory party a howling success. The Mad Dogs, I guess you'd say, are society's team when it comes to slow-pitch softball in Des Moines. They are a gang of veritable blue bloods (three Hubbells on the roster) and some of their spear carriers, waning preppies all, easing now into middle age.

Indeed, they play some softball games in the summers, but the team's raison d'etre—not many slow-pitch softball teams could get away with having raisons d'etre but this one can—has come to be the annual victory party at the grand Des Moines Club.

The latest of the bashes was Saturday night and, yes, once again that deerhead that the rest of the year hangs in quiet dignity on a Hermitage Room wall had a cigar stuck in its mouth, sunglasses put on its snout and a pair of fancy panties strung in its antlers. If pool-hall rowdies somehow got into these elegant quarters and behaved like this, the cops would be summoned. But management, realizing it's dealing with pedigrees, winks and rakes in the profits from what is the club's biggest beer night of the year.

The team traces its lineage to 1878, when, they say, F. M. Hubbell put together a ball club. He would be the great-great-grandfather of the current Hubbell players, Jim III, Fred and Mike. The story goes that one of the first of the club's games was covered by a sportswriter who reported the team played with the fury of "mad dogs." Thus the name.

They also tell you that when the modern Mad Dogs were being formed a few years ago, the 1878 roster was checked and actual heirs of the original Mad Dogs were then sought out to make up today's outfit. Charming yarn, huh? Yes, it's a wonderful story that lacks but one virtue: truth.

"The reason things like that get started," said Les Baitzer, team "owner" because he pays the entry fee into the city league, "is that several of us on the team think we actually should have been writers, and we sit around making up these stories that we naturally believe to be just cute as hell."

The Mad Dogs play an unremarkable brand of softball, usually going .500 or less and displaying little of the elan they show at partying.

Invitations to the $2,500 party, the cost of which Baitzer spreads among his 20 troops, are cleverly done. This year's invitation, for example, was a modified but official-looking subpoena from the U.S. District Court for the Southern District of Iowa commanding the guest to testify in the civil action of The Mad Dogs vs. The Des Moines Club. The invitations always include a team logo, which has the words "Madus Dogus" in Greek letters surrounding two dogs in, shall we say, a canine embrace.

The invitation is much sought after by those around town who are young, on the make and upwardly mobile. They come and engage in a lot of SOG chatter. (SOG? "South of Grand," dumbbell.) Someone the other night said it's "a little like Roosevelt High 20 years later," and in support of that point, I did hear a young beauty ask a chap, "Is that a Reichardt tie you're wearing?"

Most come dressed to kill, except for the Mad Dogs themselves, who wear their game jerseys. As you've surely concluded, there is sort of a fraternity-party aura. Boys will be boys, you know. They tell of the time at the first party when a 100-person line formed and bunny-hopped through the women's restroom.

The wildest it got Saturday was when one Mad Dog, this one wearing his full uniform topped by a World War II Nazi helmet, came racing across the room, dropped to his knees behind an unsuspecting guest and bit her on the rump.

It is a good enough time that it keeps a crowd in the Des Moines Club well past midnight, which is unusual.

But as much as these guys boast they enjoy making like "Animal House," they are reaching ages and positions which make their swashbuckling seem a touch unconvincing. The Mad Dogs, I'm betting, are not far from settling into lives of more quiet affluence.

A middle-aged columnist
takes Miss Angie Potts, 17,
to her high school prom

April 1986

LYTTON, IA. – The theme was "Remember the Feeling." And, oh, did I ever Friday night.

With Miss Angie Potts, a 17-year-old Lytton High School charmer, on my arm, I once again went through that rite of spring that is the junior-senior banquet and prom.

All the essential components were at hand in this northwest Iowa town of 370, just as I remember them being at hand the last time I went to one of these things some 20-odd years ago.

The right smell was in the air in the late afternoon – manure. It was being spread on a field south of town, and 30 mph wind gusts were fanning in what vo-ag teacher Brian Lantz called "just a little reminder that we're a farming community."

We got all dressed up, Miss Potts and I and all the other couples. And we of course exchanged flowers. When we were a half-hour early for the banquet, we killed it by doing the requisite drag down Main Street in our car, hit what they call "the turn-around" in the gravel in front of the grain elevator and then went back up Main.

We got to the banquet in the Presbyterian church basement – after waving to neighbors who were using binoculars to keep tabs on the arriving couples – and there we ate Iowa chops cooked on outdoor grills provided by the Sac County Pork Producers. Later, we moved on to the elaborately decorated Legion Hall, where enough formal and informal photographs were taken to make Kodak's stock rise.

That completed, it was time for the prom itself, although there was one more little bit of getting ready to do. Senior Jill Haden led the way in that, pulling off her high heels and pulling on her high-topped basketball sneakers, an interesting fashion mix with her pale green formal.

A DJ began spinning records. On the slow ones, the teenagers hung on to each other in full clutch and swayed. On the fast ones, everybody got outrageous enough that at one point, senior Michael

159

Todd Owen—"MTO" to everyone around here—went into a handstand and danced on his palms.

When things really started to get dizzy later, a couple of the guys gave in to a wave of high school schtick and tugged their cummerbunds up to brassiere height. I think a very few of these rascals might have slipped outside for a nip once or twice, but that kind of stuff was effectively discouraged by chaperoning faculty members.

Those who ducked outside just for cool air did notice a couple of strange cars cruising. Loads of boys from nearby Sac City and Lake View, somebody told me—probably up to no good. Soon, word spread through the dance crowd that a fight had broken out, and would-be spectators rushed from the hall for what turned out to be only a rumor—but an essential rumor if you like prom traditions.

At midnight, we all changed clothes and got together in the schoolhouse for several hours of Las Vegas–style games, movies and food.

And, through it all, these current occupants of adolescence—these 17 seniors and 13 juniors from Lytton and their dates—seemed perfectly willing to share their own special night with a middle-aged interloper who was wearing shoes older than most of them are. I refer to my tattered saddle shoes, which I wore with my black tux because they were much more comfortable and sensible than the patent leather jobs I'd rented. And they served to make the point with my Miss Potts that she'd never had a date quite like me.

This had come about, you'll remember, because a month ago, she and five of her pals, on a lark, took out an ad in their school paper. They stood somberly in a line in the photograph, wearing cardboard placards showing their telephone numbers. A caption proclaimed, "Prom Dates Wanted!"

I answered the ad. And now, even after an awfully long night for such an old-timer, I'm still glad I did it. They treated me like visiting royalty. After I wrote that I had thought fleetingly about renting a limousine because my own car has a caved-in rear fender, service station owner Otis Schultz called up the Lytton mayor and told him he would volunteer his Cadillac for my use. The mayor, Dick Maxwell, who is also a fifth-grade teacher and operator of a grocery store, came along with his First Lady, Lois, and the two of them served as chauffeurs for Miss Potts and me.

My date, the daughter of farmers Ron and Linda Potts, was elegantly turned out for the evening in a gorgeous gown in royal blue and white, the same colors as the Jeep she drives. Through the banquet and prom, she also courageously kept on her three-inch heels despite being guided around the dance floor by the klutz that I can sometimes be.

"She's a great kid," said Mayor Maxwell, "kind of the classic farm girl in that she's completely at home doing field work, but she can go inside and sew and cook, and she can also go out in public and fit right in with everybody. You don't find them much better than Angie."

Indeed, after a long night with me, and after a good-by kiss on her cheek, you know what she was going to do?

"Go home and do chores," she said.

It all happened just the way I remembered it was supposed to happen, just the way I'd want to remember it some 20-odd years from now if I was a Lytton High School kid in 1986.

I won a college scholarship because I was "a promising sportswriter." I still am, and I'll forever be a fan. Show me Iowans on the field, course, court and diamond—and the people in the stands—and I'll show you real happiness.

SPORTS

A special view of
Chuck Long's last home
football game as a Hawkeye

November 1985

IOWA CITY, IA. – There were 66,020 in Kinnick Stadium when it all came to its glorious conclusion Saturday afternoon, and almost all of them must have screamed "Rose Bowl!" at least once. But the one I enjoyed hearing it from most was 14-year-old Andy Long of Wheaton, Illinois, the youngest brother of Hawkeye quarterback Chuck Long.

Young Andy, afflicted by cerebral palsy, struggled into standing position on the yellow plastic bleachers and screamed it again and again, "Rose Bowl! Rose Bowl!" The depth of the happiness written on the face of the boy, for whom brother Chuck has always been a larger-than-life hero, was beautiful to behold.

It was like that for all the Longs, really, as they huddled against bone-rattling cold for the last football game that will bring them all together in Iowa City. They've spent an entire autumn walking on air, as everything seemed to happen just the way they felt it should happen for their celebrated Chuck and his Hawkeye teammates.

Here was Charlie Long, 47, who works in communications for Beatrice Foods in Chicago, confessing that under all those clothes, yes, he was wearing his lucky blue boxer shorts. Hasn't attending all 11 of the Hawk games been expensive? "Oh, yeah," he grinned, "we're broke, but it's been worth all of it."

Said Joan Long, also 47, "Since about the middle of the season, Charlie has been telling me this is a team of destiny, and I've been telling him I don't know how many more close games I can stand. It's been so good, and yet I'm almost glad it's over. All of the nervous times will be behind us and we can really look back and enjoy it."

Nearby were another Long son, David, 19, a U of I sophomore who is not playing football, and Chuck's girlfriend since grade school, Lisa Wells, a U of I graduate student. "See my earrings?" Lisa asked. "They're roses. Chuck bought them for me last summer when we were in Colorado. They're working, aren't they?"

Also here were Joan's parents, J. C. and Terease Hampton, of Ponca City, Oklahoma, the state that was home for both Charlie and

Joan and where Chuck was born. "When I get back to Oklahoma," Terease said, "I think I'll call up Barry Switzer, the coach at OU, and ask him if he doesn't wish now he'd had Chuck playing for him."

But Charlie immediately replied: "That would've been the worst mistake Chuck could've ever made, if he'd gone down there. You know, he wasn't recruited very heavily by the big universities, but even if he had been, there is no way he could've gone anywhere better for him than right here at Iowa. It's been a perfect match, a perfect time. Everything perfect."

There was a powerful lot of reminiscing going on as the clan sat in their 40-yard-line seats. They talked of the first game they saw here, an upset of Nebraska when Chuck was a freshman reserve.

"That wasn't just the first big college game he'd ever been in uniform for, it was also the first big college game he'd ever even seen," his father said. "He told me later that when he went out early with the receivers and warmed up, the stands were mostly empty and it didn't seem like a big deal. But then he told about coming out of the tunnel right before the game with the whole team, hearing the roar of the crowd and thinking, 'Oh my God!' "

They talked of Chuck's decision last year to pass up a fat professional contract so he could play a fifth season with the Hawks. "This was a young man who had fallen in love with this place," said Charlie. "In the end, he wanted to go the whole way here. I'd made up my mind that that's what he should do, too, but I told him I wouldn't tell him what I thought. Turned out we were both thinking the same thing."

They talked about many great games and a few disappointing ones. But they could hardly talk at all about a possible Heisman Trophy, Rose Bowl victory and national championship. "All I can say," said Charlie, "is that it's wonderful Chuck is even being mentioned, and that the team has this chance." This is a family that knows full well it has lived a storybook year, a family that wouldn't be so greedy as to expect anything more.

But I decided I was going to give them a little more anyway. Charlie Long, I said before the game, you can't imagine the joy your son has given to a state that has been dragged down and kicked so much more than it deserves, a state that is suffering the worst of times. You can't imagine the pictures of him, the talk about him and the pride in him in our small town gathering spots from corner to corner and border to border.

"I love knowing that," he said softly.

And Joan Long, I said before the game, this is a long-stemmed rose I picked up outside the stadium. It's from all of us Iowa boys.

"Thank you," she said. "I'm touched."

Not half as deeply as their family has touched us.

Hayden Fry's
weekly chore

November 1985

IOWA CITY, IA. – Give me idle time and my curiosity will lead me places I'm not supposed to be. It was that way again Tuesday here. I took some down time to attend something I've always wondered about – Coach Hayden Fry's weekly sashay with the sporting press.

I couldn't believe the jam in a room in the bowels of Carver-Hawkeye Arena. Fry's session, held late Tuesday mornings, draws at least twice as many media rats as show for the governor. There were 50 of them working 10 television cameras and three times that many tape recorders.

"And the crowd today was nothing," George Wine, Iowa sports information director, said later. "You should've seen it a couple of those weeks when we were rated No. 1 and going into the games with Michigan and Ohio State. We had 'em tripping all over each other."

The funniest thing that happened Tuesday was that the sports promoters, as they occasionally do, took advantage of the crowd of reporters to try to garner some attention for one of the minor sports – this time, men's swimming.

Before Fry came in, swimming coach Glenn Patton did a song and dance and then passed out schedules bearing a goofy photo of himself wearing an Army helmet that has five gold stars surrounding a tiger Hawk. The caption identifies him as "General Patton." Ye gods.

Fry, whom I'm accustomed to seeing only in white slacks and black blast jacket on the sidelines, arrived looking like a sartorial disciple of J. R. Ewing—sharp blue blazer, gaudy gold wristband, charcoal slacks and gray cowboy boots so elegant I salivated. Maybe you've shared my observation that during games when he wears flat-bottomed coaching shoes, he always seems to learn backwards, like he's got bricks in his hind pockets. But with those stacked heels Tuesday, he came off as one tall, erect cowboy.

The guy carries his 56 years well, although the regulars in the press corps say he's aged noticeably recently. Some say it's the big games. Others argue it's only the dippy new haircut, shorter and older-looking.

He popped a Coke, sat in the blazing TV lights and said, "Let's go." What followed were 45 minutes of Q and A about everything from crowd noise at Ohio State to quarterback Chuck Long's mental makeup during that game to the sorry plight of our farmers. The latter inspired him a week ago to add "ANF" decals to the Hawkeyes' helmets, meaning "America Needs Farmers." His voice wavered between bold bass and high whine.

The questions indicated there were some hardballers among the reporters—and some bootlickers, too. Asked what he thought of some bozo on Iowa City radio having suggested he be nominated for governor, Fry quipped, "That guy didn't bother to check the salary range on that job. I couldn't afford the salary cut." When Terry Branstad reads that line, particularly after also reading how the swimming coach thinks of himself as a five-star general, he'll surely marvel at the pretty pass things have come to in his state.

Fry was tame Tuesday, as he has been all fall. "We're eight games into the season and Hayden hasn't come in with a mad-on yet," said Al Grady, veteran columnist of the *Iowa City Press-Citizen*. "Usually, there'll be one press conference where he'll be owly, answer questions with only a yes or no and then tell us how much he hates us."

I was surprised that no one fills the role of Helen Thomas, the UPI White House correspondent, who formally opens and closes presidential press conferences. I'd assumed one of the old heads—say Grady or *Cedar Rapids Gazette* columnist Gus Schrader or broadcaster Bob Brooks or our own Maury White—would do that with Fry.

"Nope," said Schrader. "And by the way, don't lump Brooks in there with us. I've got sportcoats older than he is – and in better shape, too."

It ended with everybody eating bad roast beef sandwiches and good chocolate chip cookies as they listened to Illinois coach Mike White carry on over a speaker phone. Fry, in a chair to the side then, appeared to be near a snooze, but remember, the "Ol' Coach," as he often refers to himself, has heard all this stuff before.

Still, it's a great show, this madness football.

A golf course where the "greens" are "browns" and are well oiled

June 1982

MALVERN, IA. – Just last weekend, we watched on television as Tom Watson won the U.S. Open golf tournament and its top prize of $60,000 while playing on that breathtakingly beautiful course at Pebble Beach, California.

On Monday, a lot of Iowans will again be watching Watson. He and other top golfers will play the lush Finkbine course in Iowa City, the site of the prestigious Amana V.I.P. tournament.

Reflecting on that, it occurred to me that this might be an appropriate time to remind everybody that golf is not all Tom Watsons, big prizes, Pebble Beaches and Amana V.I.P.s. It might be a good time to take a look at how golf's other half lives. So I stopped by Fairview Country Club in Malvern, a town of 1,244 in southwest Iowa.

The course, a nine-holer on a hillside, is named well. Come here and play golf while the Mills County Fair is running on adjacent grounds and you get a fair view, all right.

Now, if your thing is total accuracy, you wouldn't say Fairview has greens. Rather, you'd say it has browns. It is one of the very few "sand greens" courses left in the state.

There is an official greenskeeper, who rightfully should be called a brownskeeper. He is Roy Wilhelm, 70, a retired farmer. He can provide details about the putting surfaces—how they consist of a layer of asphalt topped by about four inches of fine sand. The sand is oiled once a year so it won't blow away in the wind. The oil used is that saved by local residents when they drain the crankcases of their cars, trucks and tractors.

These sand greens courses were more common a half-century or more ago when Malvern and a lot of other communities were first building golf facilities. "Those were hard times," said Dr. J. A. Kline, 75, who is still practicing both osteopathy and golf here. "There wasn't money for anything better than sand greens."

Economy has always been the watchword on this course. Membership is $50 per year—for the whole family! For non-members, greens fees, or browns fees, are $2 per day. They are collected on the honor system—put your two bucks in an envelope and drop it into a padlocked box.

"We do everything we can to keep expenses down," said Ken Scott, 57, for five years the president of the private club that maintains the course. He stopped in the middle of this thought, pointed to an open-sided shelter house just big enough to cover a picnic table and said, "See, there's our clubhouse."

"There's some pressure to put in grass greens, and I'd like them, too, but we can't do it for nothing. And as cheap as it is to play here, we still have some people complain our prices are too high. To me, the view you get from standing here on this hill at sunset—why, that alone is worth the price of one of our family memberships."

Most of the labor at Fairview was and is volunteer. Years ago, whenever the fairways needed mowing, 30 or more of the members would report to the course with their push-type, non-powered mowers and have at it.

One year, someone had a bright idea that the mowing could be altogether avoided if sheep were allowed to graze on the fairways. The local newspaper, the *Malvern Leader,* carried this report on why that experiment failed: "Unfortunately, the sheep considered the sand greens ideal for their toilet needs, causing concern on the part of some members who had to either rake the greens each time of use or play through the droppings." So the sheep are gone. But players are still expected to rake the sand greens after each use.

Here's the way it works: You play a normal game of golf from the tee. When it comes time to hit to the sand green, you can be especially bold, as few balls bounce off the sand. When all players in the group have hit on, then someone grabs the heavy metal drag on the apron and makes a smooth path from one side of the sand green to the other, passing directly over the cup. You eyeball the distance your ball is from the cup and then reposition the ball on the new path, maintaining the same distance unless you are a cheat. When you putt, you have to hit the ball about twice as hard as on grass greens. When all players have holed out, someone is supposed to use the rake provided and erase the footprints in the sand.

I took my lessons on the use of Fairview from President Scott the other day. I teed it up on No. 1 and dubbed my very first shot.

"You can take a mulligan on the first hole," Scott said consolingly.

"Club rule?" I asked.

"Oh, I guess it can be," he answered.

You know, after suffering the pro tour's regimentation, Tom Watson might find some things about Fairview mighty attractive.

The way high school
sports should always work

November 1986

PARKERSBURG, IA. – The high school football season has now ended – the state championship games were played last weekend – but before we put it all behind us, the story of one late October game must be told.

What happened here between the Grundy Center Spartans and the Parkersburg Crusaders will serve as a delightful counterbalance to the ugliness and poor sportsmanship that seemed to abound in the season of '86.

This autumn had given us a lot of sorry stuff – fistfights, helmet throwing, a coach feeling he had to pull his team from the field before a game ended, one of our example-setting college coaches ordering an absolutely meaningless field goal when he was already winning by a lopsided score. Ugh.

Well, let's forget all that now and focus instead on what must go down as one of the most truly important games of the year.

And to think some were saying that the Grundy-Parkersburg encounter, which wasn't even scheduled until three days before it was played on October 28, would be a throwaway, that it didn't count for anything. As it turned out, you'll see, it counted for everything.

Both teams had narrowly missed qualifying for the playoffs. But the opponents each had scheduled for the final game of the regular season had qualified. That meant both the Spartans and the Crusaders had to decide whether they wanted to bother finding a ninth game or simply call it quits with the eight already played.

Parkersburg is coached by Ed Thomas, 36, in his 12th year here. He's built a solid program, and this team was 7-1. Grundy, equally as strong, was 6–2 in the sixth year that Don Knock, 32, has been coaching there.

Knock is a native of Parkersburg, and he and Thomas have become close friends. "In fact," he said, "Ed and his wife, Jan, are godparents for my son, Kyle."

The coaches of the two schools, located only 12 miles apart, spend a lot of time on the phone with each other during the football season comparing strategies. Their teams had never met, because they are in different conferences and because Grundy is a 2-A school and Parkersburg is 1-A.

But when they realized both were looking for a ninth game, they decided in a phone chat to finish the season against each other if their squads would agree. The players voted to play, and the game was set.

"After we decided to do it," said Thomas, "both Donny and I were a little leery. I mean, we're such good friends and we're both so competitive that we were worried how it'd go." It could not have gone better. Both coaches now say they can't recall seeing a more exciting, hard-fought football game at any level of competition.

"But the best part," said Thomas, "is that it was clean."

Early in the fourth quarter, Parkersburg led 21-7, but Grundy mounted a great comeback and tied it as regulation time expired.

A first overtime went scoreless. In the second, each scored a touchdown on the wildest of plays, and it was tied at 28. In the third overtime, Grundy kicked a field goal to win it, 31-28.

But it was then, in the aftermath, that this game became really special. The players had gathered at midfield and were shaking hands. They turned to see their two coaches engaged in a long, shameless embrace. "We had started just to shake hands, and then we both hugged each other," said Thomas. "It had been a real emotional night for both of us."

Thomas and Knock, acting spontaneously, then asked the two squads to sit together on the gridiron. Fans from both towns ringed the large huddle.

First Thomas, then Knock, talked.

"This game," said Thomas, "with all its excitement and with the way we're getting together here afterward, is what high school athletics is all about."

Knock reassured the Parkersburg players "that there are no losers in a game like this one. We all will leave here with our heads held high."

Then everyone—coaches, players and fans—got down on one knee and said a prayer of thanks for opportunities given, challenges met, values learned. It was a 15-minute scene that still gives nearly everyone on both sides goose bumps when they recall it.

Check Tom Teeple, Parkersburg barber and a football official who that night happened to be working on the "chain gang" that marks the yardage. "I wish everybody in the state of Iowa that has anything to do with high school athletics could've seen what happened," Teeple said. "For once, it was just like it should be all the time."

The best Iowa schoolboy athlete in 10 years: Aurelia's Doug Lockin

February 1979

AURELIA, IA.—He doesn't drink, smoke, chew or brag. He's thoughtful, soft-spoken, good-looking, as at ease among adults as he is among kids. He is a straight-A student, ranking No. 1 academically among the 45 in his high school class. And old-timers say he is the best all-around athlete this sports-conscious northwest Iowa town of 1,065 ever has had.

It's little wonder that the people well acquainted with Doug Lockin, an extraordinary senior at Aurelia High School, are simply unable to avoid referring to him as "an all-American boy."

It embarrasses him. "I can't say I'm like that," Lockin, 18, says.

So what is he like? What principles guide him in life? Those are uncommon questions to shoot at a teenager, the kind of test that wilts many adults.

But the boy takes the challenge, looks the stranger in the eye and, in the same tone he'd used to order steak and potatoes, says: *"I just kind of stick to the rules and do as best I can in everything I try. And however it comes out, then I do as best I can to accept it."*

He intends that as a sort of disclaimer of the status Aurelians so readily confer upon him. But darned if it doesn't come out reading like one of the canons of all-American boyism.

And why wouldn't it? Lockin, 6 feet 5 inches tall and 190 pounds, will have won 18 varsity letters by the end of the summer. He was an all-state quarterback in football on a team that won the Sioux Valley Conference and probably will win all-state honors playing for the equally successful basketball team. He is the leading scorer and rebounder on his team.

He is a reigning state champion in the high jump in track, is the top schoolboy golfer in the area and pitches and plays shortstop on the baseball team.

Some 30 colleges have been bidding for his athletic talents. And recently he took one of the standard college entrance examinations, scored among the top 2 or 3 percent of all high school seniors in America and now is being sought by a couple of colleges for their honors scholarship programs.

He's president of the youth group at the local United Methodist Church, is an active member of the Fellowship of Christian Athletes and a week ago was named the Aurelia recipient of the Daughters of the American Revolution Good Citizenship award.

He "goes steady" with a cheerleader, helps with the Scripture readings in church and gets his hair cut regularly. He doesn't even have pimples.

But Doug Conard, principal at Aurelia High, says the list of Lockin glory given here does not include what may be the boy's top quality. "I've seen kids before who have had tremendous success and have received a lot of publicity," Conard says. "A lot of them let it go to their heads. Doug Lockin is not that way. He has remained what he always was, very down to earth and caring. In athletics, he continually sacrifices himself for the betterment of the team. He has the greatest sense of values of any kid I've ever known."

But nobody's perfect, not even young Lockin.

Though he "tries hard" in choir, according to music teacher Ruth Hoferman, he is no better than mediocre as a baritone.

When he tried out for the cast of the senior class play, "Cheaper by the Dozen," he got the hook and was assigned to the stage crew.

He once got a $3 ticket from the local police officer for parking illegally on the town's main street.

His basketball coach, Duane Buttenob, occasionally wishes Doug would be a more aggressive leader. "But, I don't know, where do you draw the line?" Buttenob says. "He does so much already, and if he was yelling at the other kids all the time, maybe they wouldn't have anything to do with him."

And no one around Aurelia has forgotten how nervous "Big Lock" got when the Bulldogs made it to last year's state basketball tournament in Des Moines. "Our first game had just started, I came running down the floor and threw up right at mid-court," he recalls. "Oh!, it was awful, so embarrassing."

Oh, that more kids had such serious shortcomings, huh?

Doug Lockin, his high school days nearing conclusion, knows he has been through a golden period in his life. Asked what has been his biggest prep thrill, he rattled off several.

And the biggest bummer? He is silent for a time, then says, "You know, I can't think of anything. Maybe that's why I don't want to leave high school. One reason it's been so good is that I've grown up in this town. I have very strong feelings for Aurelia. I always said that I'd never leave here, but I see now I have to, at least to get an education. After that, if there's a good chance for me to come back here, set up some kind of business and live, I probably will."

His family is a strong, close one. "Conservative" and "traditional" are the words his father, John Lockin, 47, an insurance agent, uses to describe the clan. Doris Lockin, 41, is a kindergarten teacher here. The other children are Al, 16, a junior who is a virtual carbon copy of Doug in all activities, Brian, 10, and LeAnn, 8.

The family is proud of Doug, but hardly in awe of him. The parents say they worry about the pressure and needling that the boy's success invites—mainly from hard-charging athletic opponents, to a lesser degree from his classmates and friends here.

It'd be unnatural if Lockin's fellow students didn't occasionally weary of his accomplishments, but it doesn't happen often, says Marty Stutz, student body president. "It's funny, maybe, but I don't think there's any real resentment of him because he excels," Stutz says. "We're all so used to Doug being good in everything he does that we accept it. It's not hard to accept because he's handled it without getting conceited. For a guy in his position, there's got to be a lot of pressure. I'm not sure I could take it, but he does."

How does he take it? "I go along with the kidding," Lockin says. "I know I'm going to get it from out-of-town kids, and I try not to do anything that would make me deserve it from kids here in Aurelia. Things come easy to me—sports, books—but just because they do doesn't make me better than anybody else. I'm lucky and I know it. I try never to shut out or ignore anyone. Once or twice when I've realized I have done that, it's really bothered me."

But is there frustration in such goodness?

"Sometimes."

Does that mean he occasionally feels like grabbing a beer, standing on the main drag and announcing he's going to be bad for a while?

"I wouldn't even consider that," he says. "Maybe it'd be something more like getting wide open for a jump shot and then slamming it off the bangboard, but things have never been that bad. I can let a lot of things get built up inside me, but if I get a night's sleep I usually can see how silly they were and I forget them."

And so the legend builds in a town where, when the young kids play basketball, "a lot of times one of the guys will pretend he's Doug Lockin," according to 12-year-old Darrin Meendering. "Everyone wants to be like him when they're in high school."

What if Lockin started wearing orange satin trousers around town? Would Darrin and his buddies want to do that?

"I don't think I would," says the youngster, "but some of them might."

The best Iowa schoolgirl athlete in 10 years: Ventura's Lynne Lorenzen

March 1987

Let me take you back a year and a half to a visit a friend and I made to little Ventura in north Iowa to watch Lynne Lorenzen play basketball.

We took our snooty, city-wise kids with us.

We told these doubters that the trip through a snowstorm was worth it because "some day everybody will be able to say they saw Lorenzen play basketball on television or in the state tournament in Des Moines, but only a few of us will be able to say we saw her play on her home court."

I went on to say in a column I wrote about the trip that "if the 6-

177

on-6 game in girls' basketball is dying, as many say is the case, isn't it appropriate that in its last hurrah the 6-game has produced the best player there ever was?"

I defy anyone who watched the girls' state tournament last week to argue that Lorenzen is not the best 6-on-6 player there ever was.

E. Wayne Cooley won't. He is the boss of the Iowa Girls High School Athletic Union. He's been around since the days when the hoops were fruit baskets nailed to barn walls.

"Saturday night, after the championship game, we took our TV crew down to Babe's for dinner," Cooley said on Monday. "That's also where the Ventura team was dining, and I spoke to them." In that speech, Cooley referred to Lorenzen as "the most all-American all-American we've ever had in Iowa." Yes, he meant to say "all-American" twice.

In the championship victory over a great Southeast Polk team, Lorenzen had had a hand in all 90 points her team scored. She made 59 herself and on those she didn't score, she was credited with assists for her passes.

Cooley actually gave more of a tribute to Ventura coach Chuck Bredlow than to Lorenzen, however. "This was an occasion," he told the Ventura girls, "when a coach had figured out the perfect offense to go against one of the best defenses we've ever seen in the state tournament, and that coach was lucky enough to have players capable of following his instructions to the letter."

Cooley told me that the word had been out among veteran coaches that despite Lorenzen's presence, Ventura's forwards would not be able to handle Southeast Polk's pressure defense. The Ventura girls not only handled it, they demolished it. And that's no knock on Southeast Polk. Rather, it hails Lorenzen, who after the game was described as "all-world" by the Southeast Polk coach.

There was one magic moment in the championship game – a moment I'm going to remember forever as one of the highlights of my spectating career. It came early in the second half when Southeast Polk was making a nice run at Ventura's big lead. This was happening because Southeast Polk had switched its defense at halftime, putting a new guard on Lorenzen. The new guard was making the nation's all-time scoring leader look like a goose. Lorenzen missed two shots, turned the ball over a couple of times and then was assessed a charging foul.

Coach Bredlow, who looks not much older than Lorenzen, summoned his great star to the sidelines while a free throw was being shot. And he chewed her out like she was a green freshman in a conversation picked up by TV.

"What are you doing?" he roared. "Why are you forcing it? Just play your game!"

Lorenzen went back to the fray and proceeded to dominate like I've never seen any other athlete dominate in a game at Veterans Memorial Auditorium. I include Larry Bird, a pro player formerly of Indiana State University, among those I've seen there.

The last 10 minutes, there were 11 girls playing one basketball game. Lorenzen was playing a completely different game. She was playing herself, seeing what high levels of basketball she could reach. If there's nirvana in this game, she was there.

There's one thing about which Cooley will argue. He says it's not over for the 6-on-6 game. "We've got 71 schools playing the 5-on-5 game, and the other 410 schools insist they won't touch it," he said. "So what I'm saying is that we may some day see someone better than Lynne Lorenzen. Coaches improve, and the girls become better athletes. Yes, there may be some girl come along who is better than Lynne. But it took 20 years for us to come up with Lorenzen, who is the first player we can say is better than Denise Long. I doubt I'll live long enough to see whoever is better than Lorenzen."

I doubt I will, either, and I'm 25 years younger than he is.

A grand baseball tradition goes tumbling down— swallow that Red Man!

June 1979

It's a "different day" in Iowa high school baseball this summer, says veteran Creston High School coach Ron Clinton. "They always say if you're going to stay with coaching, you've got to adjust to changing times, and I guess this is what they're talking about," he says.

Tradition be damned, the Iowa High School Athletic Association has outlawed chewing tobacco during ball games. No one's more affected by the ban than Clinton, 43, who's in his 20th year at Creston. He characterizes himself as one of baseball's "hard core" chewers, a real Red Man man.

The coaching boxes and dugout floors were never very dusty in games involving Clinton's teams. "The Fox," as they call him, kept the ground well-sprinkled. By the late innings, he usually had gooey, yellow dribbles at the corners of his mouth—which would have made him look like a savage anywhere but on a baseball diamond, where his appearance not only was acceptable but also downright professional.

But, with the new rule, all that's in the past.

"It's traumatic," he says. "I notice I get a little shakey during the games, but I can live with it. The idea of the rule is that tobacco has no place in high school athletics, and to that, I've gotta agree. But that doesn't mean I have to like it."

For years, the athletic association has had a rule banning smoking by coaches, players and officials during high school sports events. Chewing was allowed, however. Then last fall, officials— reacting to what the association's Dave Harty said was "increasing use" by players—banned chewing tobacco, beginning this summer.

"I don't think there's been any problem with enforcing the rule so far," Harty said Wednesday. "From what we hear, there's been total compliance."

Clinton says he has been told that before one recent game in southwest Iowa, umpires visited both dugouts and confiscated what chewing tobacco they could find. "It was search and seizure," he says, "without warrants."

Then there was Monday night's game between Creston and Corning.

"John Harris, the Corning coach, has always been a pretty good chewer, and so were the two guys who were our umpires," Clinton says. "We were talking a little before the game about declaring amnesty for one night, that it could be one of those nobody-will-ever-know deals. But we all stayed clean."

He says few of his own players have ever chewed. "They've seen me get sick too many times," he says. "I've always ended up swallowing my tobacco a couple of times during the season, and after kids see how green I get, they won't even try it."

But one Creston player, he says, is preparing to have a little fun with an umpire. "He's got an old Red Man package, which he's got full of sunflower seeds," Clinton says. "He's just waiting for the first umpire to call him on it."

Could sunflower seeds be the new chew for the coach?

"Naw," says Clinton, "they get stuck in my teeth. Bubble gum might be the answer, but so far, I haven't been able to bring myself to that.

"You know, the irony about this is that the girls' athletic organization doesn't have a rule like this. We've come to the point where the girls can chew, but the boys can't. That's really something, isn't it?"

Well, it's a different day, that's for sure.

There was a time
in all of our lives
when we'd stand and chant,
"Quack! Quack! Quack!"

October 1984

While finger-strolling through the pages of "The Picture and the Pen," a glorious book of poetry and pictures published recently by two Shelby residents, I came across a great old Shelby High School cheer. Edna May Pike, 76, used it in the book as an appendix to a poem she'd written in 1925 about good ol' SHS. The cheer, which Shelby fans actually chanted back then, goes like this:

> *Boom-a-lacka! Boom-a-lacka!*
> *Bow Wow Wow!*
> *Chick-a-lacka! Chick-a-lacka!*
> *Chow Chow Chow!*
> *Stand 'em on their heads, boys,*
> *Stand 'em on their feet*
> *Shelby High School can't be beat!*

I assume the cheerleaders at Shelby-Tennant High in this more erudite age do not use that one. They should. What's more fun than the grand old cheers of the past?

> *Hipparoo! Hipparay!*
> *We're from Randolph, Ioway!*

Up the road, the fans at little Macedonia would employ their own pet nickname for their town, as they'd roar, *"Gooooo 'Donie!"*

And over at Iowa City, in the era of the Real Rose Bowls (the ones we won), the cheerleaders would form a line, move their arms in the manner of a locomotive's drive rods and yell:

> *Hoo-Rah! Hoo-Ray!*
> *I–O–W–A!*

Never to be forgotten is that classic from the northwest Iowa town, Mallard, where the teams are, of course, the Ducks:

Black and Gold!
Gold and Black!
Mallard Ducks!
Quack! Quack! Quack!

It's funny about cheers. About the time you think you've invented one, you find out someone used it decades ago. It was that way for me with *"Two bits, four bits, six bits, a dollar! All for so-and-so, stand up and holler!"* Somehow, I got the idea that originated in my own high school years, the early '60s.

But Maury White told me they were already doing it in the Neanderthal Age when he was starring for Manilla High. Then he launched into his favorite Manilla cheer:

Rickety-rackety-russ!
We're not afraid to cuss!
But nevertheless
You must confess
There's nothing the matter with us!

In a way, I suppose, cheers reflect the times. At least that's the only explanation I can come up with for the way fans at last year's Drake University women's basketball games would chant, *"Rrriiiip their arms out!"*

The quaintest of the contemporary cheers is probably one used by the swimming team at Grinnell College, where, as you know, they always do things just a bit differently. It seems 17 years ago, one of the swimmers found a plastic statue of a Buddha that bore a striking physical resemblance to coach Ray Obermiller, who is still coaching the Pioneers. From then on, Grinnell swimmers have gathered in the dressing room or at poolside before meets, put their hands on the Buddha's ample stomach and yelled in unison:

Right for might!
Might for right!
Justice for all!
Go Buddha!

"We've run into a little bit of resentment with that at some colleges with religious affiliations," said Obermiller, "but our use of it has no religious significance at all. It's just a mascot. And whoever told you that the reason we have it is because the thing looks like me, I'd like to get ahold of that guy."

It's fun to make up cheers. I've decided to work on one for St. Ambrose College in Davenport, where despite having a great nickname, the Bees, they have a bunch of boring cheers. Mine will buzz, let me tell you.

But I doubt it will gain any more acceptance than the classic I produced a couple of years ago for the Johnston Dragons, the high school team I follow. It had the fans clapping their hands five times, stomping their feet five times, screaming *"Let's all give 'em Dragon breath!"* and then wheezing out five times together at the opposition. Rejected, said the cheerleaders, who are no fun at all.

A long, long way from the big time in professional baseball

August 1981

CLINTON, IA. – Tired of hearing and reading about how everyone in professional baseball is making a killing? About the way they are pampered? About the way they whine at the slightest adversity?

Well, the other morning I was knocking around Clinton's charming old Riverview Stadium when I ran into this guy in shorts, a T-shirt and sneakers. He was sweeping away the beer cups and ticket stubs left by the fans at the previous night's Clinton Giants game.

"You work for the ball club?" I asked this janitorial-looking soul.

"Why, yes I do," he answered. "I'm the general manager."

And thus began my refresher course – taught by one Claude Augustus Stokes III, called Gus by all who know him – on how the other half lives in professional baseball.

It might seem an incredible accident that this 34-year-old Virginian could be here running a ball team in the Class A Midwest

League. After all, this is a man with a master's degree, a man who has taught the English language around the world – first in Korea for the Peace Corps, and later in Iran for the Iranian Navy. He was among the Americans ousted from that country when the shah fell and Khomeini took power.

But no accident. Stokes said he is in Clinton on purpose. He explained he is a nut for the grand old game, that he dreams of some day running a major league club, that he realized he had to start somewhere and that he heard about the opening in Clinton while he was completing his master's in sports administration at Western Illinois University.

He said he decided to follow a buddy's example and go into the business of sports after he was tossed out of Iran in February 1979. "The worst thing over there was the chanting," he said. "It really got to us a few times. But we also got a little concerned when the Iranians began marking utility poles in the areas where Americans lived."

After his return to America, he studied on the Western Illinois campus for a year, and then served last summer as a summer intern with the Chattanooga (Tenn.) Lookouts of the Class AA Southern League. In January, he signed a contract with the board that directs the Clinton club and then moved here.

The time since has seen him hustling advertisements for the outfield wall and program, coordinating travel, running special promotions, organizing the concessions and generally mollycoddling all who enter the ballpark. There are three other full-time employees and a dozen part-timers. Several board members work without pay at the games. Occasionally, someone misses work and that is when Stokes winds up doing such things as sweeping the stands.

The 18-hour workday has been common for him this summer, but as the season nears an end (this weekend's two games are the last at home), Stokes is thrilled. The Giants, who played stinko ball the first half of the season, improved in the second half. The fans kept coming out and the season's attendance is nearing 60,000, meaning the team will probably make a profit, "unless something catastrophic happens to our bus in the remaining days," he said. The profit means Stokes will receive a bonus to go along with his $800 per month salary.

"That's not much money," he said, "but I don't expect much money here. I'm not one that is motivated by money anyway. Remember, I once worked for $65 a month in the Peace Corps."

While in the Peace Corps, he met his wife, Shin, who is a nurse here. "She thinks I'm right out of my mind for putting in the hours I do for the money I get," Stokes said, "but she also knows I love to be around baseball and that this is how you have to start in this business."

He has agreed to spend another year in Clinton. Soon the Giant organization will trim itself to one person for the winter. And Gus Stokes will then work alone in the small office at the stadium, planning and organizing for another season in professional baseball's basement.

The players aren't the only ones learning about the long trip to the big time.

Sometimes being a baseball man is a very heavy load

June 1982

STORM LAKE, IA. – You've heard of the so-called white man's burden? It's that guilt trip some of us palefaces take when we chance to think of the ways we've mistreated other races over time. When I shoulder my part of that burden, it makes me feel awful.

There's another burden like that for me, too: the baseball burden. Anytime I see the grand old game suffering again I feel awful. It happened in this northwest Iowa town of 8,814 the other night.

While killing an evening here, I noticed the lights burning at the ball park, drove over and what ho! I found two games under way on adjacent diamonds.

On one, the girls of Alta High School were beating the girls of St. Mary's High of Storm Lake in softball. There were several hundred people there, some sitting in the bleachers and others ringing the outfield fence. There were cheers on every pitch, prolonged hoorahing at the end of each half-inning.

Then I walked just next door, inside the tall green wood fence surrounding the baseball field and found the Storm Lake town team, the Lakers, playing the G-Hawks of George in a Northwest Iowa Amateur League game. I counted the people in the stands, included myself to make it sound better, and came up with, uh, 14. True, it was a cool night, but it was just as cool for those noisy softball fans.

It was so quiet in the big ballpark that when one Laker walked up to bat, a fan in the stands used normal voice and asked, "What'd you do last time up?" The player acknowledged the question.

A girls' softball game drawing several hundred screamers. A few steps away, a men's baseball game drawing 14 yawners. It made me want to puke.

What has befallen the national pastime in Storm Lake? The stadium itself, once obviously beautiful, is in terrible shape. It has a ghost-town feel. The outfield fence, which sags, carries faded and peeling advertising messages that were last touched up eight years ago. The lights are weak. In a recent game, of the 48 lamps directed on the outfield, 36 had burned-out bulbs. That same night, it was dark behind the plate, too. "The catcher couldn't begin to see where the ball was," said Laker skipper Steve Brock, 29. "He didn't have a clue."

At the entrance to the stadium are two brick pillars, one of which has a plaque explaining the ball park was built in the memory of local men who served and died in World War II. If those pillars lean any more than they do already, there may be cause for another memorial—to the poor devil who gets conked on the head when they topple.

The only new, fresh, well-maintained things in the whole ball park are two Spot-A-Pots, northwest Iowa versions of the more familiar KYBOs.

"What it comes down to is that no one seems to care," said Dennis Peters, 38, who runs a CB radio shop. Oh, he cares. So does his wife, Marlys, and young Brock. The last few years, they have been town team baseball's artificial respirators in Storm Lake. They have assembled a team of skilled college players and other young men. They have taken time to sell ads to merchants, filling a score-card and helping defray expenses. Yet, they always end up chipping in a chunk of their own money to keep things going.

"That's why I gave up managing the team and now just sort of help out as a volunteer," said Peters. "I dropped about $1,000 into this the last three years. I can't afford that." Yes, he said, it hurts him, too, to look over his shoulder and see girls' softball doing so well while his game suffers.

"Maybe we're going to have to fake a fight now and then to see if it'll help draw a better crowd," joked John Schnoes, the umpire working the bases. They almost had one, no fakery involved.

Storm Lake rallied to nip George, 5–4. In the top of the ninth, the G-Hawks died on wildly disputed strikeouts. Home plate ump Curly Nelson was castigated loudly by the incensed George players as a "gutless wonder," a "disgrace to the ball park," a "homer" and a "jerk." He took the abuse and left quietly, bearing his own baseball burden, I imagine.

The grandest retirement gift
a little boy, grown old,
could possibly get

May 1987

INDIANOLA, IA. – If you're a real baseball person – whether a player, a coach or just a fan – could there be a greater honor than seeing a beautiful ball diamond named after you?

At Simpson College, in this town south of Des Moines, an honorary doctor of humanities degree will be conferred today upon Robert McBride, 63, who is retiring after eight years as the college's president, a position from which he ramrodded a renaissance in Simpson academics, facilities and finance. He'll be thrilled, of course, as will his wife, Lue, who will receive the same honorary degree.

But, bet me, Bob McBride is going to have even sweeter recollections of a ceremony held here Friday morning when they formally dedicate the baseball home of the Redmen as "McBride Field."

Forget for a moment, as he did, that this man has a bachelor's degree in philosophy, a divinity degree in Methodism and a Ph.D. in philosophy. Forget, too, that he is a husband, a father, a minister and the boss of a whole college. Remember only that he is deep-down a little boy nuts about the grand old game, but a little boy now gray, slow and bespectacled.

He'd been good enough as a catcher and outfielder in his Indiana hometown, on military teams during World War II and then on the college team at Indiana Central University in Indianapolis that he was offered a contract by the Brooklyn Dodgers. He declined it because he was by then headed into the ministry, which he considered "very fulfilling and something that was more important." But when he'd take his family to major league baseball games, he never stopped wondering what might have been.

Friday, he quietly reported – almost confided – that his .452 batting average in his senior year at Indiana Central stood as a record at that college for nearly two decades. He talked about playing with the military teams in Europe during the war and how he'd been a teammate there of several men who'd interrupted major league baseball careers to do service time. "I always thought, had I decided to go that way, I might have made it," he said.

So Friday morning, they trotted him out here, unveiled the scoreboard with the new "McBride Field" sign on top of it and then, best of all, let him not only throw some pitches but also grab a bat and take a few swings. The pitcher was Simpson's current best, Eric Sickels, a towering senior right-hander who fretted that he might unintentionally launch a beanball at his college's president.

McBride pulled it all off with commendable elan, even pointing to the outfield scoreboard before his last swing – in the "call-shot" home run manner of the immortal Babe Ruth. (The record, honestly reported, will show McBride then hit only a sharp line drive to center field, and that his head was errantly in the breeze when he did so, although he alibied for that bit of batting malpractice by saying, "When you wear bifocals, you have to hold your head that way to be able to see the pitch.")

A special highlight was Robert Larsen, Simpson professor of music and director of the Des Moines Metro Opera, leading the college choir and 200 spectators in the singing of "Take Me Out to the Ball Game," the fight song "March-on Simpson" and the alma mater "Red and Gold." Then everybody shared a "ball park lunch" of hot dogs, potato chips and lemonade.

It is of further note that President McBride, in establishing the Simpson College agenda a few years back, had given the athletic department the mission of an Iowa Conference championship, something rare in recent Simpson sports history. On Friday, coach John Sirianni had his Redmen all put their uniforms on one more time and come to the newly christened McBride Field. They handed the president the conference's first-place trophy, which they'd won one week ago.

Things like that are the reason Bob McBride and lots of others love baseball.

My favorite Iowa baseball story — a tale of tragedy, inspiration, tears, laughter and true grit

August 1977

NEOLA, IA. — There may very well be a baseball legend building here.

"Oh, it's really no big deal," says Steve Casson, 23, who's the man of the matter.

Bunk, say the fans of the local town team, the Neola Lookouts. It *is* a big deal. And fans all around the 10-team Iowa Western Amateur Baseball League, in which the Lookouts play, agree.

Three years ago, Casson lost his left leg three inches below the knee in a motorcycle accident. He says now, "My first thought was that I'd never be able to play ball again, and all I'd ever wanted to do was play baseball." So he vowed a return to the grand old game, took the anesthetic and went to surgery.

In the summer of 1977, Casson has made good on his promise. Playing on an artificial leg, he's batted .334 in 25 games and has six home runs, two of them game winners. He regularly plays first base, but he's also pitched in six or seven games.

He admits—with considerable embarrassment and only after cajoling—that there are some "storybook" aspects to his summer.

Let's start with the season opener. Casson, who also manages the team, didn't play. "I was afraid the other guys on the team would think I was putting myself in just because I'm the coach," he recalls. "I was nervous as hell. I hadn't played for three years, remember."

In the second game of the season, the Lookouts were playing at Woodbine. Again, Casson was keeping himself on the bench. But in the seventh, a Neola player was injured and Casson was forced to play first. He came to bat for the first time in the top of the ninth inning. He hit a two-run homer for the winning margin.

"I don't mean to brag by telling that," he now says, "but that one was so important to me. I just couldn't believe I hit it my first time up. It did a lot for my confidence."

Let's move on to June 1, when the Lookouts were playing at Earling. It was the top of the ninth, score tied, 8–8, when Casson socked another game-winning homer. That one even prompted mention in Father Jon Kautzky's next sermon at St. Joseph's Catholic Church in Earling. Parishioners remember Father Kautzky saying that the Casson story is a great illustration of the never-say-die kind of life we should all lead.

Now, on to Portsmouth in late July, where the Iowa Western League tournament was raging. Neola, after a fairly dismal regular season, had caught fire in the tourney. The Lookouts were in the semifinals against the powerful Westphalia Red Sox—the first-place team, one which early in the season thrashed Neola, 22–2. But this time, the Lookouts were tied with the Red Sox, 8–8, after nine innings. In the top of the tenth, Westphalia scored and was three outs away from victory.

The first two Neola batters in the bottom of the inning went down in order. Casson came to the plate. Seven hundred people were watching. He slammed the second pitch over the left-center-field fence. Around Portsmouth they say the ball traveled well over 400 feet, that it was one of the longest ever hit there.

As Casson hobbled around the bases, even the Westphalia fans cheered him. And as he approached home plate—mindful of the fact that he'd just tied the game—Casson stomped his foot and yelled: *"All right, goddammit, now let's go get 'em."*

He and the Lookouts then watched their next batter, Harley

Leaders, clout a homer for the victory. Hooray for Neola. But what about the Westphalia pitcher? "Poor guy," says Casson. "I'd never seen a head hung so low."

The Casson story is obviously amazing. But this whole league is amazing, too. Most folks knowledgeable about the game will tell you that the heyday of town team baseball—showcasing boys from 16 years old and up to men in their mid-to-late 30s—is long gone. But that's just not true in this area.

"People here like their baseball," says Mike Schechinger, 39, of Westphalia, league president 10 years. He figures strict rules have played a big part in keeping the league strong in the 30 years it's existed.

For example, one rule prohibits any team from having more than three players who are not hometowners on the roster. Another dictates that any team forfeiting a game must pay a $25 fine to the league. That pretty well eliminates no-shows.

And another rule holds that if the home team does not get a game score telephoned to league secretary Gusty Esser—a grandmother living in Earling—during the prescribed hours, there's a $5 fine.

It's a solid program—so solid that a tiny town like Westphalia (population 121) can field two teams, the Red Sox and White Sox. Woodbine (population 1,349) also has two teams, the Twiners and the '76ers. Other league entries are from Earling, Persia, Portsmouth, Neola, Dunlap and Panama. Only Dunlap among those has a population of more than 1,000 people.

Games are played on Wednesday nights and Sunday afternoons from mid-May to late August, with most of the towns hosting a tournament at some point during the season.

This season has been vitally important to young Casson. Not only has he kept his promise to himself to return to the game that is the biggest love in his life, but he also has gained confidence that he figures will be invaluable even when he's not on a ball diamond.

"Because of the severity of the injury to my leg, I hadn't been able to adjust to an artificial leg for a long, long time," he says. "I got the leg I'm using now just two months before I started playing ball this summer, and it's worked pretty well. My stub still gets irritated some from wearing it, but eventually, I think it will work.

"I was to the point where I thought I might never be able to use an artificial leg. You don't know what a pain it can be to have to get on crutches to move 10 feet. It really becomes easier just to crawl. Without an artificial leg, my mobility was so restricted." He says it took months to learn to balance himself on one foot. "I'm good at it now, though," he says. "Sometimes I think I was meant to have been born the Easter Bunny. I can hop with the best of them."

Casson worked whatever odd jobs he could find until a few months ago, when he signed on with an electronics firm in Council Bluffs. In his work there, he can sit while assembling gadgets on a bench in front of him.

After getting the artificial leg, which he straps to his body, he began practicing walking with it around his Council Bluffs apartment. Then he began thinking about playing ball once again in his hometown of Neola, just 15 miles up the road.

"The doctors told me if I really wanted to do it, I could," Casson says. "They warned me, though, that it would not be easy. My folks in Neola and the other guys on the team have made it a whole lot easier for me. Everyone's been so encouraging."

Longtime Neola baseball fan Ray Alfers says whether the team's playing at home or on the road, "the fans are pulling for Steve 100 percent. A lot of people – I guess myself included – just didn't think he'd be able to make it back like he has."

Even before the accident, Casson was a strong hitter and thrower. Added strength from prolonged use of crutches has given him even more power. The problem he has, of course, is in moving around the diamond. "I'm not the most graceful player that's ever played, that's for sure," he says, "but I do the best I can. I guess you'd say I can move at about a fast walk. If I hit a ground ball to the infield, I still get down to first base, though. Some guys figure they've got all the time in the world to throw me out, and they end up throwing the ball away."

There have been times when he's pitching that opposing batters have started bunting, testing Casson's ability to get to the ball and field it. Some league fans say such strategy is a cheap shot. But Casson himself doesn't see it that way. "I've played enough ball to know that when you're in a bunting situation, you bunt," he says, "and I don't care who's pitching. I don't want special treatment."

Oh, he acknowledges that he does enjoy what he sees as the special treatment he's been getting from the crowds. "People have really been kind," he says. "The cheers make all the aches and pains worth it. But what ball player doesn't like to be cheered?"

He says he tries to do his best to make people feel at ease when they're around him. He says he's not self-conscious about having the artificial limb, and he doesn't want others to be.

Along that line, he recalls a recent time when he was at bat in

Neola. "I hit a foul tip that hit the artificial leg," he says. "There was this hollow 'thud' sound. Everyone knew what happened, so I stepped back and yelled, 'Oh, God! I think I got a bruise.'

"Harley Leaders was standing there close, so he yelled, 'You're okay, Steve, just shake it off.'

"I yelled right back at him: 'That's just it, Harley. I can shake the whole thing off.' The crowd loved it."

As I review 10 years' worth of columns, I'm a little surprised to see how often I write about religion. Why do I? I guess it's because it somehow means a lot to me—and to most Iowans, too, thank God.

RELIGION

There are all kinds of
prayer, so what's best?
— whatever works

April 1986

SHENANDOAH, IA.—I think I pray more than most newspaper columnists in Iowa do.

Oh, there is the certain exception of Father James O'Connor, a monk in the contemplative order at New Melleray Abbey near Dubuque who also writes "Monastery Seasons" for the soon-to-be-killed *Catholic Mirror.*

And there is the possible exception of my *Register* running mate, Maury White, who is pretty devout. I know that once when he happened to be in New York City and was looking for a way to fill some idle time, he attended the funeral of Bishop Fulton Sheen at St. Patrick's Cathedral. That's a prayer-prone man.

But I do my share, and then some.

The reason this comes up now is a thought I heard expressed Monday by Bishop Maurice Dingman, boss of the Diocese of Des Moines, who was here for the same confirmation ceremony I attended at St. Mary's Catholic Church.

Confirmation is one of the sacraments for us Catholics. When I was going through it, we were told it made us "soldiers in Christ's army," but the prevailing thought now seems to be that it's more the church's equivalent of a debutante ball, a sort of ecclesiastical coming of age.

I was acting as a "sponsor" for my nephew, John Offenburger, and I scared the bejeepers out of the boy. In our faith, we are allowed to pick "a confirmation name," usually the moniker of one of the saints, and that's how our sponsors present us to the bishop for receipt of this special blessing.

John had opted simply to use John. I was kidding him beforehand that I wasn't sure I approved, and that when I introduced him to the bishop during the service, I might say, "Bishop Dingman, may I present Aloysius?" When I mentioned that, John looked at me with sufficient terror to convince me that I shouldn't.

By now, you're probably praying that I get to the point. It is this: Dingman, in his homily, said, "You know, sometimes we talk too much when we pray. There are times we should just sit quietly and listen."

But, oh, is that ever a tough nut for a rather traditional knee-bender like me to crack.

Intellectually, I recognize there must be deep value to quiet, unstructured meditation, whether in the form practiced by Christian mainliners or in the form used by the TM disciples at Maharishi International University in Fairfield. A calming and opening of the mind and spirit just have to be good.

Yet, when I try to do it, I stray. Instead of having my head engaged in anything that could be even loosely construed as prayer, I find myself thinking about the Chicago Cubs, RAGBRAI, what's for dinner, what I'll write about in my next column, and—wow, that lady over there sure is a fox.

That, I realize, is a confession of a lack of mental self-discipline. I prefer to think of it more as honesty that I need structured prayer.

Holy Mother Church made me this way. I mean, I come from the days when people actually went to confession, and for penance, we weren't told to go graze mentally but rather to hit our knees for three Our Fathers and three Hail Marys.

My roots were in a time when a good guy like ol' Johnny Hughes might well be recalling a yarn about some now-departed guy being out on a binge and break right in the middle of it to say, "and may his soul rest in peace, amen" before continuing the ribald tale.

The church bells in a lot of the more Catholic communities would ring at 6 A.M., noon, and 6 P.M., telling people it was time to say a prayer called "The Angelus," and the folks would be reciting it as they were delivering papers, serving sandwiches or finishing watching Walter Cronkite.

In that time, praying over basketball free throws was very common, although somehow no priest or nun ever clued me in as to exactly what the free throw prayer was.

That all strikes me as excessively ritualistic and slightly silly now. And, yet, I know that in times of heavy stress and serious trial, I'm very prone to think, "Where's my rosary?" That's ritualistic.

Through 38 years, I've somehow not reached that stage where I can close my eyes, spread my arms and put my mind in the sweet ether—without worrying about where my hands are and a lot of other things. OK, I'll say another three Our Fathers and Hail Marys.

I don't rule out that it works for others, but it doesn't seem to for me. And I guess that's what it all comes down to—whatever works.

The young priest who preached while wearing a Chicago Cubs cap

May 1986

CEDAR RAPIDS, IA.—St. Jude's Catholic Church, located on the west side of this city, is one of those big, mostly young and, hence, fun parishes that we knee-benders have in our large flock.

It is known to me chiefly as the home church of my little sister Chris Walsh, her husband Denny and their considerable flock of future altar boys. But St. Jude's is probably known wider in this area as the parish that each summer puts on a huge sweet corn festival, for which some members of the congregation, ahem, have coined the slogan, "Come eat our ears and drink our beers." St. Jude's, obviously, has spirit in addition to having Spirit.

The pastor is Father Gene Kutsch, who on Sunday was nursing one big honker of a cold and thus turned over preaching duties to his young associate, Father Mark Osterhaus, who clearly was having so much fun giving the homily that I found myself wanting to know him better.

"Yeah, I really do like to preach," the 31-year-old Osterhaus, a native of Maquoketa, told me later. "I suppose that means I'm a showoff in a lot of ways, but if you're going to be in front of that many people every week, you might as well like the stage."

Osterhaus came straight out of the seminary to St. Jude's a year ago. His first sermon was memorable. "I thought I should tell the people a little about myself," he said. "I wanted to let them know that my vocation in the priesthood came after sort of a wandering past. I told them how I'd taken a year's leave of absence during my time in the seminary because I just wasn't sure at that time that I really wanted to take those vows of celibacy and obedience. I felt like they were being forced upon me. But in that year away, I learned that the force there was really coming from me and God, not from anybody else.

"I also wanted to make the point with the people that I am a pretty big sports fan." So what he did was launch into a discussion about "how some guys have known since they were 5 years old that they were going to become priests. Not me," he continued. "The only thing I've known since I was 5 years old is that I am a Chicago Cubs fan."

Whereupon he reached under the lectern, pulled out a Cubs cap and put it on with his vestments.

Word spread quickly. In a matter of days, Osterhaus's big boss, Archbishop Daniel Kucera, prelate of the Archdiocese of Dubuque, ran into the young priest's parents in Maquoketa. "I hear," Kucera told them, "that your son is saying Mass with a baseball cap on."

No worry, though, explained Osterhaus. "The archbishop," he said, "is a Cubs fan, too."

I thought about Osterhaus all the way back to Des Moines Sunday afternoon, when I was listening to the Cubs drop both games of a doubleheader to the San Francisco Giants.

"Yes, that really hurt," he said later, "and you don't know the half of my pain. One of my best friends is Father Tim Casey, who's at the Basilica in Dyersville, and he's such a Giants fan that he practically wears a San Francisco jacket when he says Mass. But even though we lost the two on Sunday, we came out of the series even. We won the first two."

I instantly liked this optimist even more.

Besides his parish obligations, he also teaches theology at Cedar Rapids' LaSalle High School. In addition, he is a talented artist who earned a degree in art education at the University of Iowa and taught art at Marcus and Maquoketa before becoming a priest.

"You shouldn't call me an artist now, though," he said. "I haven't painted since I was ordained. My definition of an artist is someone who really makes it a priority to do his art, and I'm not doing that. I'm definitely no Van Gogh. I still have both my ears."

They fit on a head that looks much like that of former Hawkeye quarterback Chuck Long. "All the high school kids tell me that," he said. "In fact, they even call me Chuck Long. I've never met him, but I think he's probably much better looking than I am, and I know for a fact he's bigger."

Athletes like Chuck Long always set goals. Do priests who look like him?

"Yes," he said. "Being a priest wasn't really my idea. In fact, I did everything I could to avoid it. But it was God's idea, one I came to embrace. And now that I am one, my goal is to be a good one, a holy person, a man of God. I look at it as a 50-year type of goal, though. I've got a long ways to go."

A date with an 11-year-old girl is my introduction to the Friends

August 1983

ACKWORTH, IA. – I had a date Sunday morning with Rachael Goodhue. She is 11 years old. Stole my heart, too, the little snippet did.

If she hadn't already stolen it early in the morning with her precocious conversation and keen humor, she would've definitely captured it later when she served the cheesecake and pistachio cream pie she made for me.

I went out with Rachael Goodhue for three reasons: (1) She's a fox, (2) her name is so beautiful and (3) she asked me. She wrote me a letter saying she'd noticed that when I've written about religion, I have mentioned Catholics, Presbyterians, Jews, Methodists and others but "you said nothing about Friends [Quakers] so I am going to invite you to my church, the Ackworth Friends Church," located in this town of 83 people five miles east of Indianola.

What really turned my head in that letter was her P.S.: "You should *not* wear jeans."

Rachael lives on a big farm outside little Ackworth, which, she noted, "is just about first in the alphabetical listing of Iowa towns, and first in nothing else. There's not even a store, although Opal will sell you a little something to chew on at the post office." She referred to her buddy Opal Swarthout, 80, the postmaster. Rachael, in fact, is chummy with everyone. A talker of the first order, she doesn't know a stranger.

It is a nice life she leads on the farm with her parents, Darrell and Eve, and her younger brothers and sister, John, Thomas and Rebecca. Rachael has 4-H calves, which she named Kevin, Donald and Jeff after the hired men who work on the farm. One of them, Kevin Graham, "named a sow Rachael in revenge," she giggled.

So Rachael and I went to the Sunday Meeting of the Ackworth Friends in a beautiful structure that has 130-year-old roots. You can be certain I did *not* wear jeans.

I learned a lot about the Friends' firm principles but soft organization, their pacifist and meditative traditions, their devotion to family and home. This visiting Catholic lad felt totally at ease, but then it'd be almost impossible not to among such people of peace, among people of such a gentle, country manner. "Well," said the Reverend Erwin Cook, pastor, to a farmer Friend leaving the Meeting, "did you get enough rain to make mud?" I loved it.

And I had my date there to keep me entertained, too. I must note that, for a Friend, she did speak violently once or twice. But these indiscretions, if that's what they were, didn't fly in the face of the pacifist tradition so much as they honored her age.

There was her curt portrayal of the youngest of the Sunday School children – "the savages." And there was her whispered rage when young Lori Ruble surprised her with the news that she, Rachael and Michelle Crump would sing a heretofore unrehearsed song together during the service. "Oooooh," growled Rachael after the trio had laid an egg, "wait till I get my hands on that Lori!"

Rachael had advised me about the Friends' historical inclination toward strictness. I did have a brush with it. Our Sunday School teacher, Ethel Morgan, told me straightaway that one of her class rules is "if you lean back in your chair on two legs, you stand up the rest of the time." With six of my new, young Friends, and a teacher who wasn't kidding, all keeping watch, my chair never felt an urge even to budge a bit.

In class, we talked about Ephesians, Catholics and someone

even mentioned the Jedi. Then we broke for the Meeting itself, followed by a little fellowship in the churchyard and later a huge chicken dinner at the Goodhue farm.

It was a wonderful morning, a wonderful date. I'm pleased to be pals with the Friends.

A night singing hymns with the Methodist Men's group

November 1982

VILLISCA, IA. – It was, to say the least, a most unusual invitation.

In a clean, graceful penmanship not taught much nowadays, 84-year-old retired farmer Verne C. Watts was asking if I might come to a meeting of the Methodist Men's group in Villisca, a southwest Iowa community of 1,434.

"You could give a short talk, and you can sing as many hymns as you like with some of our good singers or by yourself," he wrote, later adding, "We will be glad to hear some of your wit and nonsense, but we will want plenty of the singing of hymns."

He said he remembered a column I'd written a year ago telling how, having grown up Catholic before the move to ecumenism, I had missed out on singing all those great old Protestant hymns. We mackerel-snappers concentrated on the heavier, longhaired, Latin stuff. And chanted.

The column went on to tell how my Presbyterian in-laws, God bless 'em, decided on some gift-giving occasion to hire their church organist for an hour for me. We met at their church, and, while she played and tried to keep a straight face, I warbled the favorites on my list of good ol' gospel gold.

But this Villisca invitation threw me into a dilemma. As I explained to Watts, when I go out to speak I get a handsome fee. I assumed it would be too much for the treasury of the Villisca Methodist Men. In fact, I told him that if they, indeed, could afford me, they should be investigated.

On the other hand, if I was going to come down here and sing to them, and if fair is fair, I'd have to pay them. Not only would I be reaping the enjoyment of getting to sing hymns, but the Methodists would be in the position of having to listen—and I'm not just bad, I'm also loud.

Besides, if you put some historical perspective to this, doesn't it seem almost absurd that a newspaperman, a Catholic one yet, would be invited to appear before a group as traditionally bluenosed as Methodists? Haven't newspapermen always been considered some of God's most original sinners? And haven't Catholics and Methodists always been sort of like oil and water?

"Just shows how broad-minded we Methodists have become," said the *Register*'s farm editor, Don Muhm, who was counseling me.

To resolve the dilemma, I waived my fee, the Methodists waived the one that rightfully would've been theirs, and we got together in the church basement the other night. If old Romans, old Wesleyans and old journalists were revolving in their graves, so be it.

Looking back, I'm not sure whether I came off as a breath of fresh air or an ill wind. Perhaps I allowed myself to feel a little too much at home. But, see, first they gave me a bowl of Izola Jenkins' oyster stew, which rivaled my mother's. Then, when I asked if Methodists are particularly known for anything in their singing, a Don Narigon yelled from the rear of the room, "Yes, being loud and off key!" Hey, just my kind of place, I thought.

Well, I got into my bag of theology and told them I believe God has a sense of humor, which is something I'm not sure had ever been said before in that church basement. When I added, "If He doesn't, then I'm in big trouble," a lot of them nodded affirmatively.

Then for some reason, I told an underwear joke. Oh, God, why'd I do it? Sometimes I think my brains are turning to mashed potatoes. It was at about this point that a few of them started staring daggers at Verne C. Watts.

Finally, I said I'd kick off the evening's singing by soloing on one of my favorites, a whimsical hillbilly hymn called, "We Need a Whole Lot More of Jesus, and a Lot Less Rock 'n' Roll." No one joined in on the chorus.

I guess the good that was done was that, having witnessed

someone so shamelessly make a spectacle of himself on a solo, the Methodist Men sang with unusual vigor when songmaster Ramon Dick and pianist Martin Hentsch led us all through such wondrous pieces as "Onward Christian Soldiers," "Nearer My God to Thee," "Are Ye Able," "Work for the Night Is Coming," "America the Beautiful" and on up "Jacob's Ladder." Of course, I got goose bumps and darned near cried at their beauty, as I always do.

Selfishly speaking, I figure I added a critical line to my eternal resume by coming to Villisca. *"Offenburger, Charles H., applying for entrance,"* I will say, hopefully years from now, as I approach the Pearly Gates. *"A repentant newspaperman. Mostly Catholic but sang with Methodists once, too. And I regret that underwear joke."*

A little diversity on the record is bound to help, isn't it?

A most unusual substitute in a Methodist pulpit

September 1986

If anybody knows where the Reverend Lee Roy Collins is, tell him to get right back home to his pastorate at the Epworth United Methodist Church in the Highland Park neighborhood of north Des Moines. There is Big Trouble.

Because Collins is on vacation, his congregation invited, uh, me to come deliver the sermon on Sunday morning. I did it under the title, "A Catholic Newspaperman in the Pulpit: What Are You United Methodists Coming To?"

Well, my 10-year-old, Andy O, and I went dressed in our golf clothes—we had a tee time 45 minutes after I was to finish—and I guess it can be honestly said I gave the best homily I've ever given.

Okay, so it was the only one.

At any rate, when I concluded, the congregation applauded. Keep in mind, these were Methodists, most of whom can still remember when they weren't even allowed to dance in public. And here they were clapping in church.

"As long as I've been a member here," Jim Walters, the lay liturgist who was running things Sunday, said afterward, "I've never heard applause in the sanctuary for a sermon."

I couldn't resist—I got right back up and said, "See what happens? You let one of us Catholics in here, and already you're starting to act as loose as we do." Next thing you know, Epworth Methodist will be running a bingo game.

"Loose" is, indeed, a good word for the atmosphere I helped create. I told them ahead of time there'd be no dickering over my fee. They were to find the old hymn, "Life's Railway to Heaven," and perform it on the morning I was there. They did.

Like me, that song is sort of hillbilly. *"Life is like a mountain railroad,"* it goes, *"with an engineer that's brave. We must make the run successful, from the cradle to the grave. Watch the curves, the fills, the tunnels. Never falter, never quail. Keep your hand upon the throttle, and your eye upon the rail."* It ends with you steering *"your train"* into the *"Union Depot,"* where you meet *"the Superintendent,"* God, who says, *"Weary pilgrim, welcome home."* I love it.

An unexpected bonus for me was the Methodists singing their "Doxology" right after they'd coughed up their offerings. That Doxology is as beautiful a piece of church music as exists—it makes the hair on the back of your neck stand straight up—as they, *"Praise God, from Whom all blessings flow; praise Him, all creatures here below; praise Him above, ye Heavenly Host; praise Father, Son and Holy Ghost."*

Choir director Harlan Gee indulged me even further by picking "Amazing Grace" as a closing hymn. That song could be secondarily entitled, "The Battle Hymn of Offenburger," particularly for the way the first verse concludes: *"I once was lost, but now am found; was blind, but now I see."*

That was the gist of my whole message Sunday morning. No, I didn't give them any hellfire and damnation. It just wouldn't be my style to preach that, probably because frequently it's my style to live it. Yeah, I told them, I'm a sinner—one who too often is the shameful model of the old-time, hard-living newspaperman. But I'm also a sinner with a keen awareness that the Big Fella is there, and that He demonstrates that He has a sense of humor in continuing to allow my existence.

Though it always gives me a case of the crawling skin when I find myself having to listen to some Born Againer "witnessing," if that's what it's called, I found myself going on to do just that. My Wake-Up call, I told them, came when I got old enough to realize it just isn't fair to expect God to be there in those times when, in deep trouble, I seek Him out in prayer. If I expect Him to be there then, then it is only fair that I be where I ought to be in normal times. And "where I ought to be" is in church regularly and being a pretty decent guy most of the rest of the time.

It seemed to play well with my audience of Wesleyans, and I was glad it did, because it was as forthright a statement of my faith as I could make.

And it all went down well for Andy O and me, too. Particularly Andy O, who told me it was "kind of nice" to be in a church without spending half the time on his knees. I'll assign him some appropriate penance for that remark.

Okay, so there are *some* Methodists who can sing on key

May 1985

FAIRFIELD, IA. – One of the nicest things about Catholicism is that we knee-benders have the sacrament of confession, through which, to put it secularly, we believe we can get immediate divine relief for screwups rather than doing an eternal slow burn once our number is called.

It's a sacrament that's fallen on hard times in the modern church. Few actually go into the little booth anymore and privately fess up to priests. Instead, most do it communally, which is to say we do it all together, which is to say it's kind of public. This, then, is a public confession.

Oh God, forgive me for what I've been saying about the Methodists.

For several years now, as I've spoken to groups, I've been getting cheap laughs at the expense of these Wesleyans. I lead into it saying that to do my job effectively, I have to experience things in different sorts of places with different sorts of people, and then learn whatever I can from being there.

Then I tell how I once spent one whole night at Peck's Tap in Libertyville and another whole night singing hymns with the Methodist Men's group in Villisca, and that I learned different things in those two places. At Peck's Tap, I say, I learned the true meaning of life – but the problem was the next morning, I couldn't remember what it was. At the hymn sing, I learned that while Methodists can't sing on key, at least they're loud, and they do all the verses.

My audiences have always loved it, at least until a day last fall when I trotted it out again while addressing the faculty of the Fairfield Community Schools in a meeting before classes started.

"I'm Martha Flinspach, junior high vocal music instructor," said a challenger after that get-together. "And I take exception to what you said. I'm also director of the chancel choir at the First United Methodist Church here, and we're going to prove you wrong." Did they ever.

After months of campaigning, Flinspach got me to this southeast Iowa town on Sunday night for the 65-voice choir's annual spring extravaganza, which is a 90-minute service of a little liturgy and a lot of music.

It was so spiritually touching, it would've swayed the souls of sailors in port on a Saturday night. But beyond the religious significance, it was also about as much fun as I've ever seen a group of people have with music – and it was all on-key. Summoned to the altar area after I'd heard the first half of it and asked what I thought about Methodist singing now, I had to cry uncle.

There were a number of top-flight soloists, including 79-year-old Helen Mitchell, who brought tears to my eyes with "Because He Lives." She approached me later and said, "Just wanted to let you know there are senior citizens in this thing, too."

And there were fantastic performances by the Huff brothers – Jon, who performs locally with a group called the "Lick Creek Boys," and David, who was home on a visit from Florida where he performs with the Miami Opera Company.

There was also a congregational sing-along during which choir members scrambled into the pews to help out us who are less talented. Intimidation is trying to sing "Lord, I Want to Be a Christian" with the golden-throated Huff brothers singing on either side of you.

And best of all, there was a four-number gig by the Fairfield Dixieland Band. They did "We've Got That Old Time Religion," "Just a Closer Walk With Thee," "Put Your Hand in the Hand of the Man" and "When the Saints Go Marchin' In."

Those seven guys did them with gusto. After one song, I actually found myself clapping and yelling, "Woo-ie!" You'd a-thought I was at a ball game. And at another point, their rhythm was so overwhelming that trombonist Ron Prill and banjo picker Merle Bates were plainly dancing in the altar area. My goodness, I thought, I can remember my mother telling me how she can remember when Methodists weren't allowed to dance anywhere, and here they were doing it right in front of Pastor Clair Odell and everyone else in the magnificent old church!

But later, Odell said all that was OK. Well, what he was really talking about was how it's OK to let music really move you. "After all," he said, invoking some pretty powerful authority, "our own John Wesley once wrote, 'Why should the devil have all the good music?'"

Oh God, it's me again – the Catholic guy. I penitently spent Sunday night in Fairfield with the Methodists. One thing bothers me. How come when You were dividing things up, You gave John Wesley to them and gave Latin to us? We still haven't gotten over it.

One Saturday's worth
of weddings at the famed
Little Brown Church
in the Vale

April 1986

NASHUA, IA. – I feel much more the whole Iowan now, for finally, after all these years of roaming the state, I have come to the church in the wildwood, the Little Brown Church in the Vale.

It was, I discovered, most of what I expected – pretty, quaint, old. The ancient walls bow. Ceiling fans spin overhead, alongside old oil lamps that have been converted to electricity. There is patterned wallpaper worn in places. The pews sag. The still-original floorboards are six inches wide and are held down by those square nails found only in our oldest buildings.

But my day here, a week ago Saturday, was not just a stroll through what was. I also was involved in the present and in the future, for nine times during my stay, I heard "the beauty of the clear-ringing bell," as 59-year-old Reverend John Christy calls it.

Each ringing means another couple has been married. In a bit of tradition at the end of each ceremony, the new spouses pull together on a huge rope that dangles into the entryway from the belfry.

I even wound up being best man in one of the weddings when a couple from Wisconsin showed up and had no one with them to be witnesses. They helped satisfy my yen to taste the tradition, so I told them to take the small witness fee the pastor said I was entitled to and use it to buy their first married drink.

The place is a veritable shrine. Whether it's a religious shrine, a tourist shrine or something even less is a legitimate question. But if legacy and visitors make a shrine – and don't they? – then this is one.

Located on a beautiful tract along the Little Cedar River two miles northeast of Nashua in north-central Iowa, the church was built between 1860 and 1864. But it was just another struggling, rural, Congregational church until it was made a legend in the first two decades of this century by the hymn, "The Church in the Wildwood."

That was sung from coast to coast and border to border in the

United States by the Weatherwax Quartet, which came from nearby Charles City and became the foremost gospel group of the era.

Sixty-five years after the song's debut, 170,000 people visited the Little Brown Church in 1985, and 850 couples were married in Pastor Christy's 10-minute nuptial service. (The rest of the 30 minutes assigned for each wedding is used for quick instructions about the procedures, photographs and the bell ringing).

Christy has performed more than 5,000 weddings in his eight years here. More than 50,500 weddings have been performed in the church's history.

An Iowa version of a Las Vegas marriage mill? "It isn't that at all," Christy said. "It's just effective time management when you consider the demand. Yes, we have to be fairly firm on our rules. But if we weren't and were trying to do this many weddings, it would quickly turn into a circus, and we're trying to preserve the atmosphere of a dignified worship service."

Christy said he gets "the feeling that a lot of these people are coming here to be married because they want a church wedding, and they are not related to a church back home. But that's OK. I will not stand in their way. I do not stand in judgment of the people who come here to be married."

He paused for a moment and then said there is one thing he probably would be judgmental about: "They've come here in pickups, and they've come on motorcycles. They've come wearing everything from the most elegant formal wear to patched blue jeans. The one thing nobody's showed up to be married in is shorts, and I sort of hope they don't."

The basic wedding fee—for use of the church and the pastor's time—is $60. An organist and soloist are available for $10 each. For $5, the service will be tape-recorded. The women's group in the congregation can be hired to put on a reception in the church basement. Modestly priced souvenirs are available, including used hymnals embossed "Little Brown Church" and banks that are models of the structure.

But even if all couples took no more than the basic service, without music, a typical year's worth of weddings would bring in more than $48,000.

It seems like a lot until Christy explains that the income pays five salaries—his; that of his wife, Marilyn, who does all the paperwork and sings some solos; a hostess's, who acts as a traffic officer between the wedding parties and the tourists; a custodian's;

and that of a man who tends the 10 acres of gorgeous grounds the church owns.

Christy is a hard-working machine of a man during the services. The words he uses – even his humorous asides to the participants – are almost exactly the same. He does have what he calls his "cheater," a little slip of paper he puts in his well-worn prayer book so he won't forget the first names of the couple he is marrying.

It is "exhausting – physically, mentally and most of all emotionally," doing up to 15 marriages on a busy Saturday, several more on other days and "usually 20 or so" on Valentine's Day.

He uses the same big, serious voice in each of the weddings – it is a voice different from the one he uses in conversation – and though he almost always uses the same words, he says that should not be misconstrued as a sign that he is untouched.

"I work very hard to stay in control," he said. "As close up as I am to these people, well, there are some real raw human emotions there, even though it is basically a very happy time for them. There are lots of tears. I'm affected, but I can't let down. I have to stay on top of things."

Not only does he administer the vows, he also is likely to be the arranger of the wedding pictures, if not grabbing the cameras and shooting them himself, as I saw him do several times.

What else did I see?

The people getting married ranged in age from 18 to 79, although the average age was early 30s, which Christy said is normal. In all but one of the weddings, one or the other of the spouses had been married before. That also now is typical.

The crowds for the weddings ranged from zero to about 50.

The brides' dresses ranged from traditional, lacy wedding gowns to a knit, pleated, flapper-like outfit.

The grooms' attire ranged from tuxedos to one man's slacks and dark sport shirt unbuttoned down to here.

As flip as some of these people were outside the church beforehand, there came during the service itself a time of incredible soberness, which is either a pat on the back for the pastor's attempt to maintain dignity or some innate realization that matrimony is very serious business.

Most of the couples decided to get married at the Little Brown Church because friends or relatives had done the same. However, Grady Malachowski of Waterloo said he and Anita did because "we saw it on the map and thought, 'Why not?'"

Among the day's tourists were Frances and Carl Hill of Maxwell, who were married here 40 years ago. Christy said that on the first Sunday of each August, about 1,000 people usually attend a reunion picnic of people married in the church.

When the organist plays "The Church in the Wildwood" as a recessional, it is an especially moving moment for anyone who knows the heritage.

Finally, there is a delightful belief, albeit naive, perhaps, expressed by all of the couples that what they've just sworn to is forever. "When I came here," Christy said, "the congregation members told me that marriages starting in the Little Brown Church last longer. Someone told me only 10 percent of them break up, although even if that was true then, I seriously doubt whether it would be now."

But listen to Linda Orozco, of Fort Sheridan, Illinois, the last of my day's nine brides. "My Mom was from Mason City, and I remember hearing my Dad saying he wished he'd been married here," she said. "So one time in 1976, I came here and sat in a pew for a while. After a time it just hit me that if I was ever going to get married, I was going to do it here because then I'd know it would last."

Here's hoping.

And the bottom line on religion today: It's good to get together

February 1983

Good morning, fellow sinners.

When you're basically a secular columnist, as I am, you open yourself to all kinds of trouble when you write about God and religion. As Lewis Grizzard, my counterpart in Atlanta, has so aptly put it, "One thing has always puzzled me: Every time I write a column in which I mention God, at least five people write me a letter and threaten to kill me."

Nonetheless, that's today's topic, even if indirectly so.

I've read there is this Iowa Pastors Conference going on in Des Moines. I must admit the first thought I had about it had to do with how dull the hospitality rooms must be at such a convention. I said I'm a secular columnist, didn't I?

The article went on to say how this is bringing together clergy from 16 denominations, and how everyone in religion is saying this conference is going to spark a whole new wave of ecumenism in Iowa. For that I say thank God! Hallelujah, even. Can I be immodest for a moment? I rather regard myself as Mr. Ecumenical around here.

Check me out: I'm Catholic. I've got a last name and a nose that probably have half the population in Protestant-minded Iowa convinced I'm Jewish. I have Presbyterian in-laws. I have dealt extensively in print over the years with disciples of all brands of religion, everything from charismatics to followers of mysterious and mystical Eastern holy men to Moonies. I am always polite when the Jehovah's Witnesses come to my door. I am on the invitation list for Monsignor J. E. Tolan's wingdings each spring, and I was the first person to sign the guest book when they built the new Baptist church in the tiny southern Iowa town of Confidence. Yes, Mr. Ecumenical here.

I have long recognized the need for ecumenism. I trace this recognition back to a time in Shenandoah when the Baptist preacher took the pulpit and railed against Catholics – while unbeknownst to him, I'm sure, his daughter was "going steady" with one. Me. Of course, we were going steady as only sixth-graders can go steady, but the incident surely deepened the paranoia I felt growing up Catholic in a town that wasn't very Catholic.

And imagine what it was like for me a couple of years later when John Kennedy was running for president. You see, not only was my family Catholic, we were also Democrats. In Page County, no Democrat has been elected to a courthouse position since the early '30s and then, I've been assured, it was just a flash of temporary insanity in an electorate gone New Deal–giddy that put one of ours in office.

I mean, nobody was hitting me over the head because I was a Catholic or denying me membership in any organization I wanted to join or telling their daughters they shouldn't go out with me. Indeed, in that era, Protestant college kids would often show how liberal they had become while away at school by attending Midnight Mass with their Catholic boyfriends and girlfriends during Christmas vacation. (Hey, this does sound like a case of paranoia, doesn't it? Well, that's how I remember it.)

It was all good for me. I learned a whole lot of tolerance back then, not necessarily because I wanted to, perhaps. In those times in that place, if a Catholic lad was not tolerant of Methodism, Presbyterianism, Congregationalism and what have you, he would've been courting social disaster – and courting very little else.

I have grown up since then to embrace a few points about religion I want to leave here today.

One, I just refuse to get too bent out of shape about it. Some of the most screwed up people I've known are screwed up over religion.

Two, there is nothing as obnoxious as a recently converted anything.

Three, when it comes to all the different denominations, our lives are richer for the diversity, which is stimulating, if you allow it to be.

Four, when you strip away all the outward trappings, we're all just folks. I really wanted to conclude this with some greater thought, but hard as I think on it, that's the best I can do. We're all just folks. It's good to get together.

You can get into scholarly arguments about what "home" is. I'm not scholarly, though. Here's what I've said it is. This might not be profound, but it's honest.

HOME

Fatherly advice to a boy heading off to kindergarten

August 1981

Dear Andy,

You are on the brink of a great educational experience.

A year ago, my boss Jim Gannon's daughter was in this same position, on the brink of a great educational experience. Jim wrote her a high-minded letter in his column, charting some of the fun, struggles and challenges she would encounter as she started college.

Son, I figure I should do the same for you—as you go off to kindergarten. This isn't going to be any cakewalk, kid. Prepare for some abuse.

You know how your big sister has been calling you "Buzzard Breath" around home? That's nothing. Wait till your new chums at school start twisting "Offenburger" into various vulgarities. The name lends itself to that. What to expect? Generations of us have been called Hamburger, Cheeseburger, Burgerwurger, Awfulburger and, of course, that grade-school special, Often-eat-your-burgers.

Some of these new friends will be a little rough—you know, cussers. They will try to teach you some new words. That doesn't bother me. But don't you be teaching them the ones you know.

While we are on the subject, you know how we sometimes have "naughty word free time" at home? There is no such thing at school. If you swear in class, be prepared to pay. And if a teacher asks where you learned that, say, "From Grampa."

You will probably be taught the words of an old song that will seem new and fun to you, "Ninety-nine Bottles of Beer on the Wall." It goes on forever. It is a wonderful song to sing on a school bus, a terrible song to sing around home. Understand?

There will undoubtedly be some squat, strong kid in your class who is mean and tough. When he gets nasty, run. Do not get into an argument about whose dad can whip whose dad. Your dad can't whip cream.

Before long at school, you will see one of your new friends come racing toward you. He will touch your shoulder, contort his face and scream something like this: *"Chrissy's germs and no re-*

turns!" Now, son, don't panic. Just pass them on as quickly as possible.

In case it should be Andy Offenburger's germs that are being passed around, well, seek out and get to know the friendly old janitor. All elementary school janitors are friendly and old. The mysterious and marvelous boiler rooms where they work are places of great warmth and comfort for little people with wounded egos.

There will be no cupping of your hand in your armpit and making the honking noise. And do not laugh out loud when someone else does it.

Do not wait too long before asking to go to the restroom.

Another rule—no showing your "Underoos" during show-and-tell time.

Ah, show-and-tell time. This will be a source of constant trouble at home. Let's have some guidelines. Things you cannot take from home for show-and-tell:

> The cat
> Your Big Wheels
> Mom
> The bullhead you caught in Minnesota
> Your cap gun
> The parakeet
> No, you still can't take the cat
> Flowers from the neighbors' gardens
> Toads

You might hear your teacher, Mrs. Ulbrich, being called "Ol' Lady Ulbrich" by some of the older, more worldly kids around the school. "Ol' Lady" is not her first name and it is not to be used when you are talking to her. You might forget and do it once. You will not forget twice.

When she astonishes you with some new fact, as she will, do not respond in your occasional manner, "Oh yeah? How do *you* know? You think you're *so* smart!" Save that for your sister.

At some point during the year, it is almost certain that some kids will say you might fail kindergarten. There is a valuable lesson here, and it is this: Sometimes people can be jerks.

No, you won't fail kindergarten. And if you are a good Andy, it won't fail you. You'll love it.

> Don't miss the bus,
> *Dad*

In life, there is occasionally great sorrow, but you *do* get over it

January 1985

Today's offering is one I'd hoped never to write. But as you probably read, I am now divorced. My "ex" and daughter are living in Omaha. My son and I still live in Des Moines. Everyone is trying to be decent and get along, although I think her parents, great people, squirm a little when I remind them that if they were my "in-laws" previously, then they must be my "out-laws" now.

Sorrowfully, divorces are pretty puny news these days. Most people's breakups are noted only in lists of small type. Those of us in the public eye know if it happens to us, our dissolutions will be dragged up from the small type and made into news stories. No matter how brief, how dryly factual those stories are, they still wound. I'm not whining; I've always understood it goes with the territory.

Rarely, though, does a principal in one of these sad situations do anything to keep it on the public stage yet another day. That is what is happening here. Why? I feel I owe it to you.

My job, per the description I came up with a few years ago, is "to report and reflect on the experience of being an Iowan." Family life has always been an integral part of that experience. That's why you've often read here about my wife, our kids, our extended families.

As I told a group of young writers in Waterloo last year, it is important for someone who writes the kinds of things I do to open himself up and share his life with his readers. Doing so in good times is a joy. Doing so in bad times is awful—but necessary if the writer really wants an honest relationship with his audience.

The last two years have been rotten for me. In the plain language you've grown accustomed to here, I got dumped. Believe me, though, I'm not blameless. There were some rather epic bursts of insensitivity on my part.

I did all I could to mend the marriage, but it became obvious I had waited until it was already beyond repair. Communication was gone; we couldn't find it again, and neither could all the counselors, lawyers, ministers, friends and family members who tried to help.

221

The psychological burden has been heavy for everyone concerned.

I know I've written columns when I should have simply taken a day off, jumped on the bicycle and pedaled off to contemplate clouds and cows and corn. Occasionally I warned my bosses I was under particularly heavy stress and asked them to watch my copy more closely than usual. They tolerated me. You tolerated me, even though most of you had no idea you were doing so.

Everyone needs an anchor. My kids, my family, a trusted old friend, a special new friend and faith have been mine; but the column often has been a lifeline, too. Four times a week it would scream at me to quit being a wimp, get up, get out and do what must be done.

The healing process is now well under way, having started when I ultimately realized reconciliation was not only unlikely but really ill advised for all involved. The financial settlement was amicable; we didn't get into wanting to "nuke each other for the ashtrays," as a lawyer friend says couples often do. The kids, now part of the large pack of youngsters from split homes, seem to be doing all right. I'm no longer the head case I became.

"There *is* life after divorce," a knowing friend advised me in the dark days. Despite my doubts then, he was right.

I feel no little shame at having taken part in something that hurts as many people as divorce does. I'm telling myself it's healthy that I feel that shame, for it's an indication that my basic, strong values are intact.

And I'm revolted by the failure and broken commitments that divorce represents. The only thing I can say to that, I guess, is that I'm going to try to do better. As I do try, you'll see the stresses, triumphs, sadness and happiness of my new life coming through in my columns, I'm sure.

If I've told you more here than you wanted to know, well, a lot of you have done the same thing to me over the years, and I listened. This time I needed you to listen. To those of you who have known the divorce was coming, I thank you for your concern.

There. Painful old business now having been properly tended, it is time to get on with reporting and reflecting on the experiences of being an Iowan. As always, I look forward to it.

And my mother gave her a plaque that said, "Those who bring sunshine to the lives of others cannot keep it from themselves"

May 1986

We don't normally run engagement announcements here.

But today I'm allowing a Des Moines couple, Dennis and Chris Peacock, to use this space to announce the engagement and approaching marriage of their daughter, Michelle.

Why?

Well, you can surely stand a little romance mixed in amongst the rest of the news, can't you?

And there's one other reason. Michelle Peacock, 26, is bright and kind and fun and gorgeous. And on an evening late in the summer, she will marry me.

Yes, you loyal readers do remember correctly—she will be my second wife. I would hope I'll get it right this time. I will be her first husband. I would hope she won't have to try again.

She is a surgical technician at Iowa Methodist Medical Center. I always tell her that means she is on life's cutting edge. It's a little bit like being tied up with me. She understands that.

At least a few months ago, when we decided to break up, she said, "Well, it's been interesting." It was one of the nicest things anybody's ever said about me. I went back after her the next day.

We met two years ago, on bicycles. *Register* photographer Larry Neibergall was shooting photos of me, in advance of RAGBRAI, riding near my home. All of a sudden, through his viewfinder, he saw this young woman on a bike go whooshing around me.

"I think I know a way to make this picture much more interesting," he said. He yelled her down, persuaded her to pose with me and a friendship was born.

That's all it was for several months. Then I came up against one of those situations for which I absolutely had to have a date. I hadn't asked anybody for one for a decade. Before I phoned her from Okoboji, where I was vacationing with my children, I got a horrible case of the shakes. I practiced asking her out on my stepdaughter, Janae. Then I drank two beers, dialed Des Moines and felt big drops of sweat running down my back. She said yes, and I almost fainted.

When I decided it was time to ask her the much more serious question about marriage, I was again very nervous. I decided I first had to discuss it with my boy, Andy O. "A new member of the team here at home," I described her. He related well to that.

Did he have any reservations? "Well," he said after a long pause, "she sure seems to want everything neat and clean around here."

We laughed together as we realized that as we sat talking about this we were both drawing pictures in the dust on the dining room table, right in front of the china closet that has my collection of seed corn caps in it. Our mutual conclusion was that we probably need whatever sharp directions she will eventually be giving us about tidiness.

The proposal, I must confess, was an act that was pure Chuck Offenburger. With another RAGBRAI approaching, she'd wanted a new bicycle. She asked me to come to Bike World to look it over. I pulled Andy out of school early, and we got there ahead of her, sneaking in a big bouquet and a bottle of champagne.

When she arrived and showed me the bike she'd chosen, I went for the flowers. I came back, handed them to her, told her the bike wasn't shaped much like a diamond ring but it was more my style and, in view of how we originally met, completely appropriate. Then I got down on my knee and asked her.

She turned bright red. "I think I can handle that," she finally said.

Hey, I asked, is that a yes?

"Yes."

I stood, kissed her and we got a round of applause from the bicycle shop staff and customers, who had been understandably startled at what was happening in front of them. "Oh man, weird — right here in Bike World!" one of them kept saying. "Wow!"

Moments later, she was helping dig a newly discovered tick out of Andy O's scalp, and then we were off to the Little League park, where she worked in the concession stand while I coached and Andy pitched. Kind of a quick introduction into Offenburger life there.

Now we're trying to plan for a whole lifetime of our own wows. OK, I write all this, and the same thing that always happens is happening. You're still wondering, "What's she really like?"

She's wonderful. And I love her.

Neil Johnson, piano teacher, has some students who are whizzes and one who fizzles

November 1984

By the time you are reading this, I will have embarrassed myself for the fifth week in a row at my piano lessons.

Yes, piano lessons.

I was supposed to know "Amazing Grace" by Wednesday evening. What I knew by Wednesday morning was cold panic.

It's a humbling experience to be a beginner at age 37. I find myself wandering around saying, "Every Good Boy Does Fine." Or, in the case of the left hand, "Good Boys Do Fine Always." How silly for a grown man to have a phobia about when I'll be forced to deal with a metronome.

But 8-year-old Andy O was starting this fall, and in some wave of trendy thought about parental involvement, I decided I should start, too.

Andy O loves it. That's because every week, our teacher, Neil Johnson, tells him he is doing fine and tells me I need more practice. The kid lords that over me. "Better practice your piano, son," I'll suggest. His answer: "Look who's talking."

Recently, he was in the family room while I was at the keyboard in the living room. I played "Jingle Bells," yelled down and asked if he recognized it. "The McDonald's song?" he said. I deserved a break that day.

Neil Johnson is a very patient fellow. I hope. At any rate, during my first lesson, he seemed to want some statement of my goals on the piano. I gave him a lofty answer about how, after all these years of singing, I wanted to learn how to read music.

Lie. What I really want to be able to do is what Bob Larson can do. Larson is an old buddy in Shenandoah. He can sprawl on his back on a piano bench so that his face is directly under the keyboard. Then he reaches out and up, crosses his hands and plays— mind you this is *upside down, backwards, cross-handed and not looking*—a perfect rendition of "12th Street Rag."

I'd also like to be able to do what the late Bill Knittle could do. He was a severely crippled man—until he sat down at a piano. He could make that sucker sing. In fact, he could make a whole bar sing. Bill for years played the Thursday night sing-alongs at the Shenandoah Legion club, where I invested so much time they once promised me clear title to two bar stools. When he'd do "It's Only a Shanty in Old Shanty Town," why, it'd bring tears to your eyes.

On a higher plane, even if it wasn't quite as much fun, I went to a Des Moines Symphony performance this fall and heard guest soloist, Alexander Toradze, a Soviet pianist of renown, keep a full house at the Civic Center absolutely spellbound with his talent. Oh, did I envy him. I reminded myself, however, that he didn't get there by being a slug at practice time.

I don't know whether I'll ever reach any of my real piano goals. It's already terribly difficult for me, and I'm barely into playing with both hands at the same time.

My music book has just a few little notes on otherwise clean staffs. One night at church choir, I glanced over the shoulder of organist Cheryl Davis as she was playing some noble fugue and was horrified to see that her music looked like the schematic drawing of a computer's intestines. I was so intimidated I thought about giving up.

I should have known it'd be like this. There was an omen. Way back when, my little sis Chris would ride her bicycle up the street to Margaret Woods' house for her piano lessons. She'd get off her bike, pat Margaret's dog, Blackie, on the head and go on in and excel. When I'd chance to ride my bicycle in the vicinity of Margaret's house, ol' Blackie would come off that porch like a snarling, Spielberg monster and chase me past the next corner. I think he knew if ever I tried that piano at his house, it'd make his ears hurt.

Well, fie on Blackie. I'm trying, and will keep trying—at least I will until the day I show up at Neil Johnson's studio and he's got some cur guarding the door.

Besides, Johnson does his teaching at Village Square Mall in the suburb of Johnston. The mall has a place with video games, pool tables, pizza and beer. Andy O and I take turns hanging out there while he takes his lesson and then I take mine. After piano, beer, pizza, 8-ball and Space Invaders, we go on to church for religious ed and choir. By bedtime Wednesdays, I'll tell you, we are more well-rounded individuals.

So here it is Wednesday afternoon, and Mr. Big Shot Columnist is sneaking out of the newsroom to go home and try to get "Amazing Grace" in order, as I promised Johnson I would.

I wonder if he'd settle for me singing it.

When an average white boy eats soul food, he pays — and I'm not referring to the tab

December 1986

"Chitterlings." Kind of a cute word, huh? But what we're talking here, folks, is hog intestines. Most black folks actually call them "chitlins," or have nicknames for them.

"More 'wrinkles!' " Nolden Gentry, a lawyer pal of mine, roared from his end of the table. "I'm going back for more wrinkles."

Ah, yes, I had dinner with black friends again the other night, meaning that only now, nearly a week later, are my innards beginning to forgive me. They don't always eat soul food, of course, but there's a tradition of having it at holiday time, and this group has made it an extra part of that tradition to include me.

I've learned a lot at these gatherings; one thing is that soul food is a little hard on my system. And, hey, I'm no sissy when it comes to exotic, ethnic food. I'm the guy who on a trip to China a few years ago was called "the man who likes everything" by Bob Ray's daughter, Vicki, and I did eat it all over there in the Orient — well, everything except something they called a "sea cucumber." After a visual exam and a sniff, I concluded they were trying to slip me some kind of worm that grows hair.

I've eaten lutefisk with the Swedes. Babe Bisignano has surely fed me almost everything Italian there is. Greek food, no problem. Ditto for Mexican and German. And there's no problem with most of what typically goes into a soul food dinner, such as the one we had at the home of my friend and neighbor, Mary Chapman.

Greens? I love 'em. Lima beans and okra are terrific, although I wouldn't want the ham hock cooked in them. I can always eat a ton of cole slaw. Corn bread that melts in your mouth is irresistible. Sweet potato pie is better than either pecan or pumpkin, two old favorites.

But it's this matter of chitlins. They take some getting used to, and I don't mean the *fact* of eating them as much as I do the *idea* of it.

Blacks, especially poor blacks, started eating them way, way back because they could get them so cheap. Indeed, they're still cheap. When you can find them in groceries today, you'll typically pay $3.50 to $8 for a bucket of 10 pounds of them. I've got a hunch that at a lot of locker plants in small Iowa towns, where there are few blacks, you could almost have them for the asking.

Which brings up two points. (1) As many hogs as we slaughter in Iowa, you'd think chitlins would be the State Dish, and (2) the reason chitlins are probably not recognized that way is that most people, I think, have second thoughts about buying any kind of meat that is sold in buckets.

Chapman went out and bought three bucketfuls to feed our dinner group of 10 people. "The big problem with chitlins," she said, "is cleaning them. You've got to go through them piece by piece, looking at every membrane and pulling off the, uh – what shall I call it? Debris? That's one bad part; it takes so long to do it. Everybody is so busy nowadays that serving them is a real feat. That's why a lot of folks don't eat them as much, but there's the other bad part, too – the smell. It's bad."

Udell Cason, who calls me his "favorite white boy," speaks just as colorfully about the smell of chitlins: "It's like you've stepped in something after a dog's been in your yard."

My wife, Michelle Peacock, said the odor is more human. "It smells like it does at work," she said, which means the surgical suite at Iowa Methodist Medical Center, where she'd been assisting on "bowel resections." Needless to say, my sweetie didn't have much of an appetite for chitlins at the party.

Gentry said that was fine "because it means there'll be more for me." His wife, Barbara, not only doesn't eat chitlins, she also refuses to fix them for him. Chapman fixed them by boiling them in a pot with crushed red peppers, onions, salt and pepper and a potato. "The potato supposedly eats up some of the stink," she said. "That's what everybody says, anyway. The potato I put in didn't seem to work that way."

But a lot of that smell does boil away. By dinnertime, you could really only catch it if you held some chitlins to your nose. I did that. It was like I'd stuck my schnoz in my shoe.

OK, after saying something like that, could I eat them? You bet. Two helpings. Loaded with red hot sauce. Delicious.

Maybe that's what got me into trouble – the sauce. For after a couple of experiences with chitlins now, I can tell you they do three things to you – fill you up, make you want to take a nap, then in the middle of the night, wake you up.

Home can be as far away as Hackensack, Minnesota, if you're with family and friends

August 1986

HACKENSACK, MINN. – There was quite the big stir this past weekend around Swanson's bait shop, which sits on the edge of this little village in north central Minnesota.

Some lucky yoho had gone out and caught a 36-pound muskie and then was immodest enough to cart the thing into Swanson's, where they were displaying it in a six-foot-long freezer barely big enough to hold it.

I thought it gauche that they'd allow the public to come in and gawk at a poor creature that had obviously either had gland problems or had been given steroids. But gawk they did. OK, so I did, too.

You don't know how badly I wanted late Saturday afternoon to saunter back in there and say, "Guys, that ain't nothin'. I just hooked a 78-pounder," which had actually happened.

"Wow!" they would've screamed. "What kind was it, then?" (True Minnesotans always put "then" on the ends of questions.)

"Well, it was a German-Irish-Swedish mix," I would've answered. "It was my boy, Andy O. Hooked him on the thumb, right alongside the nail. And you talk about your catches putting up a good fight – shoot, you've never seen an angrier catch than what I had on the end of my line! Danged near dragged me off the pontoon boat, or maybe it was more like he danged near threw me off it."

Ah, yes, Andy O and I enjoyed some father-son togetherness in our neighboring state to the north, where, given the way I acted, it's appropriate that the state bird is the loon.

We were recipients of gracious hospitality from Darrell and Barbara Allen, residents of Indianola who spend their summers in a comfy home they've built on the banks of Stoney Lake.

It's a place so very, very pleasant. Hummingbirds flit about, sucking up the sugarwater Barb sets out. Finches chase nuthatches, which in turn are skedaddled by Baltimore orioles. Ducks flock in in the evening to snatch the corn she and granddaughter Jennifer spread.

We'd come along with their son, Gordy, a good friend of mine who made the trip not just to enjoy two days at lakeside but also to retrieve his sons, Justin and Jeff, who'd been getting spoiled by their grandparents for a couple of weeks.

I wasn't the only one acting a little loony. I caught my pal Gordy eating blueberry pie and ice cream for dessert, which doesn't sound so strange until I add that the meal we'd just had was breakfast.

"Must be something about the cool, clean Minnesota air," he kept saying, explaining his suddenly huge appetite. But I knew it was more likely something about his momma's cooking.

Oh, it was a grand getaway. Eye-opening, too. Do you realize there are people up here who actually care how the Minnesota Twins are doing? A peculiar bunch, they are.

They are fully worthy of living in Hackensack, a town that winks at the real world. Its big municipal claim to fame is that it is the hometown of one Lucette Diana Kensack, said to be the girlfriend of Paul Bunyan. Was she real? "As real as Paul," is the Hackensacker's quick response.

They also keep a black bear penned up on the main drag so tourists can brag they've seen one. It eats marshmallows. And they're into avant-garde art now, what with roadside stands selling "chain saw carvings" of tree stumps.

My every trip to town, particularly to Swanson's bait shop, was an embarrassment. I didn't like it a darned bit that that place sells bait bigger than the fish I was catching. And I also didn't like how they giggled when it leaked out I was seeking bullheads. Actually, the way it leaked out was when I asked if they would do taxidermy on a bullhead. The natives are so walleye-nuts that when they're confronted with a mud-bottom fisherman, they look on him like he's got a social disease.

But we had a good ol' time—eating, drinking, swimming, boating, eating some more and airing out every possible conversational topic.

"Why do towns store water up in water towers?" Gordy Allen said to the boys at one point, testing to see how sharp they are about such matters as gravitational flow.

"So people will know what town they're in," answered Andy O, obviously thinking first about how community names are painted on.

It was time to get him out of here. He was starting to act like a real Hackensacker.

"Mr. Fiscal Responsibility" gives a big Bronx cheer to bean-counters and number-crunchers

February 1987

Tuesday afternoon and evening, I spent 90 minutes with my accountant on income taxes, came home for a chicken sandwich, then spent two hours at a financial planning seminar that my insurance agent put together.

Wednesday morning, I awoke to a call from a representative of the Des Moines chapter of the National Association of Accountants, booking me for a speech. In April. That's April of 1988.

I came away from all that with a whole bunch of thoughts, in roughly this order:

(1) Where's a cold beer?

(2) How is it that some people are so darned organized, and I can't find time for a haircut?

(3) Why is Reagan's "tax simplification" program hitting me about like the instructions to my kid's new computer do?

(4) I really should be more concerned than I am about changing my financial *modus operandi,* which has been to make a lot of money and spend all of it. And then some.

(5) There is just a heck of a lot of money being made by people who are in the business of managing money. I couldn't do it myself, but I guess I'm glad there are people who can.

It also made me think back to a meeting I arranged a couple of weeks ago with George Haws. He is my old coach in Shenandoah, although now he's relocated to Marshalltown, where he teaches. When I feel screwed up, I still go to him, always warning, "A good coach's work is never done."

In our most recent meeting, we started talking money. Keep in mind, now, this is a lifelong schoolteacher counseling a lifelong journalist.

"When it comes to money," said this sage, "I think it's a matter that there are people who are supposed to have some, and then there's us." How true.

The heck of it is, I think I'm almost proud and a little protective of being such a financial flake. What can I say? Quote Popeye? "I yam what I yam."

Tom Ahlers, my accountant, tells me one reason he consents to continue dealing with me is because he'll ask me a question such as, "How much interest did you pay last year?" and my answer will be something like, "First you tell me why I should be interested in that."

To this man Ahlers, and to my broker, Craig Johnson (who says there'd be cobwebs on my folder if it weren't for my withdrawals for cash), and to my insurance man, Bob Clark (whom I'm afraid to go hunting with anymore because I fear he'll remember my questions and then shoot me), I have long referred to myself as "Mr. Fiscal Responsibility." It makes them laugh, and that's good because these are guys who otherwise have to be so serious.

As I review my financial life, I can think of only one time when I really had money. That was back in Shenandoah in the early 1960s when I began my writing career at the *Evening Sentinel.* They'd pay me 10 cents per column inch. If the *Register* did that now, I'd get $8 a week, which is something I hope they don't start considering.

But back then, I'd get my checks, take them home and put them in the kitchen cupboard. My mother would eventually lose her patience and insist that I take those checks down and put them in the bank. She must recall those times with some chagrin now that she's in retirement and I'm still occasionally calling for a loan.

When I began keeping my own checkbook, I used it as a multipurpose sort of thing. I mean, it would always have a few real check entries, logged in the first few hours after my most recent meeting with my banker, and a lot of notes from interviews.

There are periodic embarrassments in living as I do. Or in living with me when I live as I do. I wouldn't blame my wife, Michelle Peacock, if she bought one of those ads I used to see in agate type that said, "I will be responsible for no debts other than my own."

Not long ago, she was justifiably able to explain a financial oversight on her part by saying, "Well, excuuuse me, but I've never had a mortgage before, let alone three of them."

And Andy O, my kid, is constantly nagging me with the fact that I owe him $25 (you see, he's unaware that at this writing, it's grown to $30).

Yes, all that's embarrassing. But I can always say if I die tomorrow, well, there'll be one heck of a lot of people with real interest.

Once again sitting in
the newspaper office
that knew me when

SHENANDOAH, IA. – My mother's porches needed rebuilding.

So we all showed up here Thursday and Friday and went to work. Those more skilled in our little group did the real work. I was, of course, put in charge of visits to the lumberyard, runs for refreshments and public relations. A porch redevelopment job requires a public relations person, you know.

But now here it is, late at night, and I am sitting in the deserted newsroom of the *Evening Sentinel*, the newspaper that knew me when. I was graciously allowed thinking time and writing space by Jeri Naven, one of the *Sentinel*'s newshounds.

I haven't worked here for 15 years, yet all the light switches are in the same places I remember them, there's still the bare light bulb illuminating the front door of the locked vault, and the desks are almost as cluttered as when one of them was mine.

Ever done this? Ever visited a place you once worked – and visited at a time when you're all alone there? It's wonderful. It's eerie. I can almost hear the voices of long-ago bosses yelling it's deadline time, to get my column out of the old Royal manual typewriter (still here) and into their hands. Back then it wasn't "Iowa Boy," it was "Off on Sports." Get it? "Off," as in Offenburger? A careerful of catchy column names, huh?

Over there is the telephone I used when, as a boy sportswriter, I called a girl for my first date. She said yes. I was so shook I went down to the restroom and threw up before I could smile.

And right there is the spot where, for more than 50 years, the late R. K. Tindall sat as editor. I'd been a *Sentinel* paperboy for several years before that day when, at the pimply age of 13, I showed up as one of his "reporters." He looked at me and said: "Well, I guess we'll make it work."

They probably didn't tell him about dealing with boy reporters when he was in journalism school, but they also probably didn't tell him a lot about the economics of small town newspapering. I grew to love Tindall, even though I'm ashamed I never told him so.

233

It was right on this same spot I occupy now where one morning, as I was on the phone getting the results of a basketball game from neighboring Stanton, the *Sentinel*'s big boss, the late W. D. Archie, walked up and said: "I hate sports. You had two pages of sports in last night's paper. Too much. You're fired!" The firing stuck for about 20 minutes. My admiration for the crusty old coot endures today.

And look at the vault itself, with some dippy painting on its silver door showing a gravel road leading off into a blue horizon. You don't get into the vault at night. But by going through a false ceiling in an adjacent office, you can crawl into the vault's upper level, in which the newspaper's oldest bound volumes were stored.

I can remember on hot summer nights in another time, I would walk across the alley, buy a six-pack of beer, come back and climb into that vault's sweltering upper chamber. There I would strip to my underwear, sip suds and read the paper's accounts of events in the town's earliest history. I've often wondered in later years if I left any empties up there.

There was so much that I learned here in the *Sentinel* office.

I learned journalistic responsibility. I mean – now, I can go off to some small town in Iowa, write a zinger of a story about someone and know that I won't have to face him when the story is on the street. Back when I was covering the Shenandoah School Board, I knew that if I wrote a zinger of a story about the board, within 10 minutes then–Board President Maury Reavis would be in my face. And Maury's one of my relatives.

I learned about the "war letters." Those were the letters of our biggest typeface, which, I was told, were used in the paper only when war was declared or ended – or when the Shenandoah High School Mustangs went to the state tournament.

Oh, there was that one other time when Tindall was on vacation and the substitute editor dragged out the war letters to put a six-inch headline on page one that read: "Iowa Goes Wet!"

Within the last year, the paper was sold by the Archie family, which had become through marriage the Tinley family, to one of the nation's many newspaper chains, Park Communications. I had a lot of misgivings about that. In fact, I wrote a note swearing that if Nick Partsch, the new boss, somehow messed up my paper, I'd be down to bloody his nose. In his first few months here, he's done a pretty good job, I'm relieved to say.

The phone is ringing. I pick it up. "Uh, *Sentinel*," I say, awkwardly. The awkwardness somehow reminds me I'm glad that I don't still work here. But I'll forever be glad that I once did.

The old hometown said yes
when I asked it to open
its arms to me and
10,000 friends

July 1984

SHENANDOAH, IA. – So what can I say? I mean, here we are, in the old hometown, me and 10,000 of my closest friends. Hah! The truth is it's me and 10,000 visitors who are riding bicycles on RAGBRAI, or are following along in motor vehicles, or are just in town for the party. I like 'em all, though.

I'd asked that my home folks here open their arms, hearts, homes and wallets to make this overnighter one whizbang of a stop on the route of the 12th edition of the *Register*'s Annual Great Bike Ride Across Iowa.

I'd be a liar if I didn't admit it was an emotional moment when I rode my own bike down the big hill west of this town of 6,300 to see what they'd done.

Shenandoah – sweet Shenandoah – delivered. Honest to God, they rolled out a long red carpet on the pavement at the edge of the city so my RAGBRAI pals could ride over it.

Then, the farther I rode, the better it got. Hundreds of locals who taught me, coached me, counseled and tolerated me in my youth were out there in the bright, hot sun, working themselves silly to play proper hosts to the biggest crowd that's been here since the "Shen-tennial" celebration in 1971 – and all because I said maybe the effort would be worth it.

Then I rode down main street and there were signs everywhere welcoming not just the kid, but all my friends, too.

They put my childhood home, where my mother still lives, on the official tour of the town that shuttle buses were making. "Hysterical landmark," a big sign on the house said. And my outrageous sisters had added their own banner, "Home of the Offenburger Sisters, too."

But for whatever debunking those signs hinted at, still, there was my old home, an official stop on a tour that included the boyhood home of the Everly Brothers, the current home of May Seed and Nursery boss Ed May, and the studio of artist Larry Greenwalt, whose work has graced the cover of the *Saturday Evening Post!*

When you've grown up as just another guy in Shenandoah, that is fast company.

Howard Johnson, local clothier, had my 77-year-old mother, Anna, who is one terrific sport, in his store to meet visitors. And, doggone him, he was telling that story again about how, when I was an infant, he and my brother, Tom, had tossed me back and forth until they finally dropped me – on my head.

Most of the family had returned home for the event, including Bev and Sue, two of the three outrageous sisters. Their husbands, my brothers-in-law, said they'd considered grabbing one of their kids' pickup trucks, putting two exercycles in the bed and pedaling away while someone drove them along our route, so they could brag they'd had a piece of RAGBRAI.

Brother Dan was here, too. Let me expand a bit on his appearance. He is 48 and the athletic director at Creighton University in Omaha. He'd been out in Shenandoah till the wee hours Sunday with his wife, Mary Jean, for his 30-year high school reunion. Somehow, they got up early enough for her to drive him to Glenwood, RAGBRAI's launching point, so he could make the first day's ride with me.

Now, I've made it clear that while my *Register* cyclemate John Karras does these rides in bicycling's high fashion, I go in my lawn-mowing clothes, sort of the real people's representative on RAGBRAI. Well, suffice it to say that brother Dan made me look slick.

He showed up wearing gym shorts and an old golf cap, riding one of his daughter's bicycles, a heavy blue machine with handlebar tape unraveling and flapping in the breeze. Every biker needs a water bottle, of course, so he stole one from Creighton's equipment room and used adhesive tape to hold it to his bike's frame.

Though he is a regular jogger, and thus is in good shape, his pre-ride training on this bicycle consisted of riding a distance he liberally estimated at "350 feet – two driveways down from my house and back." He spent the first 20 miles of Sunday's ride asking me to explain to him in common language how to change gears.

You know, the old boy, who was calling himself "Nebraska Boy," made it all 48 miles from Glenwood to Shenandoah. Then – and this will be proof positive that the knack of bull-malarkey runs deep in my family – you know what he did? Sat down at a typewriter at Mom's house and wrote me a three-page account of his day. I'm going to quote one part that probably should be embarrassing to me:

"I do have some advice for the *Register* higher-ups. I don't think you have to pay Iowa Boy for doing his job. He is having so much fun, he would probably do it for nothing. As a brother, it was fun to see him in action.

"For one, folks stroke him like he is important. . . . In Nebraska, we reserve that for people like Bob Devaney, Tom Osborne, Governor Kerrey and a couple of good horses at Ak-Sar-Ben.

"He is on a constant ego trip, throughout the year, I suspect, and intensively in this week of RAGBRAI. He is, after all, nothing more than an Iowa boy, yet all the other Iowa boys and girls, and their several thousand friends from out of state, treat him special. Think of how Iowa Boy felt to ride into his home town with such an entourage."

In case you can't think how that was, I'm going to make it plain. It was something that should happen to everyone. But it was most of all a feeling of deep thanks at having grown up in such a place as this, where if you don't forget *them,* they don't forget *you.*

I love you, Shenandoah. You surely aren't surprised.